The Campus and
a Nation in Crisis

The Campus and a Nation in Crisis

From the American Revolution to Vietnam

Willis Rudy

Madison • Teaneck
Fairleigh Dickinson University Press
London: Associated University Presses

Associated University Presses
440 Forsgate Drive
Cranbury, NJ 08512

Associated University Presses
16 Barter Street
London WC1A 2AH, England

Associated University Presses
P.O. Box 338, Port Credit
Mississauga, Ontario
Canada L5G 4L8

The paper used in this publication meets the requirements
of the American National Standard for Permanence of Paper
for Printed Library Materials Z39.48-1984.

Library of Congress Cataloging-in-Publication Data

Rudy, Willis, 1920–
    The campus and a nation in crisis: from the American Revolution to Vietnam/Willis Rudy.
        p.   cm.
    Includes bibliographical references and index.
    ISBN 0-8386-3658-6 (alk. paper)
    1. College students—United States—Political activity.
2. Student movements—United States.   3. Higher education and state—United States.   4. Education, Higher—Social aspects—United States—History.   5. Education, Higher—Political aspects—United States—History.   6. United States—Social conditions.   I. Title.
LA229.R85   1996
378'.1981'0973—dc20   95-45748
                                                                              CIP

PRINTED IN THE UNITED STATES OF AMERICA

To the university students and
scholars of America
who have so much to contribute
to their nation's future

Contents

Preface

How do students in colleges and universities react to social and political crises of major dimensions? How do their mentors on the faculty and the administrators of their school react to such grave challenges? Confronted with events that threaten the very social order in which colleges are trying to prepare young people for positions of service and leadership, do these educational institutions retreat to their own private "ivory towers"? Or, in such trying situations, does society expect its schools of higher learning to help resolve the crises that threaten it?

The present work seeks answers to these pivotal questions. Attention is focused on campus reactions during five crucial periods in American history — the Revolution, the Civil War, World Wars I and II, and the conflict in Vietnam. The main finding of this volume is that American students and faculty were indeed deeply involved in all five crises. Such campus activism, of course, was by no means unique. Ever since the first European institutions of higher education were founded in the twelfth century A.D., colleges and universities have been agitated, politicized, and disrupted by wars, ecclesiastical disputes, and revolutions. In similar fashion, American institutions of higher learning have been no less involved in the most challenging events of their times.

It is hoped that a historical review of college and university campuses in crisis will lead to a better understanding of the role such schools play in the larger society that sustains them. It is the principal thesis of this study that the academic community, far from being peripheral or irrelevant during "times that tried men's souls," was closely involved in each of the crises. *Academe* was a significant source of counsel and an enormously influential sounding board that helped define and crystallize national decisions and eventual actions. The colleges and universities, it will be seen, did more than merely follow established policy; they played a crucial role in shaping history.

1

The American Revolution

Politicalization

THE American Revolution had two notable effects on the nine colleges which existed at that time in the British colonies of mainland North America. First of all, the inexorable march of events during the decade of turmoil from 1765 to 1776 pushed these schools into active political involvements, try as they might to avoid them and remain detached centers of scholarship, learning, and piety. Secondly, beginning in 1776, when the war of words gave way to the clash of armies, the battle for independence inevitably left its mark on them. At that point, academic schedules were disrupted, student enrollments declined, college finances were deranged, and teaching staffs were depleted. In some instances, significant physical damage was done to the colleges due to the taking over of campus facilities by detachments of troops or to the waging of actual military engagements on or near the college grounds.

In any event, politicalization of academic institutions became more and more marked during the years of imperial crisis from 1765 to 1776. Most of the colleges of English-America came to support the Patriot-Whig side of the struggle, at first cautiously, but later much more actively and militantly. In doing so, students and professors were definitely in step with the dominant currents of public opinion in their time and place. But they also did much more. College men in many instances played an active and important part in actually articulating and defining the evolving political attitudes of the American population during these years.

The troubled state of public life during these revolutionary times certainly made it difficult, if not impossible, for faculties and boards of trustees to keep their institutions free of political controversy. Popular pressures did not permit schools, colleges, or other key institutions in society that influenced opinion, to remain neutral. In order to enforce the community's standards of political correctness, academics very often were required, like other functionaries, to subscribe to oaths pledging loyalty to the newly established Revolutionary authorities. As a matter of fact, most of the members of college communities willingly took such oaths, since they were already fervent supporters of the Patriot-Whig side. But even if they had not agreed with the majority, they were under strong pressure to conform. Those who did not fall into line were stigmatized as Tories and

3

labeled enemies of America. Those unsympathetic to the Revolution could either lie low or, as a last resort, flee to Canada, the West Indies, or England. There was an ample supply of Patriot professors and administrators ready to take their places.

By the time the Revolutionary controversy had led to a final break with the Mother Country, a politically aroused public had come to demand fundamental changes in the government of the colleges. Old charters going back to colonial times were criticized as being excessively Royalist. Changes were proposed, in some cases, to make the charters more palatable to zealous Patriots, including, in one case, a change in the actual name of the school. In another instance, the original charter was retained, serving as a general framework, but ingenious trustees worked around it to put through a profound reorganization of curriculum, degree requirements, and teaching staff.

To sum up, then, the North American colleges were all touched, in varying degrees, by the profound changes unleashed by the American Revolution. In the process, they had been engulfed by pressures leading to politicalization. In the final analysis, however, they had adjusted rather successfully to the realities of that tumultuous time. All nine of these learned institutions survived the Revolutionary era to play a role in the new order.

Student Patriots

Manifestations of anti-British activism made their appearance on American college campuses as early as the year 1764. That fall, a group of angry young men at Yale College, led by an energetic Tutor, Richard Woodhull, decided that the way to publicize their loathing for mercantilistic measures like the recently instituted British Sugar Act was to organize a boycott of English goods. "We resolve unanimously," proclaimed the New Haven collegians, "not to Drink any foreign spiritous Liquors any more."[1] Such heroic acts of self-denial, while not always carried to that extreme, emerged as a standard expression of colonial defiance during the years that were to follow.

A much more heated campaign against British enactments was shortly to commence. On 22 March 1765 Parliament approved a Stamp Act. Aiming primarily to raise badly needed revenues, this bill only added fuel to the fire in the colonies. Public forums and legislative halls all across America soon rang with bitter denunciations of the ill-conceived measure. Americans were being required to pay a tax enacted by a legislative body in which they had no representation. "No Taxation without Representation!" became the watchword of the day. Unquestionably, the colleges were in the vanguard of the heated colonial campaign against the Stamp Act. Particularly vociferous in their protests were schools that had always had a strong Commonwealth-Whig tradition. The College of New Jersey at Princeton (Princeton College), for example, converted its commencement ceremony of September 1765 into a public rally to express the repugnance that Princetonians felt for the hated law. To dramatize their sentiments, the students discarded the traditional literary topics that had always been the staple fare at colonial graduations in favor of themes considered to be more relevant to current public concerns. The Princeton commencement orators thus delivered passionate orations on subjects such as "Patriotism," "Liberty," "Frugality," and "Industry," much to the delight of a "very crowded and sympathetic audience." The young men further made their point by appearing on the platform dressed in suits of American homespun, thus showing their support for a colonial boycott of British imports. A sympathetic spectator could only commend the newly fledged graduates of Princeton College for their good judgment, not only in their choice of commencement topics, but also for their wise decision to "throw aside those articles of superfluity and luxury which have almost beggared us." This observer reasoned that: "If young gentlemen of fortune and education, many of whom will probably shine in the various spheres of public life," thus voluntarily demonstrated their convictions by their mode of attire, inevitably this would have a powerful effect on 'the lower ranks of mankind."[2]

Other college commencements in 1765 served as forums for attacks on the Stamp Act. At Harvard, for example, Elbridge Gerry, who spoke as a candidate for the Master's degree, devoted his oration to the following salient question: "Whether the new prohibitory duties, which make it useless for the people to engage in commerce, can be evaded by them as faithful subjects?" Gerry, destined in later years to be one of the influential political leaders of the fledgling American republic, answered his own question in the affirmative.[3]

At Yale College, where President Thomas Clap opposed any public defiance of constituted authority, an attempt was made to avoid controversy by canceling the scheduled public commencement. The graduates held their own private ceremony, however, at which they freely registered their objections to the latest parliamentary impositions. Meanwhile, all the tutors were departing and many of Clap's students also left the College. Facing a possible vote of censure by the governing board, Clap resigned as President in September 1766.[4]

While youthful idealism undoubtedly played an important part in motivating the campus campaign against the Stamp Act, practical considerations were evidently also involved. The Act imposed a two-pound tax on "any piece of paper on which shall be engrossed ... any degree taken in any

university, academy, college, or seminary of learning." This tax hit graduating seniors hard and seemed to them to be purposely aimed at them. It
did not then cost much more than five pounds to cover a full year's tuition
at many colonial colleges; the graduates resented the fact that they would
now be expected to come up with an additional two pounds just to get
their diplomas.[5]

The student protesters against the Stamp Act present us with an early
example of collegiate activists registering their disapproval of establishment
policy by adopting unconventional modes of attire. As one commentator
observed in 1765, homespun had become "the new collegiate look."[6] At
the College of New Jersey in Princeton, the "noble example" of wearing
only American-made clothing in public spread quickly from upperclassmen
to freshmen and sophomores. By 1770 it had practically become mandatory.
At Harvard, the graduating seniors in 1768 asked the College's authorities to exempt them from having to wear British-made academic gowns
at commencement. They were turned down. Not to be so easily put off,
the ingenious seniors did indeed wear the required formal attire at the
morning's exercises, but changed quickly and conspicuously to outfits of
homespun for the afternoon portion of the day's festivities. Yale graduates,
too, soon joined the homespun parade. Graduating seniors of the class of
1769 made a special point of appearing at their commencement with
"pride in our plain coarse republican dress."

Nor was this all. Wishing to make sure that the point of their protest
was not lost on the public, the Yale men placed an advertisement in the
local papers to explain the rationale of their purposefully unglamorous
attire. Their statement expressed the hope that "Parents and Friends may
have sufficient Time to be providing Homespun Cloaths for them, that
none of them may be obliged to the hard Necessity of unfashionable
Singularity, by wearing imported Cloth."[7]

The graduates of Rhode Island College (later to be known as Brown)
were equally determined to make a sartorial statement. In 1769 the first
graduating class in the history of that institution received their degrees
and these newly minted Bachelors of Arts — all seven of them — appeared
on stage rather determinedly in suits exclusively "of American manufacture." Even more dramatically, the presiding officer at that commencement — Dr. James Manning, President of the College — set an example for
his charges by proudly performing his duties in his own special suit "of
American manufacture."[8]

Campus Protests Escalate

On 17 March 1766 Parliament finally repealed the Stamp Act; the long
and unrelenting colonial campaign against this tax measure had at last

borne fruit. Students and professors at the North American colleges rejoiced, as did the colonial population in general. Unhappily, the era of good feeling that seemed to be dawning was not destined to last. A year later, on 28 June 1767, the British Parliament approved a rigorous new series of revenue measures, known collectively as the Townshend Acts. The legislation imposed import duties on a number of commodities that were widely used by the residents of the colonies. And these latest mercantilistic measures were not designed for face-saving purposes only. Needing additional revenues badly, the government in London obviously meant business. The new duties were to be strictly enforced by Admiralty courts aided and abetted by a significantly increased force of customs collectors. Once again, indignant protests erupted in colony after colony and once again boycotts and non-importation agreements were put into effect. As before, the college campuses mobilized to voice criticisms of British "tyranny," and students and professors alike sang the praises of American "liberty."

The commencement season had become the preferred time for the members of academe to voice their anti-British sentiments in public. Leading the way was the College of New Jersey in Princeton, which had emerged by this time as one of the most activist of the Whiggish campuses in English-America. Its 1768 graduation exercises served as a convenient forum for colonial protest. At those ceremonies one of the graduating seniors proclaimed: "It is in the Interest of any nation to have the Trade of its new Countries, as free from Embarrassments as possible." Another graduate was even more explicit in the challenge he flung at the Mother Country. "It is lawful," he asserted, "for every Man and in many Cases, his indispensable Duty, to hazard his life in defense of his Civil Liberty."[9]

Later that year, the uncompromising Scottish Whig, Rev. Dr. John Witherspoon, came to Princeton to assume the presidency of the College. Witherspoon frankly utilized the 1769 commencement to advance the cause of anti-British resistance. Graduates devoted their orations to such current issues as "The State of Political Affairs" and "The Economy." Honorary degrees were awarded to two well-known colonial activists, John Hancock and John Dickinson.[10] Two years later, patriotic themes still predominated at Princeton commencements. At the 1771 ceremonies an epic poem, "The Rising Glory of America," was presented to the audience. Written by two seniors, Philip Freneau and Hugh Henry Brackenridge, the work visualized the center of world civilization as moving inevitably from the Old World to the New. The spectators greeted "with great applause" lines such as these:

> The Ohio shall glide by many a town
> Of note; and where the Mississippi stream
> By forests shaded now runs weeping on,

Nations shall grow and states not less in fame
Than Greece and Rome of old.[11]

One of the strongest statements against the Townshend Acts was made at a colonial college, the College of Rhode Island. At that school's 1769 commencement, two of the graduates debated a proposition which certainly was daring for that time; namely, "Whether British America can under Present circumstances, consistent with Good Policy, affect to Become an Independent State?" Even the orator who spoke on the negative side of the issue included in his presentation a number of strong arguments upholding colonial rights. In turn, the graduate who upheld the affirmative made a passionate plea for American independence. This young man, one William Williams, asserted that "Their evident design is to make us slaves." But Americans would stand up for their rights, Williams declared. And they would surely triumph in the long run because they had a citizens' militia to defend themselves, not a standing army like the British.[12]

Student protestors became rather more boisterous at Yale. A rally on the New Haven town green against British policy eventually drifted over to the college's campus. There some of the student patriots decided that it would be a great idea to toast the contributions of John Wilkes, an English Radical who had written articles upholding the colonists' point of view. To do this properly, the demonstrators proceeded to drink some forty-five glasses to honor their champion. A not especially sympathetic observer on the scene reported that these students "instead of drinking 45 glasses in honor of Wilkes and Liberty ... drank themselves 45 degrees in extremo DRUNK, when they commenced BAWLING in concert just 45 times, Sometimes Wilkes and Liberty, sometimes No. 45 ..."[13]

Students from Yale and other colleges were also active at this time in a campus movement to ban the use of any paper not of American manufacture for use in college catalogs and commencement programs. The Yale class of 1768, for example, voted to require that all of their catalogs and graduate programs be printed only on locally manufactured paper. Harvard students went even further. They broadened their boycott of British products to include any local printers who were deemed to be pro-British. To implement this policy, the Harvard class of 1771 voided the contract for printing commencement programs and dissertations by graduates that had been awarded to Richard Draper, a Boston printer who was known to be pro-British. That job was given instead to a zealous Whig, Isaiah Thomas, publisher of the *Massachusetts Spy*.[14]

Even at a somewhat more conservative institution, the College of Philadelphia, students were ready to express publicly their utter detestation of the Parliamentary measures. In 1770 the Philadelphia college was headed by an Anglican clergyman from Scotland, Dr. William Smith, who had never hidden his pro-British views. Many of the institution's trustees shared Smith's outlook. Nevertheless, the school permitted four of the graduating seniors at its June 1770 commencement to openly debate the potentially explosive question: "Might resistance to the supremacy of an existing government ever be lawful?" And at the same graduation exercises a candidate for the Master's degree was allowed to read his epic poem on patriotism, a work later published in the *Pennsylvania Gazette*. In this composition, Americans were asked to stand together and never relent on the economic measures they were using to defend their liberty:

> Attend, ye Patriot Throng!
> Ye noble Sons
> Of Freedom, who, to save your
> Country's Rights,
> With rigid Self-Denial, sacrifice
> Your private Gain. ...[15]

Once again, strong American political and economic resistance had the effect that was desired. On 12 April 1770 a new British ministry headed by Lord North persuaded Parliament to repeal all of the Townshend Duties except for a tax on tea. The colonies quieted down again and student agitation, even on the more activist campuses, mostly subsided.

Conservative trustees and alumni now heaved a sigh of relief and hoped the lull in campus demonstrations would prove to be lasting.[16] This was not to be the case, however. Many merchants began to suggest that the remaining Non-Importation agreements be junked, since the repeal of the Townshend Acts made them no longer necessary. Such thinking was not to the liking of the Ultra-Whig students, however, particularly the band of militants at Princeton. These campus activists argued that dropping the boycott machinery in its entirety would be bad strategy for America and, furthermore, would constitute nothing less than a cowardly betrayal of the colonial resistance movement.

In 1770 the Princeton Patriots had a chance to demonstrate their determination to oppose, forcibly if necessary, any weakening of American resolve. Informants tipped them off that letters would be passing through their little college town between pro-Tory merchants in New York City who wanted to dump the boycotts and their counterparts in Philadelphia. The correspondence was intercepted by the students and what followed is described in a letter sent to his father by James Madison, the future President, who was then an undergraduate at the college:

We have no public news but the base conduct of the merchants in New York in breaking through their spirited resolutions not to import ... Their letter to the merchants in Philadelphia requesting their concurrence was lately burnt by the Students of this place in the College Yard, all of them appearing in their black Gowns and the bell Tolling.[17]

The students sought to extract the maximum amount of drama that they could from their act of revolutionary vigilance. They actually hired the public hangman to burn the hated letter with great solemnity in a ceremony staged in front of Nassau Hall. Apparently they intended this ominous proceeding to serve as a warning to any persons who might in the future attempt to violate the true Patriotic faith. The *Pennsylvania Gazette* noted with approval that the "hearty" men of Princeton wish to be absolutely sure "that the Names of all promoters of such a daring breach of faith, may be blasted in the Eyes of every Lover of Liberty, and their Names handed down to Posterity, as Betrayers of their Country."[18]

The already highly-politicized students of the College of New Jersey in Princeton, and like-minded undergraduates on other American campuses, were stirred up to new acts of defiance by yet another ill-conceived act of Parliament. On 10 May 1773 the British lawmakers passed the Tea Act. This unfortunate measure gave the politically influential East India Company the authority to sell its products directly in colonial markets through a select group of their own specially commissioned agents. It was a dangerous precedent from the point of view of American businessmen because it bypassed local middlemen. It implied that any British company with powerful friends in Parliament could secure a government-approved monopoly of the colonial market, undercutting the prices of American merchants.

When news of the Tea Act reached the colonies, it put the already restive Princeton students in an even uglier mood than before, if that were possible. Activists now ominously warned that any students thought to have Tory sympathies would be unceremoniously ducked under the college pump. One aggrieved student Patriot grumbled that he only hoped that two or three of his classmates, whom he characterized as "possessed swine," would be "turned off" (expelled) by President Witherspoon. The climax came when the young Princetonians, emulating Sam Adams's Boston vigilantes, staged their very own "Tea Party."[19]

In late January 1774 the outraged collegians gathered together in the school's "yard" to dramatize to the public their condemnation of the latest Parliamentary action. An effigy was brought forward of Thomas Hutchinson, the arch-Tory Governor of Massachusetts. It was adorned with a canister of tea tied around its neck and the crowd cheered lustily as it was set on fire. Charles Beatty was one of the Princeton undergraduates who was present at this occasion, and he wrote shortly thereafter: "We gathered all the Steward's winter Store of Tea, and all the students had in college, and having made a fire in the Campus, we there burnt near a dozen pound, tolled the bell, and made many spirited resolves."[20]

While all of this was going on, Dr. John Witherspoon, the stubbornly anti-Tory president of the College, said nothing and did nothing. Witherspoon saw no reason why the youthful Tea-Partyites should be disciplined. His Trustees, however, fearful of governmental disapproval, did not view the proceedings with the same degree of equanimity. Gauging the situation, the student activists for their part felt encouraged to proceed with their campaign, counting on Witherspoon's sympathetic attitude to protect them from any administrative crackdown.

The next target of the Princeton militants was located off-campus. The student crusaders decided that they must ferret out and discipline Tory-minded offenders in the town of Princeton itself. The night of 7 June, a mob of some forty students, "drest in white," decided to pay a call on a local householder alleged to be one of the obnoxious "tea-drinkers." His entire stock of the much reprobated beverage was seized and burned. Next, the youthful posse headed for the house of another local resident who, it was rumored, was a confirmed Tory. What they intended to do to this hapless individual is not clear, but in any case they found to their chagrin that the intended victim was not available. He had apparently already "made his escape." Our student observer, Charles Beatty, found this late night's activity to be nothing more than "a fine frolick."[21]

The most prominent leader of the Princeton demonstrations was a twenty-seven-year-old senior named Samuel Leake. A member of the class of 1774, Leake had a background somewhat different from that of his younger classmates. He had taught school in Pennsylvania for some time so that he could accumulate the money to come to Princeton. In a real sense, then, he had worked his way through college. He was, furthermore, a militant Whig and made no effort to hide his opinions. He seems also to have been a magnetic leader. His fellow seniors greatly respected him and willingly followed his directions at the various student demonstrations. In addition, his class showed their high regard for him by voting to select him to give the Salutatory oration at commencement. President Witherspoon warmly endorsed this choice.[22]

Serious difficulties arose regarding Leake's selection, however. At the time that the students were staging their "Tea Party," one of the most influential of the College's trustees, a local attorney named Richard Stockton, appeared on the scene and apparently "expostulated" with the young men, calling on them to end their "riotous proceedings." Samuel Leake told Stockton rather forcefully to shut up. The trustee complained that all he had gotten for his pains was "an insulting rebuke" from the mob's leader. This incident was clearly not forgotten. When some time later the board of trustees met to approve the list of nominees for the

1774 commencement orations, Leake's speaking assignment was disapproved. The board anticipated that the pro-Tory Governor of New Jersey, William Franklin, would attend the graduating exercises, as would other conservative provincial officials. It seemed politic not to offend them, and for this reason the trustees directed President Witherspoon to find another Salutatory speaker. Leake, however, refused to back down; he would not surrender his assignment voluntarily. The board struck back by barring him totally from attendance at the commencement, which meant, in effect, that he would be denied his degree.[23]

Interestingly enough, Samuel Leake's replacement at the 1774 exercises, a young man named Thomas MacCaule, made it a point to be even less cooperative with the timorous conservatives on the board of trustees than the original nominee would have been. To the great satisfaction of his fellow graduates, MacCaule delivered a fiery oration stressing the basic theme, "War must be preferred to Slavery!" Meanwhile, we may ask, what was the subsequent fate of Mr. Samuel Leake? Ironically, he received his degree in good order not much later. The political climate in New Jersey had shifted radically within a few months. The Patriot Whigs seized full power in 1775 and Samuel Leake thereupon speedily received the Princeton diploma he had earned. In later years Leake went on to have a successful career as a practicing attorney in the now self-governing State of New Jersey.[24]

Whigs vs. Tories on Campus

Though the College of New Jersey was undeniably one of the most tempestuous centers of anti-British activism during the early 1770s, it was by no means the only one. Another school in New Jersey, Queen's College (later Rutgers), supported many of the colonial protests, as did the College of Philadelphia, and the four institutions of higher education in New England — Harvard, Yale, Dartmouth, and the College of Rhode Island. At the last named school, Horace Binney delivered a stirring valedictory oration at the commencement exercises of September 1774. Speaking on the subject of "Liberty, with some Anecdotes from the present Time," Binney stressed the importance of the colonial resistance to any and all measures of British "oppression." An essential part of such resistance, he emphasized, was the development, as fast as it could be done, of a "spirit of martial heroism throughout this colony and continent." The speaker who followed Binney was even more explicit. Referring to the current political situation in America, he boldly observed that "unjust laws often impel men to make revolution."[25]

At this time only two college communities in the American colonies —

those at King's College (later Columbia) and William and Mary — remained outwardly loyal to England and to its policies. There were, to be sure, a few Tories among the students and professors on other campuses, but they remained a distinct minority. Usually such conservatives preferred to lie low, but a few came forward at Harvard College. On 9 December 1774 a couple of pro-Tory Harvard students interrupted evening prayers to make a public announcement of their disapproval of the actions of the Continental Congress. All that their pronouncements achieved was a chorus of hisses and jeers. Undiscouraged by this rebuff, the Tory Harvardians tried three months later to make a political point by conspicuously bringing British India Company tea to the college dining hall and drinking it with their breakfast. The other students responded by smashing their teacups and teapots. This tempest in a teapot might have degenerated into a free-for-all had not the faculty promptly intervened. Subsequently, the President and faculty issued a stern reprimand to both sides. The Whig students were ordered to make restitution for any property they might have destroyed; the Tory students, in turn, were directed not to bring tea into the dining hall. An appeal was made to both sides to restore the "harmony, mutual affection, and confidence within the walls of Harvard College" that should prevail "whatever convulsions may unhappily distract the State abroad."[26]

At Yale the Whiggish-minded students were no more inclined to tolerate their Tory opponents than were the Harvardians. The pro-Patriot majority were particularly annoyed by a Tory sophomore, Abiathar Camp, Jr. In June 1775 Camp's pro-British views were roundly condemned by a committee of student activists and he was asked to explain them. Camp did not respond to this request. His classmates thereupon voted to "advertise him, on the door of the Dining Hall, as an enemy to his country." They further announced that they would "withdraw from all relations with him." Camp struck back. His home was in New Haven and he was therefore able to get help from some of his pro-Tory friends among the local "Townies." These worthies beat up a couple of the Yale students who had voted to ostracize Camp. At this point, the student Whigs armed themselves with clubs and prepared to launch a counterattack on Camp and his cohorts. Only the timely arrival of Dr. Daggett, the Yale President, prevented possible bloodshed. Some time later, Camp, tired of being the campus pariah, withdrew from the College.

By this time, the New Haven school had become well-known throughout the colonies for its militant Whig bias. One of its leading alumni, a pro-Tory judge named Thomas Jones, condemned his Alma Mater as nothing more than "a nursery of sedition, of faction, and republicanism." Jones complained that Yale was now mostly remarkable not for its scholarship or learning but for "its persecuting spirit, its republican principles, its intolerance in religion, and its utter aversion to Bishops and all Earthly Kings."[27] Most Yale alumni of the day, however, undoubtedly preferred the views of John Trumbull to those of Judge Jones. The poet Trumbull, a moderate Whig, had been a Tutor at Yale during the early 1770s. He won wide fame in 1775 when he published his mock-epic *M'Fingal*, a work that poked fun at Tory attitudes and Tory politicians such as Lord North.[28]

The College of New Jersey, Harvard, and Yale were obviously militant in their support of colonial rights, and most other American colleges shared their outlook. Students, professors, and administrators were predominantly pro-Patriot and pro-Whig. Most surveys of campus opinion during these years confirm this fact. For example, a study of some 279 matriculants at the College of New Jersey in the 1760s found that only three percent could be identified as Loyalists (Tories).[29] Similarly, Samuel Morison found relatively little Toryism among the Harvard graduates of the period. Of the school's living graduates in 1776, only 196 out of 1,224, or sixteen percent, were Loyalists.[30]

Many zealous Whigs in Pennsylvania considered the College of Philadelphia to be a center of unrepentant Loyalism. This reputation was primarily due to the fact that Dr. William Smith, the head of the institution, was reputedly at loggerheads with the local Patriots. Many members of his faculty, however, were pro-Whig in their politics. This group included the College's Vice-Provost, Francis Alison, and Professors Morgan, Shippen, and Rush. The career of Benjamin Rush (later a signer of the Declaration of Independence) is a case in point. Rush, who taught chemistry at the College's medical school, wished Americans to back up their resistance to British policy by developing the production of saltpeter, which could be used in manufacturing gunpowder. Rush's advice was heeded; eventually he was appointed by the Pennsylvania Revolutionary authorities to serve as an advisor in the construction of a saltpeter works. In addition, Rush was happy to serve as physician-surgeon with the gunboat fleet that the Pennsylvania Committee of Safety deployed to defend the sea approaches to the city of Philadelphia.[31]

The situation was very different at King's College in New York City. King's College, a royal foundation, as its name indicates, remained staunchly Anglican, following the lead of its arch-Tory president, Myles Cooper. David Humphrey estimates that at least half of the school's students and alumni in 1776, as well as four-fifths of its liberal-arts faculty and most of its trustees, were firm Tories.[32] Even at such a center of royalism, however, there were Patriot professors. Robert Harpur, professor of mathematics and physics, was so well known as a devoted Whig that he was elected in 1775 to be a member of New York's revolutionary Provincial Congress. In addition, New York's Whig leadership apparently felt that

Harpur could be trusted to undertake sensitive missions for the cause, because he was appointed to be a member of New York's "Commission for Detecting and Defeating Conspiracies." In this vital post, it is quite possible that Harpur gathered inside information for the Commission on the pro-Tory activities of the head of his own college, Dr. Cooper.[33] On the other side of the political fence, however, were such King's College faculty as Samuel Closey, professor of natural philosophy, who was an Irish-born Tory, and John Vardill, professor of natural law, a polemicist who published a number of newspaper articles during 1772 and 1773 upholding the Tory cause. When the war broke out, Vardill became a British spy.[34]

William and Mary was the only other colonial college where Loyalist views predominated. The majority of the school's faculty were Anglican clergymen who had come over from Britain. Naturally these men were unpopular with the Virginia Patriots, who made it clear that they wanted all such individuals to leave the Province. This Whig attitude was illustrated none too subtly in 1775 when the Reverend Thomas Gwatkin, who taught mathematics and languages at the College, was visited "by a body of armed men." Their aim, quite frankly, was "to terrify him into compliance." Later, when night arrived, the door to Gwatkin's room was hammered "in so violent a manner as to give just cause for apprehending that the Author or Authors of this Disorder intended to break into this Professor's Bed-Chamber and do further mischief." Such occurrences alarmed the William and Mary faculty exceedingly and they felt it necessary at this time to order that "all the Arms which can be found in the College be immediately taken into Possession of the Professors." Gwatkin was not reassured, however. He decided to take advantage of an offer from Lord Dunmore, the royal Governor, to go aboard a British warship as a refugee. Eventually that ship took him back to England. Another professor with Tory opinions, Samuel Henly, soon joined Gwatkin on the warship. The two had been obliged to flee the College so swiftly that they abandoned most of their personal possessions, including books and prints.[35]

At first, there had been only one William and Mary professor who sympathized with the colonial cause. This individual was named James Madison, but he was not the other James Madison from Virginia who in later years became President of the United States. William and Mary's James Madison had been appointed professor of natural philosophy and chemistry in 1773; in later years he would become president of the institution when it was reorganized by Virginia's Revolutionary leadership. Madison had always been an ardent Whig and Patriot. In a commencement oration he had already made his position quite clear. "The authority of the People," he declared, "is the best corrective of the Disorders of the State ... We were born to be free."[36]

The Roots of Political Activism in Academe

What forces were politicizing the professors and students of the colonial colleges during the turbulent 1760s and 1770s? First of all, obviously, the onrushing march of events during these two volatile decades would inevitably foster such a reaction on the various campuses. Secondly, we should not underestimate the influence of familial example and the pull of personal association. Ideologies and political preferences espoused by the members of a student's family or by other close relatives would undoubtedly have an important impact. So, too, would views propagated by trusted classmates and other friends in the peer group.

In addition, the general drift of opinion that was already well under way on a particular campus and in the community that surrounded it was likely to have a powerful effect. Thus, students at the College of New Jersey in Princeton were under strong pressure to go one way in their reaction to the conflicts between the colonies and the Mother Country while those at King's College in New York City were being pushed in the opposite direction. Working to articulate and disseminate majority opinion on a particular campus were the speakers in student debating societies, the activists in undergraduate clubs, and the student orators at annual public commencements.

Student reactions were also shaped in an important way by their mentors — the professors and the college president. Young college men were naturally impressed by the role models set before them by increasingly politicized faculty members. John Witherspoon stands out in this company but he was by no means unique. At Harvard, John Winthrop, the professor of natural philosophy, warmly approved Thomas Paine's *Common Sense* and served in the Massachusetts Provincial Congress in 1774 and the Massachusetts Council in 1775. A professor of medicine at Harvard, John Warren, offered his services as physician to the Continental Army and later supervised military hospitals for Washington's forces. At Princeton, the Patriot cause was supported enthusiastically by Professor William C. Houston, who reinforced Witherspoon's efforts in every way that he could.[37]

Activist faculty made important contributions to the Revolution in other ways as well. They sought to mold the outlook of the young charges in their classes by means of their teaching, and they edited and revised drafts of student commencement orations to give these addresses a Patriotic direction. Cohen and Gerlach made the important point that:

> The classroom was the primary forum for shaping learning experiences and it was from the podium that the faculty strove to inculcate their particular philosophies and precepts. ...[38]

Another influence shaping the responses of college men to the events of the American Revolution was the curriculum itself. Students were reacting to the reading they were assigned and they were also reacting to reading they did for themselves outside the prescribed course of study. They were also affected by the ideas that were discussed in the disputations and oratorical exercises that were, in that day, an integral part of the required college work. Quoting Cohen and Gerlach once again,

> Many of the "self-evident" truths the students fought for ... had their origins in the college curriculum ... there was much within eighteenth-century collegiate studies from which students drew analogies to support the American cause. It was from the classic words of Cicero, Demosthenes, Plato, Plutarch, and Tacitus as well as the more modern Enlightenment writings of Locke, Hutcheson, Burlamaqui, Montesquieu ...[39]

In the formal curriculum itself, studies of what was called "moral philosophy," of the Graeco-Roman classics, and even of rhetoric, took on more and more of a political character during these years. As young Americans studied the words of ancient orators and philosophers, they very often searched these words for implications that would apply to the contemporary situation. The Marquis de Chastellux observed this American utilization of the classics and concluded that people like Sam Adams, as students, had begun "by the Greeks and Romans, to get at the Whigs and Tories."[40] Other works that were eagerly perused by students seeking ammunition for the defense of colonial rights were the volumes authored by the "Commonwealth Whigs" of the seventeenth and eighteenth centuries — political philosophers such as Milton, Cromwell, Harrington, Hutcheson, and Sidney.[41]

Many of the books referred to above could be found in the libraries of colonial colleges. The Harvard College library, for example, was well-stocked with "Commonwealth Whig" titles plus a number of the most important publications of eighteenth-century "Enlightenment" authors. Works by Voltaire and Montesquieu, as well as others by Hume, Ferguson, and Robertson, could be found on Harvard's shelves. These seminal works were definitely there but, we may ask, were students actually reading them? A study that was made of the titles listed as being charged out of Harvard's library during the 1770s indicated that a number of such works were indeed being borrowed by the students. Beyond that, we can only infer that, having borrowed these volumes, they presumably read them. Do we have any other clues? Student petitions to the Massachusetts General Court during the mid-1760s may well give us some of the desired information. The undergraduates were petitioning for restitution of volumes from their own private collections that had been destroyed in 1764 in a dormitory fire. Many of the very classical and modern works that have been specified as having possible contemporary political applications are listed on these petitions. And, finally, the notebook of a Harvard sophomore which covers the years 1766 and 1767 has been found to contain a number of references indicating considerable extracurricular reading in books written by "Commonwealth Whigs."[42]

The Outbreak of Fighting: Response of the Colleges

The Tea Act led to a dangerous deterioration in relations between Britain and her North American colonies. In Boston a mob dumped a shipment of imported tea into the harbor; the British government retaliated with the Coercive Acts, punitive measures that closed Boston's harbor and revoked the Massachusetts Charter. British troops could now be stationed anywhere in the colonies and facilities could be forcibly requisitioned to house them. The colonial response came in September 1774 when delegates assembled in Philadelphia in the First Continental Congress to consider what collective measures of economic or military resistance might be necessary to oppose the latest British measures.

By 1775 the controversy within the British Empire was rapidly drifting out of control. A possible military confrontation loomed ominously on the horizon as London poured troops into the American colonies to enforce its authority, and the colonists, in turn, hastily organized peoples' militias to defend local rights. College campuses were by no means isolated from the escalating crisis. Student activism now entered into a new and critical phase. American undergraduates were in the forefront of the movement to defend self-government against King and Parliament, by force if necessary.

As early as 1769, or perhaps 1770, students at Harvard College had established the first organized militia company to make an appearance on an American campus. The motto of the student organizers — *Tam Marti quam Mercurio* — led spectators to refer to the group as "the Marti-Mecurian Band." In the fall of 1771, no less than sixty-one young Harvardians were following the prescribed drills and military exercises of this local "swagger company." Dressed in long blue coats faced with white, along with fancy breeches, white stockings, and three-cornered hats, the student militiamen attracted a good deal of attention in Cambridge. They stored supplies of arms and ammunition in Hollis Hall in case these were ever needed by the corps, but, alas, all these weapons and bullets were confiscated in 1775 by the Massachusetts Committee of Public Safety as it girded for a possible British attack.[43]

A student cadet corps also surfaced at the College of Rhode Island.

These undergraduate volunteers played a key role at the College's 1774 commencement as they escorted the Governor of the Colony to the ceremonies and later performed drill formations on the campus green. A local newspaper remarked that the student cadets secured "universal approbation" from the spectators, thoroughly convincing them that "Americans are no less capable of military exercises than Europeans."[44]

Students of the College of New Jersey also moved in June 1774 to form a militia company. Charles Beatty became a member of this unit, and he congratulated his comrades-in-arms for being "willing to fight and die in defense of *your* Liberties, and the liberty of *your country*." The young gentlemen seemed to be quite proud of their fancy uniforms of green, yellow, and white, but they were somewhat annoyed that they had not been issued "more than half enough muskets to arm their ranks properly."[45] Beatty found, however, that the spirit of the group remained good, notwithstanding. "You need not speak here," he reported, "without it is about Liberty — Every man handles his musket and hastens in his preparations for war."[46]

At Yale, students were similarly stirred to martial action. A campus militia unit was organized in February 1775, the reason being, it was stated, that "now our liberties are at the crisis."[47] Two individuals, described as "regular soldiers," helped train the collegians, their services being paid by contributions from the members of the company. In March of that year a Yale student reported that:

The MILITARY ART just begins to dawn in the generous breasts of the Sons of Yale ... College Yard constantly sounds with, *poise your firelock, cock your firelock*, etc. These warlike noises are continually in College.[48]

Finally, in mid-April 1775, the event that had long been expected but nonetheless dreaded took place. Open warfare erupted between colonial militiamen and British soldiers at Lexington and Concord in Massachusetts. The controversy between home country and colonies had moved from the political and economic sphere to the arbitrament of arms. What now were the colleges to do? They could no longer temporize; they must face current reality, unpleasant as it might be.

Commencement season in 1775 became a time to stand up and be counted. In New Hampshire, even the attempt to hold a public graduating ceremony, given the gravity of the times, was severely criticized. At Dartmouth College in August 1775 a number of graduating seniors denounced the school's scheduled commencement, maintaining that the outbreak of hostilities made such public displays irrelevant.[49] At the College of Philadelphia, on the other hand, commencement exercises were held, as scheduled, shortly after news arrived of the battles at

Lexington and Concord. However, disregarding the presence of the pro-British Provost, William Smith, the orators of the day took advantage of the occasion to make strong Patriotic statements. Benjamin Chew, the class Valedictorian, reminded the audience that even imperial Rome had fallen from "the summit of human glory" because of her arrogance. Such evils, Chew warned, might bring about a similar fall in modern times. The College of Philadelphia, he concluded, must always work "to train up a succession of patriots, sages, and lawgivers, to support and dignify our great American cause."[50]

Even at William and Mary, where Tory sympathies among faculty members were strong, patriotic sentiments were quite evident in the student body. After Lexington and Concord, students from the College joined the local militia to help patrol the streets of Williamsburg. And later, when the academic year came to an end, a number of William and Mary students enlisted in the Continental Army that was now being formed. One of these young student-soldiers was James Monroe, destined to be President of the United States.[51]

American College Presidents Confront Revolutionary War

The key campus personalities who shaped institutional responses to the Revolutionary crisis were of course the college presidents. Most of these educational leaders sympathized to a lesser or greater degree, as the case might be, with the agenda of the Whigs and Patriots. To be sure, few American college presidents were as active, or for that matter, as influential politically, as Dr. John Witherspoon, the energetic and combative head of the College of New Jersey.

Witherspoon was an active Patriot long before independence was declared. As early as mid-summer 1774 he asserted that America must:

> Declare a firm resolve never to submit to the claims of Great Britain, but deliberately to prefer war with all its horrors, and even extermination, to slavery; to resolve union and to pursue the same measures until American liberty is settled on a solid basis. No colony shall make its separate peace.[52]

No less militant in public statements, though not as well known to the public, was James Manning, head of Rhode Island College. Manning readily agreed to the request of his graduating seniors in 1775 to cancel the school's public commencement as a gesture of austerity and defiance. He then took advantage of the occasion to state his convictions on the crisis confronting the colonies. "Though the Din of Arms," he said, "and the Horrors of Civil War, should invade our hitherto peaceful Habitations;

yet even these are preferable to a mean and base submission to arbitrary Laws and Lawless rapine."[53]

At tiny Queens College in New Brunswick, New Jersey, the acting President, Jacob Hardenbergh, was so active in stirring up support for the Revolution that the British finally felt obliged to announce a reward for his capture.[54] At Harvard, two of the three men who served as president during the Revolutionary years were self declared Patriots. Samuel Locke was forced out of office, to be sure, for alleged indifference to the American cause as well as for sexual indiscretions. His successor at Harvard, Samuel Langdon, a close friend of John Hancock, preached extensively in favor of colonial rights. Even that did not prevent Langdon from being forced out of office in 1780 on grounds of "impiety," "heterodoxy," and poor performance as educator and preacher. Much more successful was Rev. Joseph Willard, Langdon's replacement. Willard, an ardent Whig and Patriot, addressed a group of army recruits from Massachusetts in 1781 as follows:

> The cause in which you have engaged is so good, so important and laudable, that it reflects honor upon any name to be enrolled in the list of American troops whose commander is the great, the virtuous and intrepid Washington.[55]

The president of Yale College, Ezra Stiles, was clearly just as strong a supporter of the American cause as his more vocal colleagues on other campuses, but he felt that it would be unseemly for him as a clergyman and an educator to play an active role in politics. Stiles assumed his position at Yale in 1778, and thereafter worked strenuously to safeguard the valuable books, papers, and scientific equipment of the College from British attack. But meanwhile he confided only to his diary the loathing he felt for British actions and the happiness he experienced at the news of American victories.[56]

The head of Philadelphia's college at this time was not troubled by scruples such as those besetting Stiles; instead, Dr. William Smith's big problem was that he made his political views entirely too well known to everyone. A bluff, hot-tempered man, Smith never was renowned for shyness or discretion. His greatest difficulty in that troubled Revolutionary time, however, was that his loyalties were perceived as being unmistakably divided. In the early years of the controversy with Britain, Smith, despite his status as an Anglican clergyman, was a loud supporter of the rights of the colonists to self-government. As the conflict escalated into an all-out civil war within the British Empire, however, Smith confronted a powerful dilemma. He loudly proclaimed that the Americans must defend their rights even by armed resistance, if necessary, but he could not bring himself to support outright secession from the "Mother Country." The

Provost's ambivalence on the hotly disputed question of American independence already became clear as early as 1775. In that year, he stated in public that "the din of arms . . . where Liberty dwells, would be preferable to the nightingale's song in vales of slavery." But on another occasion, Smith also advocated

> the maintenance of Religion as the true way of restoring our lost peace, preventing the further effusion of kindred-blood, and healing our country's wounds, upon a true plan of Constitutional Liberty, which can only stand upon that just subordination to the parent state, which is for the mutual interest of both parent and children.[57]

As 1776 wore on, it became obvious that Philadelphia College's Provost, like a number of the more conservative American Whigs of the time, was willing to battle for colonial rights, even by force if that regrettable alternative turned out to be unavoidable, but only from *within* the British Commonwealth. His views were made unmistakably clear when he published a series of letters (using the pseudonym "Cato") in the *Pennsylvania Gazette* during the months of March and April 1776. Smith's letters were purposely designed to contradict the major premises of Thomas Paine's eloquent pro-independence pamphlet *Common Sense*, which had just been published in Philadelphia.[58]

Smith had thus made himself extremely well-known, if not notorious, to all militant Whigs in town. Just before the British army occupied Philadelphia in 1777, the Patriot authorities placed the Provost under house arrest as a security risk. Later, he was released and permitted to return to his duties as head of the College. In 1779, however, as we shall see, Smith was legislated out of office by the new State government when a sweeping reorganization plan for the Philadelphia school was approved and promptly implemented.[59]

For two other presidents of American colleges the problem in 1775 and 1776 was not divided loyalties but loyalties that the majority viewed as "politically incorrect." The heads of King's College in New York City and William and Mary College in Virginia were uncompromising Tories; having bet on the losing side in a time of Whig revolution, it was inevitable that they would have to go.

The Rev. Myles Cooper, an English-born graduate of Oxford University and a "High-Church" Anglican and royalist, was the head of King's College during these troubled years. Since coming to King's, his supreme goal had been to make that college into a bastion of British royalism and Anglicanism in the New World. During the early 1770s, Cooper emerged as the leader of a small group of arch-Tory pamphleteers and satirists who regularly published their diatribes in the city's newspapers, defending

Parliament and the royal prerogatives as strongly as they ridiculed the alleged stupidities they acidly attributed to Whigs and Patriots. The latter, in turn, were infuriated by these attacks, charging that they were inspired by royal officials.[60]

After the fighting erupted at Lexington and Concord, the ideological and political struggle in New York reached a new and dangerous level. Extremists among the Patriots, known as the "Sons of Liberty," asserted that they had uncovered evidence suggesting that Cooper and four other prominent local Tories had secretly appealed to the London authorities to send British troops to New York City to suppress "disloyal" elements there. At this point an ominous public letter was sent to Cooper and his associates warning them: "The injuries you have done to your country do not admit of reparation. Fly for your lives, or anticipate your doom by becoming your own executioners."[61]

Cooper decided under the circumstances that it might be wise to seek safety by temporarily taking refuge on a British warship that was anchored in New York harbor. He wanted to get back to his duties at the College as quickly as possible, however, and after a while he made the mistaken assumption that things had calmed down sufficiently for him to do so. His miscalculation nearly cost him his life. About midnight on 10 May 1775, an angry mob of upwards of four hundred "Sons of Liberty" marched on King's College. Their openly announced goal was to kill the "arch-traitor," Myles Cooper. While the mob was breaking down the College's gates, a young graduate student rushed to President Cooper's bedroom to waken him and warn him of his peril. In the meantime, two young King's College undergraduates, Alexander Hamilton and Robert Troup, succeeded in delaying the attackers for a few minutes by giving impromptu speeches in front of the main college building. Hamilton and Troup praised Liberty and American rights but pleaded with the mob not to do anything rash that would discredit the noble Patriot cause. This tactic gave enough time for a half-dressed Cooper to flee for his life via the school's back door. When the members of the mob finally reached his room, bayonets at the ready, they found that their prey had escaped. Cooper reached a friend's house near the Hudson River that night and was able the following day once again to reach the sanctuary of the warship. This time he stayed on board and eventually sailed back to England.[62]

In sharp contrast to the combative Cooper, John Camm, a mild-mannered fellow Anglican clergyman who had become President of William and Mary College in Virginia, made no effort to intrude himself into local politics. Camm did not, like Cooper, carry on a propaganda campaign for the royal cause, nor did he seek in any way to politicize his institution. Despite this caution and discretion, Virginia's most active Whigs and

Patriots were not appeased by him. They had determined that they could not have someone with Camm's admitted Tory sympathies in such an influential position as the head of the colony's only institution of higher learning. To be sure, Camm's silence in 1775 enabled him to survive for a time while Patriot mobs were frightening two of his more outspoken Royalist colleagues into fleeing, posthaste, to England. But in the months that followed, even the gentle Camm could not avoid an ultimate showdown. When militant Whigs solidified their dominance on the College's governing board, they grew increasingly hostile to the largely powerless President.

One thing Camm now flatly refused to do. He would not obey a directive from the new board that he repudiate openly and publicly the authority of King George III's government. Camm maintained that the College's original charter prohibited him from making such a statement. The board thereupon voted in October 1777 to remove him from the Presidency for alleged "irregularities" and replaced him with James Madison, the enthusiastic young Patriot and Whig who was then serving as Professor of Natural Philosophy and Mathematics.[63]

Politicizing the Colleges: The Question of Loyalties

The Revolutionary conflict was both a civil war within the British colonies in North America and an anti-imperialist crusade by these very same colonies seeking national liberation. A political upheaval as fundamental and complex as that was bound to create agonizing problems of conflicting loyalties for many people. To deal with this problem, the Revolutionary authorities in many instances devised stringent measures to enforce pro-Patriot conformity and ferret out opponents of the new order.

The principal means of ensuring ideological purity was the loyalty oath. A number of the newly independent states resorted to such tests of allegiance, requiring all persons in responsible positions to subscribe to them. This type of legislative enactment usually applied to the professors and trustees of colleges, as well as to other key personnel in the society. In New Jersey, for example, a loyalty oath was approved by the new state legislature in September 1776 which specifically applied to the faculty and trustees of the College of New Jersey as well as to other persons. Long renowned as a hotbed of Whig activism, the Princeton college's teachers and officials gladly took the oath.[64]

The legislature in Pennsylvania passed a very similar loyalty oath bill in June 1777. All adult citizens of the now independent Commonwealth were required to subscribe to a statement by means of which they would expressly "renounce and refuse all allegiance to George III, his heirs, and successors." The Patriot leadership in Pennsylvania was particularly interested in seeing whether the Provost, faculty, and trustees of the College of Philadelphia would subscribe to the new enactment. Provost Smith and his governing board had long been suspected of lingering Tory sympathies. The Provost did subscribe to the oath, but he still was considered by many of the leading Whigs as their enemy. He was listed that summer, for example, as one of forty-one persons whose support of the new government of the State was most questionable.[65]

Members of teaching staffs at other American colleges were in like fashion asked to prove their allegiance to the Revolution. At Harvard College, for instance, the governing board was directed by the Massachusetts House of Representatives in October 1775 to appoint as instructors henceforth only persons "whose political principles they can confide in." Nor was this all. The Harvard Corporation was also told that it must now "inquire into the principles of such as are now in office, and dismiss those who by their past or present conduct appear to be unfriendly to the liberties and privileges of the Colonies." In order to satisfy this demand for ideological purity, the Harvard trustees appointed a committee of investigators, headed by James Otis. The committee got to work, but no faculty member was dismissed as a result of this state-ordered inquisition. The committee reported that it had summoned a number of faculty members to testify before it, but that all the declarations of political principles that had been made to it by the professorial witnesses were found to be eminently satisfactory.[66]

Restructuring

For Patriot activists, the next step logically after imposing loyalty oaths on academic institutions was to reorganize and restructure those found to be insufficiently Revolutionary. Militant political ideologues were sure that prewar centers of pro-British conservatism such as King's, Philadelphia, and William and Mary remained nests of Toryism after 1776. Sweeping plans were formulated to shake up such obdurate institutions and make them more conformable to the new power structure. It is particularly noteworthy that these plans anticipated the emergence, many decades later, of the state university movement in America. During the Revolutionary years, however, such ambitious schemes for public higher education ran into a number of insuperable obstacles. Effectively blocking their implementation were stubborn realities such as the general public's aversion to paying taxes for any purpose, no matter how worthy; the suspicions and jealousies of the various religious denominations; and the struggles for power of rival political parties and competing political leaders.

The most extensive restructuring plans for colleges surfaced in three former colonies-turned-independent-states, namely, New York, Pennsylvania, and Virginia. Let us examine the New York situation first.

There, in 1775, King's College suffered through very difficult times — its president having fled to England and its public commencement canceled. Most students dropped out at this point; and when British troops occupied New York City in 1776, the College was converted into an army hospital. After the war ended in 1783, a public debate ensued over the question: What should be done with King's College? The school had been chartered originally by the British Crown and had always received generous support from Anglican, pro-Royalist individuals. Radical Patriots demanded that, as a consequence, this Tory citadel par excellence be thoroughly reconstructed and made into a state institution serving all the people. At first their arguments carried the day. A bill was passed by the state legislature on 12 May 1784, "granting certain privileges to the college heretofore called King's College, for altering the name and charter thereof ..." The institution was to be reopened for instruction under a more fitting patriotic name — "Columbia." Legal title to the college and its properties was to be transferred to a newly established state education commission — "The Board of Regents of the University of the State of New York."

Proponents of the 1784 blueprint hoped that it would pave the way for the emergence of a secular, state-controlled institution of higher education in New York State. No such development took place, however. The alumni and friends of the old, pre-1776 Anglican college remained highly influential and were quite strategically placed in city and state government. Conservative political forces allied to them staged a surprising comeback in the later 1780s at the expense of the radicals. Taxpayers were alarmed when they were told that they might end up paying much higher levies than before to finance a grandiose state venture in higher education. Defenders of the status quo warned that the 1784 bill had made no improvement but instead had created a cumbersome, bureaucratic, and inefficient structure in the educational field. The upshot of this campaign was that the state legislature in 1787 passed a new bill which substantially reversed its action of three years before.

This 1787 measure transferred control of the little college in New York City back to the original King's College governing board. That board, it is true, had reorganized itself to some extent by dropping all members who remained unrepentant Tories, but it still was dominated by Anglicans (now known as Episcopalians). The new Columbia, in other words, was not going to be radically different from the old King's College. The keynote now was continuity, not academic revolution. This dominant theme was symbolized rather nicely by the choice for president put through in 1787 by the restored board. The appointee, William Samuel

Johnson, not purely by coincidence, happened to be the son of King's first president, the Reverend Samuel Johnson. A prominent Episcopal layman, William Samuel Johnson was deeply conservative. He had not originally been a supporter of American independence, but later played an active part in Connecticut's affairs and was one of that State's delegates to the Constitutional Convention in 1787. Under his cautious stewardship, Columbia continued to be, as in colonial times, a small, privately endowed, liberal arts college. Despite its strong ties to the Protestant Episcopal church, representatives from other religious denominations were elected to its board of trustees and young men from New York City's diverse groups were admitted to its classrooms.[67]

The effort to reconstruct colonial colleges resulted in a much more heated and long drawn-out controversy in Pennsylvania than was true in New York. Perhaps this happened because the affairs of the College of Philadelphia became deeply entangled in the rough-and-tumble struggles and infighting of Pennsylvania politics during the Revolutionary era.

The War for Independence brought radical leaders to power in Pennsylvania, men who were deeply suspicious of the Province's old-line aristocrats, believing them to be inflexibly pro-British and pro-Tory. Those radicals wished to construct a future Pennsylvania that would be populist and egalitarian, free of any taint of British influence. As in New York, the ultra-Whig Revolutionists were initially successful, carried along by the dynamic of the precedent-shattering events of 1776. In that year, as a matter of fact, they were able to secure enactment of a State Constitution for Pennsylvania that, without question, was one of the most radical, ultrademocratic state charters of its day.

In their zeal to root out conservatism and Toryism, the radicals (or "Constitutionalists," as they came to be called) viewed the College of Philadelphia with great suspicion. Provost Smith and his trustees, they knew, had been of doubtful loyalty to the cause of American Independence.[68]

The British withdrew from Philadelphia on 18 June 1778, and the refugee radicals and Constitutionalists returned to the city in a bitter mood, anxious to settle old scores. A list was quickly compiled of outright Tories and of those who had "collaborated" with the British during the military occupation. Those on the list found to be guilty of such crimes could be tried for "high treason" by local justices of the peace and their estates were to be confiscated by the public authorities. An extralegal "association" of more than 180 vigilantes was encouraged to aid the courts by ferreting out evidence against such "traitors" and finding witnesses who would be willing to testify against them.[69]

Against the backdrop of this local "Reign of Terror," the Pennsylvania legislature turned its attention to the affairs of the highly suspect College of Philadelphia. Provost Smith and his teaching staff had taken the required loyalty oath, and at this time—the fall of 1778—they were making strenuous efforts to reopen their college for instruction. The Constitutionalists, however, were meanwhile readying an all-out attack on the institution. Their first step was to induce the Assembly to launch a full-scale legislative investigation of the College. The investigating committee collected a large body of documentary materials pertaining to the founding, the history, and the current operations of the College of Philadelphia. When all of this was reviewed, the legislative investigators submitted a final report condemning the school as an enemy of "the common cause," whose trustees had repeatedly demonstrated "an evident hostility to the present Government and Constitution of the State."[70]

After further legal and parliamentary maneuvering, the Pennsylvania Assembly responded to the pressures that had been applied to it by voting overwhelmingly, on 27 November 1779, to reorganize the old College of Philadelphia and, in effect, to create a new and very different type of institution in its place. This reorganized school was to be known as "The University of the State of Pennsylvania" and it was to take control of all the assets and properties of the pre-existing College of Philadelphia. A new board of trustees was established to manage the affairs of the new university, a board that included among its members a number of public officials. To no one's surprise, these trustees were now all Patriots and firm Constitutionalists, including such eminent public figures in that camp as Joseph Reed, President of the State's Executive Council, and the scientist, David Rittenhouse. The new university was promised financial aid by means of an annual appropriation of monies from the public treasury. Inevitably, the services of Provost Smith were dispensed with, and he was replaced by a colleague, John Ewing, professor of natural philosophy at the old college and a prominent Presbyterian minister in Philadelphia. Rittenhouse was appointed Vice-Provost.

Supporters of the reorganization bill in the Assembly insisted that, in spite of the many changes that had been instituted, the Philadelphia college's 1755 charter had not been abrogated, but was simply being amended. The institution founded by Benjamin Franklin in colonial times, according to this theory, continued to function without substantial interruption, but had simply been brought into closer harmony with the democratic forces let loose by the Revolution.[71]

Joseph Reed, who became the president of the new university board, declared that the institution from its inception had been "founded on Principles of universal catholicism, embracing all Professions of the Christian Religion." With the recent changes, he pointed out, the school had gotten an interdenominational board of governors, an interdenominational faculty, and an interdenominational student body. Like Reed, the other Constitutionalist leaders of Pennsylvania endorsed the idea of state-supported higher education that would seek to diffuse science and learning to all people qualified to profit from it. In a very real sense, their program reflected the outlook of the eighteenth-century Enlightenment. They desired an educational system that would further, not hinder, their version of a grand republican experiment. The break with Britain, they believed, gave Pennsylvania a chance to realize the ideal of a commonwealth without an entrenched hereditary elite. Chartered corporations protected from public control—such as the Bank of North America, for example—were opposed to "the spirit and policy of democracy." Special privilege of all kinds, including that of the old chartered private College of Philadelphia, undermined equality and popular government. Even though independence had been achieved, such private monopolies helped maintain "an indirect, yet firm aristocracy over the state, before we be aware of the mischief."[72]

Inspired by lofty ideals of this kind, the University of the State of Pennsylvania held its first public commencement in 1780 on a date chosen for its symbolism, 4 July. Twenty-three graduates received bachelor's degrees. In addition, the university awarded eight honorary degrees, one of which was bestowed on Thomas Paine, hero of the radical Whigs and Constitutionalists. Provost Ewing appealed that day to the newly-fledged graduates to seek to be "all heart and all soul" in support of the glorious principles of the American Revolution."[73]

Even as Pennsylvania's grand school for republican virtue began its career, forces were working to undermine it. One unfavorable circumstance that quickly became apparent was financial: the university's expenses during the 1780s regularly exceeded the amount of money that the legislature was willing to appropriate for it from tax-raised public funds. Perhaps even more ominous, the balance of political power in the state began to shift in a way that boded no good for the school's future. Beginning in 1780, a coalition of conservative forces started a strong comeback. This political counterrevolution in Pennsylvania hoped to destroy the power of the Constitutionalists and, in so doing, revoke the radical state charter that they had introduced in 1776. It soon became clear that one of the major objectives of the conservatives (or "Republicans," as they were now called) was to do away with the University of the State of Pennsylvania, an institution that they regarded as the chief ideological base and training center of their Constitutionalist enemies. Disaffected Anglicans, Quakers, and Presbyterians, conservatives who had not wished a complete break with Britain, and all Pennsylvanians who distrusted what they viewed as the excessive "leveling" provisions of the 1776 constitution joined to build up the power of the new conservative party.[74]

The 1780 elections ended in a deadlock: the Conservatives won control of the Assembly but the Executive Council remained firmly in the grasp of the Constitutionalists. New elections in 1781 did not alter this standoff, which continued for a number of years. William Smith, tired of waiting for reinstatement, moved to Maryland, where he soon busied himself with the establishment of a new institution — Washington College. He continued, however, to bombard the Pennsylvania authorities with angry protests denouncing his removal from the leadership of the College of Philadelphia. Friends and sympathizers among the Republicans brought Smith's petitions to the attention of the Assembly in 1784, but no action was taken.[75]

Year after year conservatives in the Assembly brought forward bills to resurrect the College of Philadelphia and each time they were blocked, in one instance due to the absence of a legal quorum, which resulted from the withdrawal of a number of Constitutionalist members. The restoration project, nevertheless, remained high on the Republican party's agenda. The 1788 elections gave that party a larger, more secure majority in the Assembly. As a result, a bill was finally approved on 6 March 1789 restoring to the original College of Philadelphia all the properties and privileges it had secured under its pre-existing charters of 1753 and 1755. Dr. William Smith was jubilant when he heard the news; he immediately moved back from Maryland to celebrate his triumph and to resume his old position at the now restored College.[76]

The College's governing board began to function once again and elected ten new trustees — all wealthy and conservative Pennsylvanians — to participate in its proceedings. Once again, Dr. Benjamin Franklin was named to be the honorary president of the board and in deference to his advanced age, the trustees agreed to hold their meetings at his home.[77]

The old College had won complete vindication — or had it really done so? In actuality, the legislation of 1789 had done little more than create a difficult and anomalous situation. The old foundation had indeed been restored but the new state institution had not been abolished. Forced out of the building it had occupied for a number of years at Fourth and Arch Streets, the state school simply moved to Masonic Hall. Later it relocated in a new building on Fifth Street that had just been constructed for the American Philosophical Society. "Only dubiously capable of supporting a single college," Russell Weigley comments, "Philadelphia now had two rival colleges within a few blocks of each other."[78]

This awkward situation could not last for long. Financial realities forced both sides, despite their bitter quarrels in the past, to seek a solution at the conference table. There were simply not enough available students to keep both schools in business and there were not enough funds, public or private, to support full programs at the rival institutions. It was difficult to do, but a deal was finally hammered out. The two competing boards of trustees would be replaced by a new unified governing board of twenty-four members. The old boards would each be permitted to nominate twelve members to the new body. The faculties of the two colleges would be merged. The combined institution of higher education that was to emerge from these compromises would be known as "The University of Pennsylvania" (the phrase, "of the State of," which had so annoyed conservatives, was now quietly dropped). The settlement ended the cold war in Pennsylvania's realm of higher education but it was hardly welcomed by William Smith. Once again the controversial Provost was out of a job: the new board had chosen Dr. Ewing, head of the state university, to be the new Provost of the unified University of Pennsylvania.[79]

Compromise had become inevitable, of course. It meant, however, that the full potential of the original ambitious plan for a secular, publicly controlled institution would not be realized at that time. Despite its imposing title, the University of Pennsylvania remained for many years a small, traditional, privately controlled liberal-arts college "with strong Anglican overtones."[80] Franklin's pioneering plan of 1749 for a secular, utilitarian institution remained only a precedent for possible action at some future date while "the democratizing possibilities of state sponsorship," one commentator notes, "of initiating the American state university movement — were lost."[81]

During the Revolutionary years, politicizing currents engulfed Virginia's old chartered college in very much the same way that they had battered the colonial schools of higher education in Pennsylvania and New York. There was a significant difference, however. At least initially, it appeared that more educational change was being achieved in the Old Dominion than was the case in the other two states. The reasons for this difference were twofold. First of all, the people who sponsored the reorganization plans in Virginia had more political clout than their counterparts in New York and Pennsylvania and were seemingly more ingenious in implementing their program. Secondly, Virginia's reformers had Thomas Jefferson as their leader.

Even before the final break with England occurred, prominent Virginians were voicing their dissatisfaction with the fact that only a narrow and traditional classical curriculum was made available at William and Mary College to the young men of the Commonwealth. These critics called for a broader, more diverse course of study, making available history, modern literature, and natural sciences. They emphasized the pressing need for high-level professional training in law and medicine so that Virginians would not have to travel to distant locations to receive it. They demanded that the College's Grammar School for younger boys be detached from the main campus so that a more mature atmosphere for learning could predominate.[82]

The repeated appeals for reform before 1776 went unheeded by the William and Mary faculty and trustees. Most of the College's faculty was made up of English-born Anglican clergymen, graduates of Oxford, who insisted that the curriculum should adhere to the traditional lines of the program that they themselves had pursued. It should be rigidly classical, they believed, and all studies must be strictly prescribed. Modern literature and thought, and modern science as well, had no place in their concept of a proper college. As for specialized studies and professional training, these should be undertaken only after graduation from college.[83]

The result was an impasse in the pre-Revolutionary period that was exacerbated by a number of bitter disputes, both political and ecclesiastical, between the College and its entrenched group of English-born clergymen, on one hand, and the province's Legislature, representing the views of most native Virginians, on the other. The basic issue came down to the question: Who shall rule the College? When the Commonwealth declared its independence from England in 1776, the critics of William and Mary at last had an opportunity to achieve their goals. By 1777, most of the strongly loyalist faculty had fled, retired, or been dismissed. Tory members were expelled from the school's governing board. William and Mary was now firmly in the hands of the Patriot-Whigs. The revamped Board of Visitors was in a position to be able to reform and revitalize ("new-model") the demoralized, financially embarrassed college. As we have seen, the first step in the restructuring process was to make James Madison the new president of the school. Madison was so enthusiastic in his Patriotism that his sermons regularly pictured God's realm as a celestial republic, not divine monarchy! Such a man would be quite agreeable to having the new public authority, as embodied in the legislature of the self-governing Commonwealth of Virginia, assume the ultimate control over William and Mary.[84]

All of this might offer promise for the future, but what of the present? William and Mary College in 1777 and 1778 still desperately needed an immediate increase in financial support, as well as additions to its faculty and student body. Recognizing this, the Visitors asked the legislature to give more money to their school. At first, their requests were turned down. The auspices seemed to improve markedly, however, when Thomas Jefferson, a strong supporter of the College, became Governor of the State. Jefferson did not disappoint his reformer friends. During the year 1779 he proposed a remarkable series of legislative acts to the people of Virginia, acts that were designed to revamp the whole educational system of the Commonwealth from primary to graduate school. Universal elementary education was to be the foundation stone upon which the rest of the pedagogical edifice would rest. Upon it, in turn, would be a group of state-sponsored secondary schools giving scholarships to the brightest students of the State. These "high schools," or "academies," would prepare students for admission to a radically transformed William and Mary College. That old colonial institution would become a great state university; nonsectarian, publicly supported, and available to a number of poor but able students who would attend on state scholarships. The state university would also be useful to the community because of the great variety of new and specialized courses it offered, along with diverse pre- professional and professional programs.[85]

Jefferson's far-reaching proposals were brilliant, but, like the earlier appeals by the Visitors, they fell on deaf legislative ears. No state monies were appropriated to finance the ambitious proposals (Jefferson had even projected a so-called "State Library" to meet the needs of scholars, literary people, and scientists in what was to be essentially an institute of advanced study). The problem was that in those troubled times of war and revolution, Virginians were in no mood to pay greatly increased taxes to support grandiose educational and cultural programs. Furthermore, "Dissenters" (i.e., Presbyterians) in the State — no negligible group — were afraid that institutions such as Jefferson proposed might end up strengthening their Anglican rivals. These suspicions were not allayed by the fact that James Madison, Patriot and Revolutionary reformer though he be, had found it expedient to seek ordination as an Episcopal clergyman before he was permitted to assume his duties as President of William and Mary.[86]

What, then, was to be done? Jefferson and his friends handled the situation by turning to an ingenious strategy. As Governor, Jefferson had an ex-officio seat on the Board of Visitors. Using this position as his base of operations, he undertook to achieve what he had proposed, with the full support of his fellow Visitors, by manipulating and stretching to the utmost the powers already granted to the Board, under the old colonial charter. In this same year of 1779, the Visitors, under Jefferson's direction, issued a number of new decrees, revitalizing and restructuring the College while at the same time taking steps to cut down on expenses and save money.

The original charter had authorized the College to have seven professorships; the Visitors cut back that number to six by abolishing the chair of "Divinity" (i.e., theology). Jefferson had thus succeeded in killing two unwanted birds with one stone. He reduced expenses and at the same time realized his longstanding ambition to make his Alma Mater more of a purely secular school. The Visitors discovered that another chartered professorship they wished to abolish or transform, the Brafferton chair, could not so easily be done away with because it was financed by a separate endowment that Jefferson hoped to retain. The Brafferton grant had been intended to support missionary efforts to convert the

Amerindians. Jefferson and his colleagues wished to shift the major focus of the professorship from Christianizing the tribes to collecting and studying anthropological data about their traditional beliefs, folklore, and languages. The remaining five authorized professorships were totally rearranged to follow the curricular plans that Jefferson had specified in his legislative proposals. The five fields that were now assigned professors were as follows: (1) Law and Politics; (2) Medicine and Anatomy; (3) Natural Philosophy and Mathematics (i.e., the natural sciences); (4) Fine Arts, Moral Philosophy, and "the law of nature and nations"; and (5) Modern Languages. This comprehensive reorganization of the College's course offerings was supplemented by the decision of the Visitors, already mentioned, to get rid of the Grammar School (or secondary education division) at William and Mary.[87]

Jefferson and his colleagues had achieved a number of important objectives with their William and Mary reforms of 1779. They had introduced university-level instruction for the professions of law and medicine. They had introduced the systematic study of modern languages and literatures as an integral part of the American college curriculum. They had severed the close ties that had existed since colonial times between the College and the established Church of England. And they had moved to foster a more mature and scholarly atmosphere on the William and Mary campus by closing down the preparatory program for younger boys. Jefferson had gotten most of what he wanted, though not everything (his proposal to have additional professorial chairs in History and the Ancient Languages was not implemented).[88]

At the same time, the Visitors took action designed to relieve some of the economic difficulties besetting William and Mary. They hoped, first of all, to save money by reducing the number of professorships. Then, they believed, it would be possible to put a further cap on expenses by abolishing the College's "Commons" (i.e., campus dining hall). The Visitors hoped that this action would force the school to give a contract to a private operator who would be responsible for providing meals for the students. In turn, the students would then directly pay the contractor for their meals and the College would no longer be involved in this expensive operation. Another major economy move by the Visitors was their announcement that, in most cases, professors' salaries would no longer be paid from College funds. The professors would have to obtain their compensation by charging the students fixed tuition fees (one example might be a payment of a thousand pounds of tobacco per year from each student). Nor was this all. The Visitors also planned to save money by changing the student scholarship system. Scholarships were now to be put on a so-called "self-sustaining" basis, which meant that a scholarship student would receive money equal only to a five-percent return on the principal of the original grant, no more. And, finally, to ensure that their directives would be strictly followed by the College administration and staff, the Visitors mandated a major change in William and Mary's governmental structure. In colonial times, the College had been almost entirely self-governing; following the precedents of colleges at Oxford, all major internal decisions had been made by the group of Anglican priests who constituted its faculty. The Visitors now decreed that all future questions involving curriculum, appointments, or any other College matter would be decided only after due consultation between President and faculty on one side of the table and a standing committee of six Visitors on the other. Thus, ironically, a century of collegiate self-government at William and Mary had been ended, largely due to the fundamental changes that had been brought about in Virginia as the result of a democratic revolution.[89]

Not only did the American Revolution usher in more state control of Virginia's higher education (or, put another way, a larger role for representatives of the people); it let loose strong forces of nationalism and nativism. Patriots demanded that any new professors hired to replace the late unlamented teachers who had come over from England be native-born Americans, preferably, Virginians. And, indeed, this was the direction taken by the governing board. All the new members of the staff were native-born with one exception, Carlo Bellini. Bellini, who was hired to teach modern languages, was an Italian friend of Thomas Jefferson.[90]

Once in place, the new faculty introduced sweeping changes in William and Mary's internal procedures, changes that were in close accord with Jefferson's concept of the proper way to offer collegiate instruction. For the 1780s these were radical ideas, unprecedented in institutions of higher education either in America or England. One of the new provisions permitted students to be admitted to William and Mary without demonstrating proficiency of any kind in Greek or Latin. Another regulation abolished all residence requirements for earning a baccalaureate. In addition, it was announced that students would no longer be required to follow a single, prescribed curriculum while in college; they were free to enroll for whatever classes they desired or they could select a specialized professional field, such as law or medicine, and take the courses that were required to attain that particular degree. Furthermore, students would now attend as many or as few lectures as they desired, and do so in any order they chose. There were no longer to be examinations that must be passed for individual courses, but students desiring a college degree in a special field or profession would have to pass a rigorous general examination in the field before they could receive a degree in it.[91]

All in all, the restructuring of William and Mary College in 1779 and 1780 constituted the most far-reaching and innovative change that had ever been undertaken in any eighteenth-century American college or, for that matter, any institution of higher education in the entire English-speaking world of that day. Without question, Jefferson's new-modeled William and Mary deserved to be called The Revolutionary College.

Despite all that had been accomplished at Williamsburg during the Revolutionary years, Thomas Jefferson subsequently became more and more disenchanted with his creation. Eventually he became so disappointed with the way things were going at his Alma Mater that he led a successful campaign for the establishment of a completely new state institution, the University of Virginia.

What had soured Jefferson on William and Mary? For reasons beyond its control, the restructured College never attained the intellectual stature for which he had hoped. The Virginia legislature never gave the school the financial support it needed. The large number of state scholarships that Jefferson felt were vitally necessary were never provided. The under-girding network of elementary schools and Academies that he considered essential was never established. As a result, the pool of properly prepared students for which he hoped never materialized. Even some of the curricular reforms proved illusory. George Wythe's law department did high-quality work, but many of the other subdivisions existed only on paper. It may well be that the private tuition fee system of compensation for instruction undermined academic standards at the school.[92]

The inability of the Virginia reformers to realize quickly the full implications of their far-reaching plan does not diminish the historical significance of their work. They had established a precedent of tremendous importance in the history of higher education in America.

War's Heavy Hand

"May you never be alarmed," wrote President Manning of Rhode Island College to a friend in England (it was November 1776), "as we have been, with the horrid roar of Artillery, and the hostile Flames, destroying your Neighbours Habitations! ... You will not think it strange that the Colleges have suffered greatly, by this tremendous Convulsion."[93] Dr. Manning did not in truth paint the picture darker than it actually was. The Revolutionary War confronted the colleges of North America with the very real possibility of irreparable disruption and physical destruction.

Seven of the nine colleges in the colonies were occupied by military forces at one time or another as the fighting spread. Five had the misfortune of being seized first by one side and subsequently being taken over by the other. College buildings were prime targets for the marauding armies because they were often the largest and most solidly built structures in their communities. The British, French, or American military for this reason were very likely to covet such buildings for use as army barracks, military hospitals, headquarters for commanders and their aides, or even fortified strongholds. Students and professors, meanwhile, were dispossessed and scattered to the four winds. Books and items of scientific equipment were looted, damaged, and stolen, or, if practicable, hastily evacuated and hidden in the countryside. Sometimes battles engulfed the school itself, as happened most notably at Princeton. In retrospect, the nine colleges were probably fortunate just to have survived the war so that they could regroup and rebuild for another day.

When actual fighting commenced in the Spring of 1775, college schedules were inevitably affected, sometimes rather thoroughly disrupted. Students were allowed to leave in advance of the appointed time for summer vacation and public commencements were canceled. Four of the nine colleges made no effort to hold formal graduation exercises. This decision was made not only to satisfy student and alumni Patriots who demanded it as a gesture of protest, but also to avoid the possibility of violence should royal officials insist on attending the proceedings.[94]

The news of the outbreaks at Lexington and Concord created, as might be expected, much consternation and apprehension, but also much excitement on most campuses. Typical, perhaps, was the reaction of a Yale undergraduate who jotted down in his diary:

> Today tidings of the Battle of Lexington, which is the first engagement with the British troops, arrived in New Haven. This filled the country with alarm and rendered it impossible for us to pursue our studies to any profit.[95]

The following day, the Yale faculty decided that it would be best, under the circumstances, for the students to leave the College and return to their homes. This action was taken two weeks before the students were scheduled to begin their Spring vacation. The faculty also canceled commencement; it was not until 1781 that Yale was able to hold graduation exercises once again.[96]

Harvard also called off its 1775 commencement; its faculty was acutely aware of the fact that the Cambridge, Massachusetts, area had narrowly escaped being the scene of a major military confrontation. This became a possibility when Lord Percy in April 1775 led a force of British regulars across the Charles River to Cambridge from their base in Boston. Seeking hostile militiamen and hidden munitions in Lexington, Percy halted his detachment at the Cambridge Common and asked local residents to suggest which would be the best route to reach his objective. None of the Harvard College students he quizzed and none of the Cambridge householders on the scene seemed to know the way. At this point. a Tutor from the College, one Isaac Smith, well-known locally as a Tory sympathizer, stepped forward and gave the British commander the information he was seeking. Smith later explained that he had to do what he did because he "could not tell a lie" (subsequently he found it quite expedient to abandon his Harvard post and flee for his life to England). In the meantime, Percy's column did march on toward Lexington; along the way his troops joined up with the main British force that, after skirmishing with the colonial militiamen, was retreating to Boston from that town. As it happened, the British line of retreat bypassed the center of Cambridge. This was fortunate for Harvard College because, had it been otherwise, a bloody battle might very well have erupted in the College Yard. Massachusetts militiamen, prepared to fire on the hated Redcoats, had entrenched themselves in the various Harvard College buildings. No one can say with certainly what would have happened had the British come that way. The British never came, however, and there was no Battle of Harvard Yard.[97]

Harvard's wartime travails were far from over at this point. Its American defenders created a new set of problems. Washington's continental army, besieging the British in Boston, demanded that Harvard's buildings be made available to serve as barracks. The Massachusetts Committee of Public Safety agreed to satisfy this demand and told the authorities of the College that they must dismiss their students in advance of summer vacation and evacuate the premises. The Harvard Corporation did as it was told but was not quite ready to shut down completely. Plans were made to reassemble in the little town of Concord, and in October 1775 about half the usual college enrollment showed up there to begin a new term. They were, according to Samuel Morison, "boarded in taverns, which displeased the faculty, or in private houses, which delighted the Concord maidens; their favorite walk with student lovers, a secluded lane, is still called the College Road."[98]

The British evacuated Boston on 17 March 1776; by late June, Harvard was back in operation at its campus in Cambridge. The school's buildings were soon found to be "greatly defaced and Damaged." This apparently was a going-away present from the "friendly" troops who had been quartered there while they were defending the Province. Harvard billed the Commonwealth of Massachusetts 450 Pounds Sterling to compensate for this damage; it took two years for the College to collect the money.[99]

The College of Philadelphia was another American institution of higher learning that was obliged to watch helplessly as the importunate demands of war disrupted its work and ruined its facilities. During the Fall of 1775, American militiamen from neighboring Chester County marched onto the campus and took over the buildings to be used as billets. The militia did leave a few of the available rooms for use by the College, and Provost Smith and his staff tried to conduct classes in these limited quarters.[100]

As the war ground on, the burdens on the College of Philadelphia became ever more onerous. In December 1776 the trustees complained that with more than 150 militiamen billeted on them, anything like quiet study was becoming impossible. The following January, Provost Smith and his faculty felt constrained to register a formal complaint with the Council of Safety, the highest Revolutionary authority in Philadelphia. Smith charged that troops had repeatedly broken into College rooms; that the school's yard was crowded with horses and wagons; that "some violent Young Men calling themselves Deputies of the Barracks Masters" had forced open "Lecture Rooms, and even Bed Rooms"; that without any written authority and that "without a moment's previous Notice" the staff was ordered "to remove Books, Papers or Furniture" not "even allowing Time to send for the Keys"; and that "before we could well clear away the dirt and filth left by one set of Soldiers, ... another set has been forced upon us."[101] The Revolutionary leaders appear to have been profoundly unimpressed by the College's petition.

As the war ground on and on, problems multiplied for heads of colleges, for professors, and for trustees. One of the most serious of these was the question of enrollments. The college population from 1776 though 1782 inevitably shrank, as students, and some faculty members as well, abandoned the classroom for the battlefield. This trend certainly weakened the colleges, but it might have been much worse in its effects. There was no mass exodus from the campuses such as occurred at the colleges in the Confederacy during the Civil War. And the authorities never imposed a system of nationwide mass conscription such as the one that prevailed in America during its involvement in twentieth-century global wars. A saving grace for the colleges of the Revolutionary era was the very influential tradition, inherited from colonial times, that deemed it appropriate to give college men blanket exemptions from military service. This pattern apparently developed at a time when many college students were destined later to be clergymen and when many of their teachers already were ordained ministers.[102]

A study that was made of alumni records during the Revolutionary period came up with an estimate that despite the liberal provision for exemptions, at least twenty-five percent of America's college students and graduates were in some branch of military service during these years.[103] This is certainly an impressive total.

Some of the college volunteers underwent great privations. Some witnessed horrible carnage on fields of battle. A collegian from Queens College sent back to his friends a graphic account of what he had witnessed at Saratoga:

What Scenes! The Woods on fire, the mountains Belching Smoak and flames. The Roaring Artillery shaking the worlds Around us.[104]

In addition to declining enrollments, the colleges during the war years had to confront the challenge of plagues and epidemics from time to time. Epidemics of smallpox and typhus seem to have struck the campuses with greater force because of the disturbed wartime conditions. Both Yale and Harvard had to shut down temporarily during these years because of dangerous plagues. There were, furthermore, other emergencies confronting the colleges, which arose because the fighting disrupted vital supply lines. Examples of this type of problem would be the difficulty of obtaining adequate supplies of firewood to heat college buildings and the scarcity of food needed for the student dining halls. Then, too, the financial stringencies brought on by the war made it very difficult for college administrators to meet their obligations. Wartime currency inflation undermined the ability of governing boards to compensate their faculty adequately or to pay pressing bills. Textbooks, too, were in increasingly short supply. The Harvard faculty sought to cope with this problem in an innovative way. In 1778 it petitioned the State government for permission to sequester books from the confiscated libraries of Tories.[105]

The wartime travails of academe are graphically revealed when we review the difficulties experienced by the College of Rhode Island during these challenging times. In December 1776 an American militia force was hastily mobilized in Providence in order to confront a rumored attack on the city by a British naval expedition. President Manning reports what happened next. Since these militiamen were "unprovided with Barracks they marched into the College and dispossessed the Students, about 40 in number." For the next five years, Manning states, "... the course of Education in the College ... were in a great measure interrupted ..." It was not until the spring of 1780 that the soldiers finally evacuated the building. But seven weeks later, they were replaced by another military detachment. The Comte de Rochambeau's French naval expedition, coming to the aid of the Americans, demanded that the college structures be made available to it for use as a hospital for servicemen. This request was approved and again Rhode Island College was under military occupation. It wasn't until two years later — in May 1782 — that the French finally departed. President Manning gives us a graphic description of what they did when they were in residence at the College. They had added

A House of Office at the North End with a Vault 15 Feet deep under it ... from which Addition, the intolerable Stench renders all the northern Part uninhabitable.

Another Gallic "improvement," according to Manning, was "an Horse Stable built from the East Projection to ye North End by which the House is greatly weakened." In 1782, the President reported, "The

Corporation have ordered the augean Stable cleansed ... It is left in a most horrid, dirty, shattered Situation."[106]

Yale College was probably more fortunate than its neighboring institution in Rhode Island. Though its student body and its book collection were scattered again and again by wartime alarms, the New Haven school's buildings were never appropriated by the military. Nevertheless, Yale had a narrow escape from total disaster during this time. The British eventually launched a major attack on the port and city of New Haven and the buildings of Yale College could very easily have been burned and destroyed.

The Yale authorities had anticipated that something disastrous might happen and began during the Spring of 1777 to ship books and scientific apparatus to the countryside for safekeeping. At the same time, students were directed to leave New Haven and reassemble for classes in such nearby towns as Farmington, Glastonbury, and Wethersfield. British naval forces were known to be lurking offshore and might launch a hit-and-run raid at any time. The months went by, however, and no raid occurred. This emboldened the Yale faculty to allow the students to return to the New Haven campus during the latter part of 1778. That this was a mistake was made evident the following Summer. In early July 1779 the British fleet made a powerful attack on New Haven. Yale's president, Ezra Stiles, directed the students to flee for their lives. He also hastily packed up whatever important College papers and records he could take with him as he departed for a safe refuge.[107]

Watching the skirmishing from afar as the British landed in New Haven, Stiles saw flames shooting up and feared that Yale College's buildings must certainly have been destroyed. The President noted in his diary that the invaders had perpetrated a deliberate campaign of "Plunder, Rape, Murder, Bayoneting, Indelicacies toward the Sex, Insolence and Abuse and Insult toward the Inhabitants in general."[108]

The British eventually withdrew and returned to their ships. Stiles, full of foreboding, returned to his campus and discovered that the College had somehow escaped destruction. Edmund Fanning, a Yale graduate and zealous Tory, was a son-in-law of the commander of the British raiding force. Fanning had served as a colonel in the attack on New Haven. He later claimed that he had personally dissuaded the British commander from burning down the College or the city. Fanning's role may not have been as crucial as he made it out to be, but evidence exists that he and other persons on the expedition who were Tories and Yale alumni may indeed have succeeded in restraining indiscriminate looting by the invaders or wanton destruction of Yale's properties.[109]

There were a number of other American colleges that felt the sting of war and its aftermath during this troubled time. In the Middle Colonies, no less than four schools—King's College, Queens, the College of New Jersey, and the College of Philadelphia—were located squarely in the path of the contending armies, as the British concentrated their forces in the strategic New York-Philadelphia corridor and the Americans tried to repel them.

King's College tried to continue its work in the difficult period following President Cooper's enforced flight to England. This was not easy to do and finally, on 6 April 1776, New York's Committee of Safety told the College's faculty that they had just six days to clear out. American troops had decided they needed the King's College building. The school's acting president canceled commencement, sent the few remaining students away, and hastily moved the college library and scientific apparatus to New York's City Hall, presumably a safe place to store these vital possessions. The College itself was converted into a hospital for soldiers.[110]

In September 1776 Washington's forces were driven out of New York City and General William Howe's British detachments took possession of the town. Fortunately for King's College, there had been no fighting directly in the city, and as a result the school had escaped serious damage. One group of soldiers had left but very soon another military unit took over. The British decided that they, too, found it convenient to use the College as a military hospital and so they now appropriated the premises. The school's building continued to serve this function until the end of 1783. Unfortunately, during this same period the College's books and scientific equipment, which had supposedly been securely stored away for the duration, became casualties of war. Judge Thomas Jones, a local Tory who was unlikely to be publicizing information that would reflect unfavorably on the forces of the King, reported in disgust that unruly British soldiers had managed to break into City Hall expressly to loot. These Redcoats, apparently permitted to run wild by their superior officers, had seized books, pictures, and scientific instruments belonging to King's College. Judge Jones reported, furthermore, that "the books were publicly hawked about the town by private soldiers."[111]

Howe's army crossed the Hudson and moved into New Jersey in November 1776, pursuing Washington's fleeing Continentals. Queen's College and the College of New Jersey were now in imminent danger. Queen's generally had a bad time of it during the war, forced as it was to close down twice as approaching armies scattered both students and teaching staff. This was now the second time that the College had been obliged to suspend operations. A number of Queen's College students, angered by the threat of military occupation, announced at this point that they were volunteering for service in the Continental army. They would, they declared, assist in every possible way "their Countrymen to repel an Enemy endeavoring to establish a system of Tyranny and Oppression."[112]

Queen's neighboring institution, the College of New Jersey at Princeton, was also repeatedly disrupted by developments resulting from the war. A number of Princeton students left the school in early 1776 to serve in the American forces. Then, in late November, as the King's legions rolled southward through New Jersey, the College authorities feared for the safety of their institution. President Witherspoon hastily closed down the College, dismissed the few students who remained on campus, and quit the premises as quickly as he could. By December 7 the British had reached the little town of Princeton and placed Nassau Hall under military occupation, turning it into a combined barracks and stable. Inevitably, some books from the library were stolen or destroyed at this time, but the celebrated "Orrery" (David Rittenhouse's intricate mechanical model of the solar system) was placed under special guard as a result of orders by the British commander, Lord Cornwallis.[113]

On 3 January 1777 Washington launched a daring counterattack on the small British unit that had been left in Princeton as a garrison. During the fighting that ensued, the American forces found themselves obliged to shell Nassau Hall. Three cannon shots hit the building, one of which damaged the Prayer Hall and, ironically, passed through a portrait of King George II, which was hanging there at the time. The British garrison finally surrendered and the Battle of Princeton was over. The American triumph was short-lived, however. Cornwallis dispatched his powerful main force to Princeton and chased Washington's hit-and-run detachment out of the town. This time, though, the British general decided not to stay in the small New Jersey village. He much preferred New Brunswick for his main base in the Province. The enemy occupation of Princeton had lasted just one month.[114]

As the residents of Princeton went back to their homes and the students returned to their college, they were disheartened and angered by what they found. Benjamin Rush described the scene this way:

"Princeton is indeed a deserted village. You would think it had been desolated with the plague and an earthquake ... the college and church are heaps of ruins, all the inhabitants have been plundered."[115]

The Redcoats were gone, but the Continentals who replaced them were hardly an improvement. Thomas Wertenbaker describes these local Patriots as behaving "more like a swarm of vandals" than like the defenders of American liberty. These Revolutionary soldiers:

amused themselves by playing with the "Orrery" until the delicate machinery was so badly deranged that it could never be entirely repaired. They used benches and doors for firewood, ripped up the floors, punched holes in the partitions, ruined the organ.[116]

In March 1777 President Witherspoon took a leave from the Continental Congress so that he could return to Princeton and assess the situation. Once there, the President shipped whatever books remained to places in the surrounding countryside. He made a valiant effort to revive the school, issuing a public announcement inviting students to come to the College in July. Few showed up, however. In any case, all plans for getting the College started up again had to be shelved. It was learned that, beginning in October, Nassau Hall would be needed as a facility for sick soldiers.[117]

It was not until late in 1778 that the Hall became available for instruction again. The facility was so damaged at that point, though, that few lectures or recitations could go on. Repairs were made as soon as was practicable, and eventually students began to return. Only eighteen were enrolled in 1780, but by 1784, with the end of the war, the total had climbed to sixty-eight. Like Harvard, the College of New Jersey sought compensation from the government authorities for the many thousands of dollars worth of damage to its property that had occurred during the war. It took some time, but the United States Congress, perhaps cognizant of Dr. Witherspoon's manifold services to the American cause, did finally agree to pay restitution for what Princeton had suffered. When the government's payment arrived, however, it was found to be entirely in depreciated currency![118]

The College of Philadelphia's faculty and trustees had struggled valiantly in late 1776 and early 1777 to keep their school functioning in spite of the militia that was quartered there. Matters only got worse that spring as the local Revolutionary authorities began mobilizing resources to confront an anticipated British assault on the city. On 28 June 1777 the trustees finally gave up on their futile struggle and voted to shut down the College. Late the following September, General Howe's British troops marched into Philadelphia. The College's main building was now converted into a British army hospital. All that Provost Smith could do at this point was to address a petition to Howe, entreating him to order that the College's valuable scientific equipment, including a second Rittenhouse "Orrery," be protected from harm. This done, Smith took refuge on an estate located on an isolated island in the Schuykill River.[119]

In June of 1778 a new British commander, Sir Henry Clinton, decided to withdraw the King's forces from Philadelphia to what he felt was a more secure base in New York City. Washington's troops marched back into Philadelphia and soon thereafter Provost Smith returned to the College. In early 1779 the trustees were able to report that twenty-two undergraduates and forty medical students were in attendance at the school. By this time, however, as we have noted previously, the College of Philadelphia was becoming the centerpiece of a fierce power struggle between the two principal political forces in the city.[120]

Much farther South, another institution of higher education, the College of William and Mary, seemed to be in a more fortunate position than its fellow schools to the north. William and Mary was situated so far from the main theaters of war that it took for granted it should be able to carry on its normal activities without interruptions stemming from military operations. That happy state of affairs came to an abrupt end, however, during 1780 and 1781. The British high command decided at that time that it would be helpful for purposes of diversion to open up a Southern front. Royal forces accordingly moved south, raiding Richmond, moving on to Petersburg, and fortifying themselves in the Yorktown Peninsula. William and Mary College was now to experience a taste of war. Cornwallis's legions, on their way to Yorktown, camped near Williamsburg in June 1781. The College was not yet directly threatened but the faculty thought it best to close it down temporarily.[121]

British soldiers were all about the College's building, and there was some pilfering. President Madison, for example, discovered that his barometer and thermometer had now mysteriously disappeared. The real trouble for the College, however, occurred only after the royal forces had finally marched away. Washington's army—a coalition of French and American troops-arrived in Williamsburg in September 1781. The French soon made clear that they must have William and Mary's buildings to use as a hospital for their men. While they were taking over the College's facilities for this purpose, many more of the school's books and scientific instruments simply vanished. Then, on 19 October 1781, it was learned that Cornwallis's entire army had been forced to surrender at Yorktown. Taking this dramatic news as their cue, the William and Mary faculty politely asked the French to evacuate their campus as quickly as possible. But Washington, afraid of offending his French ally, temporized. The Comte de Rochambeau, commander of the French contingent, had apparently made it clear that his forces were not ready to go; they would have to remain in their quarters in Virginia at least through the winter of 1781–82.[122]

This decision proved troublesome for William and Mary College. On 23 November 1781 a large fire broke out in its premises, burning down a wing of one of its buildings. President Madison's remaining collection of books and scientific apparatus was irretrievably lost. Fortunately, the College's main edifice suffered no major damage. There was nothing to do now but wait for the French guests to depart. This finally happened in June 1782. William and Mary's professors returned to the campus a couple of months earlier to get ready for resumption of instruction and were clearly not sorry to see the visitors go.[123]

The American Revolution and the Colleges: An Evaluation

It was the ninth of July 1776. A special celebration was being held at the College of New Jersey. That night, Nassau Hall was "grandly illuminated, and INDEPENDENCY proclaimed under a triple volley of musketry, and there was universal acclamation for the prosperity of the UNITED STATES."[124]

How appropriate it was that America's independence be celebrated on the grounds of the little Presbyterian college in Princeton, New Jersey. Without question, that school had played an important part in helping to bring about the world-shaking event ever associated in subsequent days with the fourth of July 1776. The College's students had made known their commitment to American self-government with campus rallies, demonstrations, and effigy burnings, with boycotts of British imports, with symbolic wearing of American made homespun, with fiery commencement orations, and with brisk militia drills. Their activist president, Dr. John Witherspoon, backed up in most instances by his faculty and trustees, had been in the forefront of the Patriot movement in both the Province and throughout the thirteen colonies.

Britain's Coercive Acts in 1774 had shaken Dr. Witherspoon out of his carefully cultivated public posture of scholarly civility and clerical impartiality, making him henceforth an explicit and outspoken Patriot. During the tumultuous years that followed, the good Doctor with the strong Scottish burr emerged on the continental scene as a prominent Whig leader, United States Congressman, uncompromising advocate of a total break with Great Britain, and eager signer of the Declaration of Independence. No college president of his day did as much, and risked as much, to ensure success for the American Revolution.

Witherspoon's fervent Presbyterian and Scottish "Common Sense" philosophy seemed to undergird his militant Whiggish leanings. At Princeton he unabashedly used the course in "Moral Philosophy" that he taught to a generation of devoted students to make them antiroyalist and anti-Tory. In June 1775 he was already telling the people of Princeton that one must accept the possibility of "a lasting and bloody civil war." And he added that "it becomes those who have taken up arms, and profess a willingness to hazard their lives in the cause of liberty to be prepared for death" (later his own son was killed in the war).[125]

An enthusiastic supporter of Thomas Paine's pro-independence arguments in the powerful essay *Common Sense*, Witherspoon served on some one hundred and twenty committees during his years in the Continental Congress, including the Board of War and the commission that conducted the vital negotiations that gained France as an ally. Underlying all of his actions was the conviction that he articulated in May 1776 in a sermon that he delivered at Princeton:

There is a decisive proof of the impossibility of these great and growing states, being safe and happy when every part of their internal polity is dependent upon Great Britain. ... When the branches of the tree grow very large and weighty they fall off the trunk.[126]

Witherspoon's Princeton was obviously highly politicized but, as such, it was representative of American colleges, rather than unique. From Dartmouth in the far-off mountains of New Hampshire to William and Mary in Virginia's old colonial capital, collegians involved themselves more or less actively in the controversies and conflicts of the stirring eighteen-year period stretching from 1765 and the Stamp Act to 1783 and the final settlement with the Mother Country. On these campuses, Patriot-Whigs usually outnumbered Tories and loyalists. At most of them, too, professors, presidents, and trustees ultimately joined their students and college alumni in taking a stand for American rights. The young college people of the 1770s were hardly professional politicians, but they made a significant contribution to the Revolutionary movement through their demonstrations, boycotts, orations at public commencements, and local drill companies. Later a number of them made an even more direct impact through service in the Continental army.

Campus activism in the late twentieth century came to be associated in the minds of many people, justly or not, with violence. How violent were the college activists of the American Revolutionary period? It is obvious that their protests, while passionate and strong, were never as explosive as those of the Vietnam era, nor did their actions match, in their own century, the savagery of the "Reigns of Terror" that occurred during the French Revolution. As a matter of fact, the collective actions of student and faculty Whigs during the 1760s and 1770s never attained the level of violence displayed beyond college walls by "Sons of Liberty" zealots who destroyed Tory property and threatened Tory lives. This does not mean, however, that campus Patriots played an insignificant role in the Revolutionary movement. Of course, they cannot be said to have stirred up colonial resistance single-handedly. Their contributions, however, in preparing public opinion for defiance of British measures and, ultimately, independence, were crucial. These men of academe — students, instructors, college presidents, alumni, and trustees — amounted to much more as a group than merely a sounding board for community sentiment. Instead, they comprised an influential elite that led the way in formulating colonial demands and eventually in crafting proposals for a new political entity in North America. It is difficult to visualize an effective American Revolutionary campaign without this supremely important collegiate component.

Campus contributions to the American Revolution loom as all the more remarkable when we realize that many of them were spontaneous. Collegiate activism during those times was mostly local rather than national in scope and it never conformed to a coherent central plan or strategy. No national student or faculty political action group existed to direct and coordinate local campus demonstrations. There was no academic equivalent of the Continental Congress in Philadelphia. For that matter, the Tory minority on the campuses had no central association or unified strategy either.

One of the most important contributions to the Revolutionary cause from academe was ideological. The reigning ideology that swayed American Revolutionary leaders was a combination of the so-called "Commonwealth Whig" political philosophy of the seventeenth century and the "Natural Rights" concepts that came straight from the eighteenth-century Enlightenment. In turn, this ideology was propagated by lectures of professors in the colonial colleges, by the sermons and "Moral Philosophy" courses given by the presidents of those colleges, and by the assigned and extra-curricular reading that the students in these institutions were doing. In addition, the addresses that were delivered at meetings of college debating societies and at public commencements tended to reinforce the American Revolutionary ideology. The message was simple and direct: Governmental tyranny must be resisted; limited and representative government must be defended at all costs; liberty and virtue must be upheld by any and all means. This was both God's Will and man's Natural Right.[127]

Recently some have argued that the campus militants of the Revolutionary era were not radicals at all. This argument is based on mistaken assumptions. It maintains that college radicals during the American Revolution are misnamed because their movement did not include a generational protest and because it did not clash with authority figures on their individual campuses or in the colonial political establishment outside.[128] Such a definition of radicalism during the Revolutionary era is much too narrow. Why should the absence of internal turmoil within the Revolution's ranks detract from the significance of its commitment to change? Was campus participation in a major anticolonialist war diminished in its importance because the young freedom-fighters of the 1770s attacked the British Empire instead of their own parents or other local adult authority figures? It is incomprehensible that the contribution of the colleges to the American Revolution should be regarded as relatively minor because the committed student Patriots of the day did not mind fighting for their cause side by side with their professors and because they did not feel it was necessary to burn down their campus buildings or battle local townsmen or militiamen to prove their radical credentials. They seemed much more interested in fighting alongside such comrades-in-arms to liberate America from British domination.

The spirit of the young student activists of the Revolutionary decades is summed up much more helpfully by a contemporary observer. Andrew

Eliot, a Tutor at Harvard, expressed his admiration for what the young men of the colleges were trying to achieve:

> The young gentlemen are already taken up with politics. They have caught the spirit of the times ... Their Tutors are fearful of giving too great a check on a disposition, which may, hereafter, fill the country with patriots ...[129]

When all-out war erupted between Great Britain and her American colonies, the members of college communities paid dearly for their devotion to their country's liberties. War's heavy hand came down forcefully on most of them: buildings were taken over, campus facilities were damaged or destroyed, instruction was interrupted, colleges were emptied of students, and faculty went into the military services. In spite of all such discouragements and menaces, ambitious reformers formulated plans during the darkest days of the war with the aim of transforming and radically restructuring America's colleges when peace returned.

At last, in 1783 word came that a peace treaty had been concluded with Britain and that America had formally achieved its independence. As the news reached the several campuses, joyous celebrations were held at colleges from one end of the North American mainland to the other. What was the keynote of these victory celebrations? Perhaps Ezra Stiles, President of Yale College, put it into words as well as any leader of an American institution of higher education at that time. Asked by Connecticut's state assembly to deliver an "election sermon," Stiles responded with an oration entitled "The United States Elevated to Glory and Honor." His principal thesis was that America had been successful in defeating a powerful monarchy because of its superior virtue and because of the help of Divine Providence. Now she had an obligation to serve the world by providing an example of how a democratic republic could function successfully. This could be done only if she developed an educated citizenry. "The cultivation of literature," said Stiles,

> will greatly promote the public welfare ... there should always be found a sufficient number of men in the community at large of vast and profound erudition, ... to illuminate the public councils, as well as fill the learned professions with dignity and honor.[130]

Thus, at war's end, Ezra Stiles, equally with such Revolutionary leaders as Thomas Jefferson and Benjamin Rush, advanced the proposition that the ultimate triumph of America's experiment with independence and republicanism depended essentially on the education of its citizenry. Like Jefferson and Rush, the president of Yale was saying that the highest possible standards of training in schools, colleges, and universities were essential so that the new society could produce a "Natural Aristocracy" (in contrast to the old elite of birth and wealth) to lead it in a constructive and wise direction. Higher education would thus make the success of the American Revolution certain and secure.

2
The Civil War

American Colleges in the "Middle Period"

COLLEGE life in America from the 1780s to the 1850s was marred by intermittent riotous behavior. An undeclared war raged between students and faculty. Professor Benjamin Silliman of Yale found the cause of this sad state of affairs to be what he termed the country's predilection for excessive, unchecked democracy.[1]

Andrew Dickson White of Cornell added that the restrictive college government of the time helped foster campus unrest. Professors all too frequently were expected to act like policemen or spies, treating undergraduates as if they were dealing with mischievous schoolchildren. An additional factor, as Seymour Lipset notes, was the resistance of mid-nineteenth century students "to the efforts of the schools to impose a traditional, uncritical religious outlook on undergraduates receptive to the intellectual challenges to orthodox Protestantism."[2]

For fifty years, therefore, student activism in America turned inward. Rather than debating national political issues, collegiate rebels expended their energies fighting against compulsory chapel and unsatisfactory dining hall conditions. Frankly, some college presidents during these years preferred it that way. Francis Wayland, head of Brown University, for one, felt it to be his duty to shield students from becoming distracted from studies by outside political controversies.[3]

National political issues, under these circumstances, were debated, if at all, by college students in "literary societies," which were purely extra-curricular organizations. Such questions were not considered part of the curriculum nor were they used as topics for commencement orations. A classic illustration of the ostrichlike attitude of pre-1850 American colleges may be found in their reaction to the explosive questions of slavery and slaveholding. Powerful forces in American society opposed any public "agitation" of this touchy subject. During most of this period antislavery views were considered by large numbers of people to be extremist and subversive. Many college officials, influenced by this conservative outlook, were occasionally under pressure to suppress antislavery organizations or publications in order not to offend potential contributors.

During the 1830s, when the issue of abolition of slavery first began to surface, a small minority of student zealots, many of them at Middle-

Western evangelical colleges, began to take a public position on the question. The relatively small number of incidents that resulted from such efforts provoked the wrath of nervous college authorities. At Western Reserve College, a small group of students who dared to express antislavery views were summarily dismissed for "disruptive" activities. At Amherst, a student antislavery society was immediately shut down. At Marietta, militant antislavery undergraduates quit the school, complaining that the administration discouraged discussion of the issue. Some faculty members, too, were dismissed for expressing antislavery views. At Granville College in Ohio an instructor was fired for this reason. And at Harvard, Karl Follen, a faculty member active in the New England Anti-Slavery Society, was dropped from the staff. College presidents, like professors, were not immune from such treatment. The head of Miami University in Ohio was asked to leave by trustees who objected to his antislavery opinions.[4]

In general, college faculties in the more conservative Northeast, writes Arthur C. Cole, took a much dimmer view of public "agitation" of the slavery question than did their counterparts in the West. President Theodore Woolsey of Yale was one of the few prominent educational leaders in the East who risked public condemnation by openly denouncing the Fugitive-Slave Act and other proslavery laws. And in the Middle West, radical antislavery clergymen from New England were the ones founding colleges as part of a home-missionary crusade to "redeem" the region and rescue it from "unbelief, barbarism, and cruelty." Some of these schools were considered, by conservative Easterners, to be "hotbeds" of antislavery propaganda. The first real challenge to academic caution and timidity came in 1833, when the Oberlin Collegiate Institution first opened its doors. There is no question that, for that time, Oberlin College was absolutely "unprecedented in the ... English-speaking world."[5] Here was an institution of higher education that was both co-educational and completely unsegregated racially. To make it even more notorious, Oberlin's leadership favored a total and uncompromising abolitionism. Revivalistic Congregationalism prevailed at this unique school. Its leading spokesman, the evangelist Charles G. Finney, inspired a whole generation of students and faculty to do battle with slaveholders and slavery, as well as with the Devil.

Oberlin turned out to be immensely popular. The school's enrollment by 1850 soared to over twelve hundred, a new record at that time for college attendance.[6] A number of other newly-founded Middle-Western schools joined Oberlin in acquiring a reputation for uncompromising antislavery activism, noble in the view of some, treasonable and criminal as seen by others. One of the best-known was also a Congregationalist institution, Illinois College. Its president, Lyman Beecher, collaborated closely with Elijah P. Lovejoy, the militant abolitionist, who was later killed by an enraged mob in Alton, Illinois. Beecher's successor at Illinois College, Julian Sturtevant, although a strong advocate of freedom, sought to moderate the extreme stance that had come to be associated with the institution.

Conservatives in Southern Illinois, many of Southern origin, were not appeased, however. They charged that faculty members at the College continued to indoctrinate young minds with "pernicious" antislavery opinions and that, even worse, some Illinois College professors were involved in unlawful and "criminal" activities, to wit, sheltering runaway slaves and spiriting them North along the Underground Railroad. Charles Rammelkamp, who wrote a history of Illinois College, states that the antislavery attitudes of the school's professors impaired the growth of the institution during the midnineteenth century. "Indeed, there are those who assert," he writes, "that had it not been for the antislavery position of the College, it would have grown into one of the largest colleges in the state." Similar militancy was manifested by the faculty at another Illinois school, Knox College in Galesburg. Outraged pro-slavery advocates charged that President Jonathan Blanchard of Knox and his faculty had turned Galesburg into the most important "station" of the Underground Railroad in the state.[7]

The Colleges React as the Nation Drifts toward Civil War

By the 1850s, as the greatest national crisis since the Revolution confronted the American people, there was a marked increase in campus involvement in such heated issues as states rights and slavery. No longer could the nation's institutions of higher education turn a deaf ear to the furious debates about America's destiny that raged across the land. Following the Mexican war and the controversial Compromise Acts of 1850, what had previously been the concern of a few extremists began to challenge the major political forces of the country. Concepts of what was appropriate for discussion by college students would have to change.

The passage in 1854 of the Kansas-Nebraska Act, repealing the 1820 and 1850 compromises between the North and South, unleashed a storm of protest in Northern colleges. Condemnation of the measure was especially strong at the small denominational schools founded as a result of the New England home-mission movement. Such a place was Marietta College, where an anti-Nebraska protest meeting was held on 3 July, 1854. The assembled students passed a number of resolutions at that meeting that, in the words of a local newspaper, were "red-hot and anti-Nebraska." The students also voted that, "as a mark of utter detestation of the Bill and its upholders," they would "toll the chapel bell one and one-half hours." And, as if this were not enough, they further directed that the national flag on the school's main building be covered with black crepe. One of Marietta's resolutions asserted that "the national honor has been sullied, plighted faith broken, and the legislative hall disgraced ..."[8]

Marietta College by this time had become one of the most vociferous centers of "free-soil" sentiment in the Middle West, but anti-Nebraska meetings were held at many other schools. In Lewisburg, Pennsylvania, a gathering assembled on 21 February, 1854 to express the community's loathing for the Nebraska measure that opened up western territories to slaveholding. This rally attracted the active support of President Howard Malcom of Bucknell University and two of his senior professors. When protests proved ineffectual and the hotly-debated measure was enacted by Congress, a second meeting was assembled in Lewisburg to denounce the action. This rally, with three representatives from the University speaking, was held in the Bucknell chapel.[9]

A number of other colleges joined the anti-Nebraska campaign. Ohio University professors and trustees, for example, spoke at a protest rally held on 13 March. The speakers launched blistering attacks on Senator Stephen Douglas, chief sponsor of the bill. A second anti-Nebraska mass meeting was held in Athens in July and, once again, Ohio University participants made forthright speeches, excoriating Congress for passing such a measure. Led by the academics, the rally passed resolutions that slavery be prohibited in all United States Territories and that the Fugitive Slave Act be repealed immediately.[10]

The sectional crisis became even more menacing in 1856, complicated by the politics of an election year. Preston Brooks, a Congressman from South Carolina, savagely attacked antislavery Senator Charles Sumner in May of that year, almost killing him. An indignation meeting was held immediately at Amherst College, a school in Sumner's home state of Massachusetts. Faculty members joined students at the rally, castigating "Bully" Brooks as unfit to sit in the United States Congress. After the speeches, an effigy of the hated South Carolinian was solemnly burned.[11]

The presidential election later that year carried the polarization of public opinion still further by pitting the radical "free-soiler," John C. Fremont, as the Republican candidate against the cautious, pro-Southern Democrat, James Buchanan. Anti-slavery academics worked hard for Fremont's election. At Bucknell, Professor George Bliss distributed to the newspapers texts of two letters he had composed to aid Fremont's candidacy.[12] The president of Illinois College, Julian Sturtevant, was hardly nonpartisan. Sturtevant, a close friend of Abraham Lincoln, worked zealously all through the fall of 1856 for Fremont's local campaign organization.[13]

Like Illinois College, the other Middle Western schools bearing the imprint of the missionary abolitionists were outspoken in their condemnation of Southern slaveholders. The president of Wabash College in Indiana published an article in 1857 that denounced all those who attempted to defend slavery. "The Christian religion," he wrote, "does not authorize such power" as is concentrated in the hands of slaveholders.[14]

Antislavery zeal could, under certain circumstances, lead to infringements of academic freedom. Earlier, abolition-minded students had found that their opinions were suppressed by college authorities. Now, at some schools, the situation was reversed. William Springer, a junior at Illinois College, prepared an address in 1857 for a convocation of his class that questioned the value of militant agitation as a means of getting real reform accomplished. His supervisory professor, who was uncompromisingly abolitionist, would not approve the oration for delivery. The whole junior class thereupon appealed to the President of the College to allow the speech to be given, but the latter allowed the professor's ban to remain in effect. Springer's friends then showed up at the "Junior Exhibition" and distributed printed sheets to the audience summing up the arguments the student would have made if he had been allowed to speak. Infuriated by this challenge to faculty authority, the trustees voted to expel Springer. Many years later, long after the end of the Civil War, Springer was elected a member of the United States Congress. Illinois College then tried to make amends for the incident by giving him an honorary doctorate, the highest award it could offer.[15]

Some governing boards of Northern colleges were more tolerant of slaveholders than militantly pro-abolitionist Illinois College. In Maine, conservative trustees of Bowdoin College decided in 1858 to award an honorary LL.D. to Senator Jefferson Davis of Mississippi, later President of the Southern Confederacy. This action proved to be a serious embarrassment for the school during the postwar years, making it difficult to extract state aid from the legislature.[16]

Talk of possible war between North and South led students in the 1850s, as in Revolutionary times, to form campus military companies. Skeptics dismissed these developments as motivated solely by a desire to attract "the admiring glances of the young ladies." The reasons were more serious and compelling than mere martial display, however. One perceptive contemporary saw the phenomenon as an ominous offshoot of "the militant attitude of the sections on the slavery issue."[17]

Lew Wallace, later the famed author of *Ben Hur*, showed his artistic flair in his plans for the "Montgomery Guards" in Indiana. This militia unit sought to emulate the élan of the colorful French Zouaves of Crimean War fame. They wore colorful uniforms modeled on those of the Zouaves and attracted considerable attention as they marched and countermarched smartly through the streets of Crawfordsville. A number of students from Wabash College were members of Wallace's unit.[18]

Similar military preparations occurred in other parts of the state. In South Bend, upper classmen at Notre Dame formed a militia in 1858 called the Continental Cadets. "It may have been the presentiment of war to come," writes the historian of Notre Dame, "that stimulated this flurry of military activity."[19]

As the sectional disputes grew more bitter, reactions on college campuses reflected different gradations of pro-Southern or pro-Northern sentiment, depending on the geographical location of the schools and their ideological orientation. At one institution, however, circumstances led to a much more even division of opinion on the issues of the day than at most other places. This school was the College of New Jersey at Princeton.

During the first half of the nineteenth century, young Southerners had come to Princeton in great numbers; some estimates maintained that nearly half of the College's enrollment in those days was composed of students from slaveholding states. As late as 1860, Southern young men still comprised at least a third of the student body. Their presence may have given Princeton somewhat of a southern flavor and undoubtedly had an effect on the school's reaction to sectional issues.[20]

At times the Southern undergraduates were able to attract support from sympathetic Northern classmates. Such was the case in 1859 when the Southern contingent organized a demonstration protesting John Brown's raid on Harper's Ferry. Brown had failed in mid-October 1859 to set off the slave revolt he desired. Captured by Virginia forces, he was put on trial for treason. Although hailed as a Christlike martyr by Northern abolitionists, he was found guilty and hanged on 2 December, 1859. The following evening, Princeton students from the South staged a march up Nassau Street denouncing Brown and all abolitionists like him. Joined in this march by sympathetic Northern classmates, they carried signs proclaiming: "Down with Seward," "Down with Henry Ward Beecher," "Down with John Brown, horse thief, murderer, and martyr." The President of the College ordered the young men to return to their rooms immediately. These orders were not too efficacious, however. Later that night some of the pro-Southern students took to the streets again. They quickly attracted an unruly mob of spectators, which gathered in front of Nassau Hall and amused itself by setting fire to effigies of Seward and Beecher amid many "groanings and cheers."[21]

The Colleges Confront Secession and War

The national election of 1860 dramatically illustrated the degree to which American public life was being polarized by sectional conflict. The college campuses at this time reflected rather closely the divisions of opinion in the larger society. In the majority of the free states, campus opinion was overwhelmingly pro-Lincoln. In the slave states, it was almost impossible to find students or professors who endorsed Lincoln. Indeed, at many Southern schools voices were heard declaring that the slave states should withdraw from the Union if Lincoln and the "Black" Republicans won the contest.

There were many examples of pro-Lincoln sentiment at Northern colleges. At Bowdoin, an informal poll showed 135 students favoring the Republican candidate and only 35 supporting his Democratic opponent, Stephen Douglas.[22] At Harvard, 74 seniors listed themselves as Republicans, 23 as Constitutional Unionists (supporters of the moderate candidate, Senator Bell), and 9 as Democrats.[23] At Mount Holyoke, 246 young ladies were for Lincoln and 32 for Douglas.[24] Faculty members, too, were involved in electioneering for Lincoln on Northern campuses. At Bucknell, Professor George Bliss was busy "canvassing" for the Republican ticket.[25] At Ohio University, a number of faculty members were active in the "Central Lincoln Club."[26] At Oberlin, the campus newspaper grudgingly endorsed Lincoln as "certainly better than any Democratic candidate," but still considered him to be weak and evasive on the slavery issue.[27]

Collegians in the South were also deeply interested in the outcome of the election. Two student societies at the University of Virginia put themselves on record as recommending that the South secede if Lincoln should win. The faculty of the University was more cautious, however, endorsing secession only if it became absolutely necessary to preserve Southern liberties. Many students agreed with that proposition. An informal poll of the entire student body at Charlottesville revealed that the majority favored a moderate "wait-and-see" attitude.[28]

In colleges and universities of the lower South, campus opinion was more extreme than in Virginia. William Tecumseh Sherman, later the renowned Union general, assumed the presidency of Louisiana State University in 1860. He soon discovered that anti-Lincoln sentiment was becoming so rabid that most of the students were hot for immediate secession.[29] When Lincoln was elected president in November 1860 America moved into a dangerous "Lame Duck" period — the four months between the election of a new president and the departure of the defeated administration. During these critical months, several states of the lower South seceded, setting up their own Confederate government. Most colleges followed this disquieting sequence of events closely and nervously. The possibility of war and catastrophe became very real.

Yale students, although increasingly fearful that a brothers' war might occur, were not ready to accept disunion in order to avoid such a tragedy. When a few undergraduates from the South hoisted the white Palmetto flag of South Carolina onto a tower of Yale's Alumni Hall, other students promptly tore it down.[30] At Oberlin, a traditional center of abolitionist sentiment, students and faculty were not willing to purchase peace by accepting a compromise. Resolutions forwarded to Washington in February 1861 stated that Oberliners opposed any concessions to "traitors in arms against the Union."[31] And at Marietta college, literary societies debated topics such as: "South Carolina ought to be kicked out into the ocean," and "Should the Southern Confederacy be speedily reduced to a state of subjugation to the Union?"[32]

At some Northern schools, campus opinion was somewhat more cautious. At Indiana University, where border-state views were prominent, many students hoped for some last-minute compromise. A mass meeting on 2 February 1861 endorsed the Crittenden Compromise, then being debated in Congress, as a useful vehicle to appease the slave states. The climate of opinion at the Indiana campus, by the way, was quite similar to that of much of the southern Middle West. There was, to be sure, a determined minority at the University that was opposed to any deal with "the slave-holding power."[33]

At the University of Michigan, campus opinion at this time was just as bitterly divided as at Indiana. Conservative views predominated among the townsmen of Ann Arbor and people in the surrounding countryside. At the university itself, a considerable number of students shared this outlook. These undergraduates were doubtful that the country should risk provoking a civil war over the slavery issue.

The prevailing campus attitude at Michigan came to the surface during a disturbance that erupted in January 1861. Parker Pillsbury, a radical abolitionist from New England, came to Ann Arbor to speak at a local church on the controversial theme, "No Union with Slaveholders." Pillsbury was met at first with an avalanche of boos and jeers; then the audience became so violent that the speaker was obliged to flee for his life, jumping out of one of the windows in the rear of the church. The incident greatly mortified some University of Michigan people. They feared that reports of the disturbance would severely damage their school's reputation. To counteract such unfavorable publicity, it was decided that another prominent abolitionist should be invited to come to Ann Arbor and speak his mind freely on the slavery question. The speaker invited was the well-known antislavery crusader, Wendell Phillips. He agreed to come and deliver an address at an Ann Arbor church. To insure that this time there would be no disruption of the proceedings, a large force of "husky seniors" was recruited to guard the building. And a historian of the university notes: "When the last hoop skirt had gone, the church was still standing. The Class of 1861 had won its first victory of the war. Mr. Phillips had to run a gauntlet of sarcasm and threats from invisible students hiding in the shadows, but he was not molested."[34]

Not surprisingly, the rapidly worsening crisis accelerated the formation of drill units on the campuses. At Harvard a volunteer company was formed in 1860–61, with a French officer giving instruction in military maneuvers.[35] At Trinity College in Hartford, the Graham Guards, a campus military outfit, was organized about this time. The unit got its rifles from the Connecticut State Arsenal.[36]

On the eve of the attack on Fort Sumter, tensions in many areas of the country reached almost unbearable levels. In the border states, this period of waiting and worrying was particularly nerve-racking. Leaders of higher education in Maryland sought to keep as low a profile as possible. The president of the College of St. Joseph assured the public that three-quarters of the students at his small Episcopalian school were pro-Union. Nevertheless, he wanted to make sure that all "discords and distractions" would be kept out of the college. To do so, he imposed a ban on St. Joseph's students; they were not to make speeches or write articles about current political questions.[37] At the Maryland Agricultural College (later the University of Maryland), the situation was somewhat more difficult. The majority of the school's trustees were slave-owners who sympathized with the Confederacy. In addition, many of the students on campus came from slaveholding families. The institution's administrators sought nevertheless to follow an official policy of noninvolvement as best they could. Maryland's president implemented this policy by making a public announcement stating that: "In the lecture room and in the literary societies, as also in social intercourse, mere political issues and questions are practically ignored."[38]

No such scruples troubled students or professors at schools in the deep South. There, opinion was practically unanimous that the North was the aggressor and must be resisted; it was believed there was no alternative to secession from the Union. And when secession came, the colleges and universities quickly fell into line. Many of them responded as the University of Mississippi did, removing all United States flags from the premises. At Mississippi, too, the new militant mood led to the burning of books from the libraries of campus literary societies that were alleged to be pro-abolitionist.[39]

As the crisis deepened, Southern students followed the example of their Northern counterparts and formed campus military companies. The South had always had a large number of military academies. One of the most famous of these, Virginia Military Institute, had sent a number of its cadets to join other state militia forces in repelling John Brown's raid in 1859.[40]

Many other colleges in the slaveholding states prepared rapidly for a possible war. At the University of Georgia, the streets resounded with the marching feet of parading members of the college's militia—outfits such as the Athens Guards and the Troup Artillery.[41]

At the University of Virginia, members of the Sons of Liberty and the Southern Guard donned picturesque uniforms and practiced the manual of arms on the University Lawn. In February 1861, at a time when the State of Virginia had *not* yet officially seceded from the United States, someone hoisted the Confederate flag on the roof of the Rotunda, the renowned building designed by Thomas Jefferson.[42]

In Alabama, the Governor and legislature decided as early as September 1860 to convert their state university into a military academy.[43] Other universities in the South followed Alabama's example; anticipating imminent hostilities, they began to militarize themselves. In December of 1860 the University Greys prepared for action at the University of Mississippi, while a military company was formed in the same month at South Carolina College, which quickly enrolled a major portion of its student body.[44]

The belligerent spirit that manifested itself on Southern campuses in late 1860 and early 1861 was summed up by Merton Coulter as follows:

> ... the hated Yankees dwindled into pygmies too insignificant to be regarded at all, unless with contempt. Yankees knew nothing about guns; Southerners were born marksmen. ... Now the South would have its independence, and if the North wanted war the South would accept it. The University campus had never before known the intensity of excitement that now swept over it.[45]

One of the most wrenching developments at Northern colleges during these months was the mass exodus of Southern students from their campuses. Hundreds of young people were involved, the majority hoping to reach their homes in the slave states before the outbreak of war cut them off from a chance to return. Anxious parents demanded that their children come home. Patriotic Southern men felt that it was their duty to get back to their native states as quickly as possible to help defend them from invasion.

Sometimes the panicky exodus assumed almost mass proportions. In 1859, two hundred medical students from the South who were attending school in Philadelphia left for Richmond by special train, impelled to leave by news of the John Brown raid. Another highly publicized withdrawal was the departure of a number of cadets, all of Southern origin, from the United States Military Academy. These young men felt constrained to give up their hopes for careers as U.S. Army officers in order to make themselves available, if need be, for the defense of their native states.[46]

More usual, however, were quiet leave-takings of small groups of students—five, ten, even twenty—departing without fanfare and without ceremony. From Harvard, from Yale, from Ohio University, from Princeton, from dozens of other schools in the free states, little groups of Southern students left, most of them never to return.[47]

The poignancy of leave-taking was heightened when Northern classmates accompanied the departing Southerners to the railroad station. Sometimes the farewells were tearful. At Princeton, an account left by a student recalls:

> There was a closer grip of the arm as we sauntered to Jug Town or Rocky Hill, there were many sad scenes at the railroad station by the canal, as our Northern groups gave farewell — generally a hug — as the ... train creaked its fatal echo of goodbye.[48]

At Miami College in Ohio the separation was especially painful. Two groups of student volunteers left the College on the same morning, riding together to Hamilton on the same train. Then they had to part, one group going north to Camp Jackson for service in the Federal army, the other entraining for Cincinnati and their homes in the slave states.[49]

Not all departures were tearful, or even cordial. Some Southerners left in an angry, confrontational mood. This was certainly true in the case of a student named Bullock enrolled in the Medical School of the University of Pennsylvania. When news arrived of the outbreak of fighting at Fort Sumter, Bullock, who later served the Confederacy as a naval officer, confronted his startled classmates and announced in a loud voice: "I am going to leave for home at once to fight for my own state and to have it out with you fellows."[50]

Very different in spirit were the statements jotted down by departing Southern students in an album kept by a Northern classmate, Francis B. Sellers, '61, Dickinson College. Two of the most moving farewells were the following:

> If I wear the "Phi Kap" badge, don't shoot me, Frank. Yours Fraternally, H. Kennedy Weber, Baltimore.
> ... Though I am a secessionist, yet I am your friend. May prosperity attend you in all you do, except in making war upon the South. Yours Fraternally, Cyrus Gault, Jr., Baltimore, MD.[51]

After Sumter: The Colleges at War

When Southern troops attacked Fort Sumter on 12 April 1861, the time for debate by students and faculty was over. The outbreak of the long-dreaded war between North and South forced people on the campuses to transform words into actions, to take stands that many had hoped would never have to be taken.

Students, shaken by the sudden rush of events, found it difficult to keep up with their studies. A young man at Oberlin wrote to his brother:

It is in the midst of the most intense and alarming excitement that I address you these lines. WAR! and volunteers are the only topics of conversation or thought. The lessons today have been a mere form. I cannot study. I cannot sleep, I cannot work, and I don't know as I can write.[52]

At many Northern colleges, classes were immediately canceled when news arrived of the attack on Fort Sumter. At Princeton, however, President Maclean announced that classes would be held as usual. Many of the students simply ignored his dictum. Instead, a group of under-graduates from the North climbed up to the roof of Nassau Hall, pulled up the bell rope, and hoisted a United States flag over the famous building. Administrators tried to get them to come down, but they refused to do so. Fortified with a hamper of food, "beverages of questionable sort," and a few harmonicas, the young demonstrators remained on their high perch for a while. Meanwhile, the Southern students on the campus made a special point of showing up conspicuously for their scheduled classes. They soon found out, however, that this tactic was not working very effectively. At that point the Southerners changed their strategy and staged a raucous pro-Confederate rally on the College lawn. By the evening of April 14, a standoff between the two sides was eased and a possible riot was prevented by a "treaty of peace." The two bands of student demonstrators then headed for the Princeton Inn together to celebrate the settlement properly.[53]

At Colby College in Maine, military drill began the very afternoon that news of Fort Sumter reached the school. "Many students enlisted at the first opportunity," recalled a member of the Class of 1863. "My class ... which entered with fifty men, went down to only eight at graduation."[54] Farther west, the grim news had a similar effect at the College of Miami in Oxford, Ohio. That campus first learned about Fort Sumter on 13 April. By noon, anxious students were gathering in the college chapel for an emergency meeting. Ozro J. Dodds, editor of the school paper, pushed his way to the podium. "I do not know how you feel," he shouted to the milling throng of undergraduates, "but as for myself, I have determined to offer my services to the Governor of Ohio." Loud cheers filled the room, and soon Dodd was busy writing down name after name of would-be student volunteers. By the end of that day he had collected 160.[55] At Marietta College all classes, along with morning prayers, were canceled. According to the faculty minutes, the college had also "given leave of absence to a number of students ... to go as volunteers. It was voted to give permission to the students to form a military organization."[56] Oberlin, for its part, canceled a standing rule of the College that forbade students to participate in military organizations. Within a few days, over 150 students enrolled in a campus military company.[57]

In the South, similar decisions had to be made quickly by students. Was it proper, they wondered, to remain at college when they might be needed to defend their state, even possibly their own homes? J. R. Cole, a senior at Trinity College in North Carolina, faced this dilemma in mid-April. His military company, the Guilford Grays, had ordered him to report for duty immediately. Cole actually had no desire to leave college and he was not even sure that the war was necessary. He felt, however, that he "had enjoyed with it [the military company] the pleasures of peace and social companionship; and I must share the fate of the company, whatsoever it might be." John McKnight, a fellow student, stopped by his room. Cole asked his visitor, "What are you going to do, John?" McKnight's reply was: "Whatever you do." Cole then stated emphatically: "I am going." "Then I'll go too," said McKnight. Two hours later, Cole recalled, "we were on our way to our company, and the war."[58]

When Virginia voted to secede from the Union, the cadets at the University of Virginia were ordered immediately to leave for Harper's Ferry.[59] The cadet corps at South Carolina College had already been mobilized before 12 April. Wishing to participate in the imminent attack on Fort Sumter, the corps left Columbia without authorization but arrived in Charleston too late to accomplish its purpose.[60] At the University of Georgia, fourteen members of the Junior Class left for the army as soon as they learned of the outbreak of fighting.[61]

Student Enlistments

When war began, dire predictions were made that colleges would be forced to shut down, at least for the duration of the conflict. The Civil War was indeed a major disaster for higher education, but this was true mainly in the South. The situation was quite different in the North. On some campuses, to be sure, conditions were undeniably grim, but the overall situation was more favorable. Not only did higher education survive in the free states; by 1865 it had attained a stronger position than it ever had before. How are we to explain this turn of events? Perhaps three principal factors were involved. First of all, most colleges in the Northeast and Middle West were located at a considerable distance from the main war zones, while Southern schools, by contrast, were generally situated squarely in the midst of these dangerous areas. Secondly, Northern institutions were usually more successful than their Southern counterparts in readjusting courses of study and admissions policies to facilitate survival under difficult wartime conditions. On the whole, Northern schools were more flexible and experimental than were Southern ones. The introduction of coeducation in certain wartime Northern colleges is a case in point.

Finally, and perhaps this is the most important factor that was at work, Northern colleges were able to tap significant financial resources. The fratricidal conflict triggered a huge economic boom in the North, much of it in war industries. The Southern economy, on the other hand, was ruined by the war. In the North, increased funds were available to subsidize higher education. In the South, there was little or no money for colleges or universities.

From the very beginning, college officials tried to prevent a mass exodus of their students. They often drew a distinction between undergraduates who had not yet reached the age of eighteen and students who were older. Their argument was that the younger boys should stay in college and continue their education. This, for example, was the approach employed by President Pugh of Pennsylvania State in 1861. To this end, he was reported to have offered, "words of caution and advice" to his students.[62] In similar fashion, the Oberlin faculty stated its conviction that "those under age should not go without the consent of their parents and that the weak and sickly should be weeded out ..."[63] The trustees of the University of Rochester made a special point of praising "the judicious course of President Anderson in restraining the natural enthusiasm of the young men and persuading them to persevere in their college course."[64]

In the Middle West a number of faculties were anxious to "restrain youthful enthusiasm." The authorities of the University of Wisconsin were eager to persuade one E. G. Miller, leader of the University Guards, to remain in college, believing that his decision would have an important effect on other students. Miller made up his mind, however, to volunteer. "When they ask me fifty years hence," he said, "where I was during the rebellion, it won't sound just right to say 'grinding Latin and Greek at No. 11, North College.'"[65]

In the South, too, some college presidents tried at the outbreak of the war to cool youthful ardor. At Trinity College in North Carolina, President Braxton Craven appealed to students to try to at least complete their college studies before going into the army. One student recalled that Craven had beseeched him at length not to go, "telling me that all the plans I had ever formed would be overturned, and nothing would be as I wished, that the war would be no child's play, but a long and desperate struggle."

Sometimes it was the parents who took the initiative. At the University of Mississippi, for example, a group of anxious parents wrote to the faculty in April 1861 stating their desire that those of their children who were under eighteen years of age be dropped from the membership rolls of the institution's military company. They were afraid that otherwise these minors might be mustered into the Confederate armed services in the near future.[66]

In the North, when President Lincoln issued his appeal for seventy-five thousand volunteers on 15 April 1861, many college students responded. At Rutgers College, eleven undergraduates left school immediately. At Lafayette, a number of students took similar action.[67] At Amherst, sixty or more undergraduates, stirred to action by a fiery sermon, made a decision to leave for the army at once.[68] Many students at Bowdoin similarly opted to heed the President's call. Forty-eight seniors graduated from the Maine institution in 1861; of that total, twenty-two soon departed to fight in the war.[69]

Enrollment statistics at various Northern institutions made the picture rather clear. Princeton's registrations dropped in one year from 314 to 221. Union College's enrollment declined in the same year from 390 to 294. The student body at Rutgers had shrunk to just 64 enrollees by the year 1864. The University of Rochester's enrollment also declined markedly. Dickinson College's student body was reduced by one-half during the war years. And Lafayette, which had registered some 87 students in 1861, had only 19 remaining on its campus in July 1863.[70]

Harvard, the nation's oldest institution of higher learning, enrolled twenty-four hundred students in April 1861; of these, five hundred volunteered for service when the war broke out. By 1865, ninety-three Harvardians had died in the service.[71] Samuel Morison calls attention to an interesting fact: "Among the graduates and undergraduates who did join the Union forces, the fatalities were proportionately three times greater than those suffered by the Harvard contingent in the World War." He finds these grim statistics particularly remarkable because

Public opinion in the North did not require students to take up arms, as in the [first] World War; there was no mass movement into the army or navy, and draftees who hired a substitute were not despised ... No fear of being charged with cowardice, no public compulsion or worked-up propaganda, compelled these men to serve on either side.[72]

In the Middle West, the quick mobilization of volunteers led some communities to arrange for a ceremonial send-off for the student soldiers. Wallace Chessman describes one such leave-taking in that fateful spring of 1861. The ceremonies happened to take place at Oberlin in Ohio but they could just as well have been held at many another Middle-American town with a local college, and probably were:

Town and gown turned out en masse at the railroad station as the hour drew near. The recruits marched down and drew up in order, sober, tight-lipped, their new silk flag flapping smartly before. Professor Ellis addressed them briefly ... and they were commended to God in prayer led by Professor John Morgan, the pastor of the First Church. Then, to tears and waves and shouts of

farewell from the "immense crowd," the Oberlin company was off, some . . .
never to return, others only after a long period of service and imprisonment.[73]

Meanwhile, college enrollments in the area were dropping fast. Marietta's
student population decreased by 36 percent between 1861 and 1864.[74]
Indiana University "did little more than keep its doors open."[75] In
1863, Indiana enrolled its smallest number of students since 1840.[76] The
University of Wisconsin also experienced heavy losses.[77] Oberlin lost 147
students to enlistments during 1861 and 1862. The Oberlin school's catalog
for 1862 summed up the situation most succinctly: "War, for the time
being, is fearfully adverse to the prosperity of this college."[78]

At Wabash College, thirty undergraduates volunteered immediately
when Lincoln issued his April 1861 appeal, and many more joined up in
the months that followed. By 1864 the school's graduating class totaled
just three.[79] A similar rush to enlist occurred at Illinois College; before
the war was over, 240 of its students had left to defend the Union.[80].

Later in the war, students sometimes signed up for emergency service.
Thus in 1864 when Governor Brough of Ohio appealed for volunteers to
defend the state against a possible Confederate raid, half the students at
Muskingum College joined the emergency force.[81]

Grinnell, a small college in Iowa, was practically wiped out by the war.
Its 1865 catalog stated that, by that year, some eighty-one young men,
almost the entire masculine enrollment, had left for the army. A reminiscence from those times fills in the details:

> In 1861 there was a freshman class of twelve. But then the war came. Soon all
> but two were in the field. Other young men came, but their minds turned feebly
> to Latin and Greek, while their thoughts were following those who had enlisted
> in their country's cause. Sometimes the recitation room had no place for the
> lesson either for student or teacher . . . One after another was missing. Where
> gone? To the war. As . . . the call for men became more urgent, twenty-six
> enlisted at one time, their teacher at the head. The time came when all the
> male students of military age were bearing arms.[82]

Conscription and the Colleges

As the war dragged on, the colleges, already decimated by student volunteering, were threatened by a new challenge, the draft. When the glamour
of enlistment wore off and hope for a quick victory faded, volunteering
inevitably slackened. The need for soldiers remained greater than ever,
however, especially after Antietam, Fredericksburg, and Chancellorsville.
Both sides were consequently obliged to resort to the highly unpopular
expedient of conscription to replenish their armies.

The North moved in March 1863 to address this critical situation. Congress enacted a bill at that time instituting a national system of conscription. To be sure, this measure had a limited impact; it would go into effect only if local districts failed to fill their manpower quotas. The bill was nevertheless severely criticized as an unwelcome departure from the American tradition of defending the country by a force of citizen volunteers. By 1863 most of the idealistic, antislavery college men had enlisted in the war; those who remained on Northern campuses tended to resent the government's new policy bitterly.

The response to conscription at Yale College makes for an interesting case study. While by no means representative of all Northern campuses, it gives us a clue to the mood that had developed at many war-weary colleges. In New Haven, as elsewhere, there had been the usual enthusiasm for volunteering during the first two years of the conflict, but that eagerness and dedication had died down considerably. Campus opinion now saw no special dishonor in evading the draft by whatever means possible. In this respect, the response was remarkably similar to the one that developed among many college students a century later during the Vietnam war.

It is most instructive in this connection to peruse a list of potential draftees that was published by a New Haven newspaper in July 1863. The paper listed the draft status of all Yale students who had been selected for military service. Of the seventy-eight young people listed, only thirteen ultimately went into the army. The others were legally exempted from the draft for one reason or another. The New Haven newspaper explained how these Yale men were able to escape conscription. The excuses that were employed included the following: (1) nonresidents of New Haven; (2) age under twenty (the draft began with twenty-year olds); (3) disqualifying physical disabilities; (4) only sons who were the sole support of their parents. In addition to being members of these four exempt groups, Yale men could avoid the draft by hiring substitutes to serve in their place, a perfectly legal expedient. It was also legal to pay the government a fee of three hundred dollars in order to gain draft exemption.[83]

Some of the Yale students who avoided military service during the Civil War were destined in later years to attain national, even international, prominence. In this distinguished company were such graduates as William Graham Sumner, the noted sociologist; and J. W. Gibbs and O. C. Marsh, both eminent scientists. When Sumner graduated from Yale in 1863, he immediately left for Europe to do post-graduate work and did not return to his native land until the war was over.[84]

Yale was apparently not the only Northern college where students used a number of expedients to escape the draft. At Trinity College in Hartford, for example, many students were reported to have found legal technicalities quite useful to avoid military service. The College's historian notes that the use of such ploys produced no protests or outbursts of patriotic indignation on the Trinity campus.[85]

At this time, poor workingmen who could not afford to go to college were not able to use the available legal expedients to exempt themselves from conscription. Earning a dollar or so per day, as most of them did, they did not have the three hundred dollars necessary to buy exemption. Ultimately they responded to the draft with anger and violence. In July 1863 a series of bloody draft riots terrorized New York City, Philadelphia, and Boston. Federal troops had to be brought in to suppress the mammoth New York uprising. In New Haven, rumors swiftly spread that a similar outbreak was imminent. It is ironic that some of the same Yale students who did not wish to leave college to donate their services to the Union army were anxious to join a local militia that would have the mission, if necessary, of defending the city and the Yale campus. They had no scruples whatsoever about fighting marauding antidraft "Townies" who were, as one analyst puts it, "the laboring classes of Broad Street and Grand Street."[86] There definitely seemed to be elements of "town vs. gown" in the attitude of these Yale undergraduates, and perhaps some aspects of class war as well.

The problem remains, however: why were so many Yale students averse to serving in the Union army? The factor of personal security and career plans immediately comes to mind. Then, too, many of them may have been opposed politically to Lincoln's Republican administration and its antislavery policies. Ellsworth Eliot's study of Yale during the Civil War era presents another explanation. The Yale men were reluctant to serve in the Union army, he theorizes, because the conflict was a fratricidal conflict, not a foreign war. They wanted no part of a conflict in which brother killed brother and classmate was obliged to murder fellow classmate.[87] His explanation may sound plausible but, then, it is difficult to explain why students from the same institution reacted so differently during the American Revolution. That struggle, after all, was as much a civil war in the colonies as it was a colonial campaign for independence from the Mother Country.

An anonymous commentator in the *New York Times* in July 1864 advanced a somewhat different explanation to justify the reluctance of some college men in the North to fight in the war:

> There are those who think that it would be far better that these young men who are in college were fighting in the field, but more careful thinkers feel that never more than now do we need to have a body of young men thoroughly educated for the responsibilities of civil life ... Let us not then, while we honor the brave youth who are gaining the victories of war, depreciate those who are preparing for the victories of peace.[88]

In the Middle West, too, there was a deep aversion to conscription at many colleges. The situation was eased somewhat, however, by the fact that the draft was scarcely ever enforced at these schools in middle America. It was mainly used there as a weapon to boost volunteering. At Ohio University, for example, a frequently heard argument was: "It would be humiliating if, to fill its quota, the country had to resort to a draft." In this connection, in August 1863, a large poster was tacked up in Athens, Ohio, where the university was located, announcing to students and townspeople alike:

> LAST APPEAL and Best Opportunity to avoid the CONSCRIPT LAW and secure the Bounty, 2d OHIO REGIMENT HEAVY ARTILLERY—a most desirable branch of the service and stationed near home.[89]

A similar approach was employed at Muskingum College. The whole emphasis there, too, was on volunteering. The students were given to understand that the most honorable solution to the manpower problem would be for sufficient numbers of young men from the college and from the local community to enlist so that the draft would never go into operation.[90]

There was an undercurrent of violent opposition to the draft, however, in many rural areas of the state of Ohio. This was undoubtedly generated by widespread local disapproval of the Republican administration in Washington and of "Mr. Lincoln's War." People in the college towns of Southern Ohio heard reports of bands of Peace Democrats, popularly known as "Copperheads," meeting secretly in the surrounding countryside and plotting to disrupt the draft. At one time several companies of the Ohio militia were mobilized to guard against possible draft riots. The college campuses, however, were never active centers of opposition to the draft or to other wartime measures of the government in Washington.[91]

Colleges Battle for Survival

Faced with wartime shortages of students, colleges had to locate substitutes in order to survive. Where were such replacements to be found? A number of institutions hoped to obtain them by expanding their preparatory (secondary school) departments. These subdivisions were populated by youngsters under military age and if enlarged sufficiently, might compensate for the loss of enrollment.

Valparaiso University in Indiana, for one, pursued this survival strategy with a fair degree of success. Its Preparatory Division grew considerably during the war years.[92] In similar fashion, Bucknell University found now that its preparatory department was extremely useful. During the summer of 1863, at a time when the institution's liberal arts college and theology school were forced to close temporarily, the preparatory school continued to function with a large enrollment.[93]

Colleges resorted to other expedients as well in their effort to attract "substitute students." Even before the outbreak of civil war, colleges in the Western states were beginning to introduce coeducation in their classrooms, something that was still considered inconceivable in more tradition-minded Eastern schools. During the war years, these pioneering Western institutions were in an excellent position to increase female enrollments even more, thus compensating for the steadily decreasing male registration. Oberlin, a trail-blazer in the field of coeducation, expanded offerings for women considerably during the war. For the first time in the school's history, Oberlin's female contingent outnumbered its male counterpart.[94]

Other colleges in Ohio followed Oberlin's lead. One of them, Mount Union, subsequently reported that it was able to survive the war primarily because of its female enrollment.[95] Another Middle Western school, Grinnell, admitted its first group of coeds in 1861. This was done despite vociferous opposition from Grinnell's male students. The experiment was successful as a survival expedient, however. "It was the women students," writes John Nollen, "who kept the College going during the four years of the Civil War."[96]

Valparaiso University was known during the Civil War as Valparaiso Male and Female College. But as more and more women were admitted, the school "had by now become almost a women's college, perhaps because its coeducational policy made it suspect to men in a day when coeducation was still a novelty."[97] The University of Wisconsin, undiscouraged by such reactions, pursued a similar policy. Its trump card was its teacher-training program. Anticipating that this subdivision would now be in an excellent position to attract increased female enrollments, Wisconsin expanded its role in teacher preparation. There was, in any case, an urgent need for such a program; many of the state's male schoolteachers had left to join the army and replacements had to be found as soon as possible.[98]

Another important source of substitute students was provided by returning army veterans. A number of these who had been to college before the war wished to go back; others were interested in beginning their college training. The colleges, in turn, found that they could perform a patriotic service while at the same time adding badly needed students.

Middle Western schools were the leaders in providing courses for veterans. Indiana-Asbury College, for example, announced in August 1864: "All worthy returned soldiers who come well recommended will be admitted on free scholarships." Interested individuals were advised to apply for grants before the beginning of the fall semester.[99] Valparaiso University also granted scholarships to veterans for free tuition, but the grants were limited to those who had been wounded.[100]

A number of Ohio colleges took steps to attract veterans. Ohio Wesleyan registered so many of them in its Class of 1868 that it came to be known as "The Soldiers' Class." It became the norm now "to see a student who had lost an arm or a leg in the fighting." Ohio University, like Valparaiso, admitted wounded veterans without a tuition charge. Wabash College, going one step further, made arrangements for wounded veterans to take college work while still convalescing. A special fund was set up to help pay the living expenses of such persons while they attended college.[101]

The movement to provide a college education to veterans was substantially encouraged by pioneering state legislation that anticipated in some respects the "G. I. Bill of Rights" of World War II. In 1864 the legislature of Ohio passed a bill that required all state-supported schools, such as the College of Miami and Ohio University, to admit veterans free of charge. These discharged soldiers would have to be residents of the state to qualify. Furthermore, they were required to provide proof that they had entered the service as minors and subsequently had been honorably discharged. Those who qualified were eligible for free tuition for an amount of time that equalled the total military service they had performed by their twenty-first birthday. This act was later amended in 1866 to provide state compensation to all colleges and universities that were providing free tuition to student veterans.[102]

Enrollment shortages were not the only problems causing difficulties for administrators and trustees during the war. Fiscal emergencies also provoked serious concern. Such problems were interlocking: smaller registration meant decreased revenue from tuition fees: Wartime inflation, at the same time, meant that the schools had to pay more for supplies and services even though they had less money on hand to do so.

The situation was worst at small, marginal institutions that were operating "on a shoestring." Few of these smaller schools had a permanent endowment that yielded steady income. They had to depend on a shrinking tuition base as their debt burden increased.

Such circumstances inevitably produced discouragement, even panic. At Indiana-Asbury, so many students left the school that the president issued a public statement saying: "As the idea is abroad that we have suspended, allow me to say that this is incorrect."[103] At Illinois College, enrollment dropped to just forty-five in 1863, prompting the school's president, Julian Sturtevant, to muse: "College became rather a dull place to teachers that lectured to empty seats and to the few students who were hindered by various considerations from going to the war."[104] At

Antioch College, conditions became so discouraging in 1862 that the president, Rev. Thomas Hill, felt that he should resign; most of the members of his faculty did the same thing. The presidents of Denison University and Heidelberg College also resigned about this time, explaining that economic circumstances caused by the war made it impossible for them to support their families.[105]

In July 1862 Bucknell University reported that its debt had increased to $16,377, "all of which was bearing interest."[106] The University of Wisconsin's fiscal situation was somewhat better than this. Its Regents reported a deficit of only eighteen hundred dollars in 1865, adding the reassuring information that "they had on hand nearly enough wood to carry them through the ensuing winter."[107]

The rampant price inflation sweeping through the North seriously complicated the financial picture for many colleges. Soaring prices made it virtually impossible for faculty to support themselves on prewar salary scales. But to increase faculty pay to decent levels the hard-pressed schools would somehow have to find additional funds, a nearly impossible task.[108]

Most items in college budgets now steadily increased in cost. At Ohio Wesleyan, the price of such a mundane service as cutting the campus grass had tripled between 1861 and 1863. The cost of butter for the Ohio Wesleyan dining hall had gone up from ten cents a pound in 1862 to twenty cents in 1864; the price of a dozen eggs had more than doubled.[109]

Professors reacted in diverse ways to wartime inflation. At Bucknell, when the faculty petitioned the trustees for salary increases, their technique was rather shrewd. Pastors from local Presbyterian and Methodist churches were induced to appear at a board of trustees meeting to present an appeal "from the pastors and churches of Lewisburg to raise the salaries of the Professors." The trustees responded grudgingly; they were not especially happy at being pressured in this manner. Only very small pay increases were granted and these were limited to the lowest paid members of the staff. In addition, all faculty members got a hundred dollars cost-of-living payment.[110]

It wasn't easy, but faculty members won salary increases at a number of other campuses during these years. Indiana-Asbury College, for example, had stubbornly held the line on salaries for a long while, but finally yielded in 1865 and granted an increase in faculty pay.[111] Marietta was obliged to move in a similar direction in 1864. The school's trustees declared at that time: "In consequence of the greatly increased expense of living, and encouraged by the favoring Providence of God in largely increasing our funds over the past year ... [it is resolved] to add to the salaries of the President and Professors and the permanent Tutors fifteen per cent."[112]

Schools were forced to resort to various stratagems to survive the financial crunch. In one case, a college (Ohio University) dealt with financial stringency by not appointing a replacement for a professor who had gone into the service.[113] In another instance (Ohio Wesleyan) one of the Tutors was persuaded to return to his farm temporarily so that a faculty member could retain his position.[114] At Lafayette College, the situation deteriorated so badly by 1863 that the school's trustees were obliged to make an urgent appeal to their teaching staff, pleading for sacrifice so that the institution might survive. The professors were told that regular salaries could no longer be paid and they were asked to help keep the school "in operation during the coming year, at such compensation as the Board may be able to give."[115]

As the Civil War neared its end, faculty demands for increased pay and restoration of salary cuts grew more insistent. A number of schools were forced to take action on this matter. At Denison University, the trustees in 1864 reversed a 15 percent cut in faculty pay that had been made two years earlier. Similar action was taken at Otterbein College in 1864, whereupon several trustees resigned "in protest against the extravagance of the proceedings."[116] At the University of Wisconsin a novel procedure was followed in 1864: faculty salaries were cut across the board but each professor was granted a share of the student fees that were collected for his courses.[117]

Some colleges were able to reduce wartime deficits with contributions secured from special fund-raising campaigns. Such campaigns proved in some instances to be remarkably successful; the wartime economic boom made increased funds available. At the College of New Jersey, writes Thomas Wertenbaker, "the trustees saw that many persons were reaping rich profits from the war and were indulging in extravagant and lavish expenses." They concluded therefore that the hour had struck to launch a major fund-raising campaign. Their reasoning proved to be correct: by 1864 they had raised one hundred thousand dollars for Princeton.[118] Other colleges accumulated much-needed resources through very similar campaigns. During the final months of the war, both Bucknell and Denison were able to raise additional funds by making special emergency appeals. Each school obtained over one hundred thousand dollars to add to its endowment.[119]

The War Menaces Northern Campuses

At the outbreak of the war, some observers in the North feared that military operations might cause serious damage to college properties and disrupt academic routine. In actual fact, very little physical destruction occurred. Few schools in the Northeast and Middle West were as close to the battlefront as were their Southern counterparts. Nevertheless, there was always an outside chance that desperate Confederate raiders might break through Union lines and swoop down on an undefended campus.

That very threat seemed to materialize in the Fall of 1862, when Lee's army advanced Northward; potentially his troops might reach southern Pennsylvania, where they would menace a number of colleges. As news of Lee's invasion spread, some students left their campuses, volunteering for emergency militia duty. Twenty Dickinson College undergraduates and a dozen students from Lafayette were excused from their classes to join the defense effort.[120] As far North as Princeton, students were caught up in the excitement of the hour. An urgent proclamation was tacked up in front of the Princeton library, calling for volunteers to come to the defense of their country.[121] As it turned out, student help was not needed in this instance. The Union army stopped Lee's drive in Maryland, at Antietam Creek, and the college volunteers returned to their classes.

Farther west, there were also alarms at colleges, because, it was reported, General Kirby Smith's Confederates might make a diversionary advance north of the Ohio to take pressure off Lee. The Governor of Ohio issued an urgent appeal for militiamen and dozens of students responded. At Oberlin, the departure of the college's militia unit "left some classes without a single male student."[122] These "Squirrel Hunters," as the volunteers were called, converged on Cincinnati, where emergency fortifications were being hastily constructed. None of these martial preparations proved necessary, however, because the Confederate forces never crossed the Ohio River.[123]

A few days later, however, panic set in at Ohio University. Word arrived that a small Confederate raiding party had somehow managed to get across the river. A large group of students hastily gathered on the campus, "fire bells rang ... two companies were quickly formed ..."[124] This also proved to be a false alarm, however.

Much more serious was the potential threat to northern colleges that materialized in July 1863. General Lee, deciding to make one last desperate effort to break the military stalemate in the war, led his main army northward once again. Very soon the Southern troops were fanning out across much of southern and central Pennsylvania. There was a real danger at this point that the colleges along the invasion route might be damaged as major battles raged.

Governor Curtin of Pennsylvania appealed for sixty thousand volunteers. From colleges all across the state students and faculty answered his call. At Gettysburg College, half the student enrollment volunteered.[125]

Dickinson College in Carlisle, Pennsylvania, which was directly in the path of the Confederate advance, fell into the hands of Southern troops. After a brief battle, the Confederates were driven out of town but soon fought their way back, shelling the Union troops who were entrenched in Carlisle. One of the shells tore through the roof of Dickinson's South Building, hitting a beam, but did not explode. Another hit a recitation room in East College, destroying three windows. This projectile "tore out several cubic yards of stone work, wrecked the woodwork, recitation benches, desks, and tables . . . "[126] Eventually, the Confederates withdrew from the area, and Dickinson College, surveying the damage, tried to return to normal.

The two opposing armies groped for each other over the rolling Pennsylvania countryside; they found the confrontation they had been seeking at the little college town of Gettysburg. The fateful battle there began on 1 July 1863 and raged on for two more days. Incredibly, on 1 July classes were held as usual at Gettysburg College, beginning at the customary time, 8 A.M. Normal routine soon proved impossible to maintain, however. Union signal corps officers showed up to make a survey of the surrounding terrain. The sounds of battle grew louder and louder until finally the school's president, Dr. Baugher, was forced to give up. Baugher decided that he had better dismiss the class he was trying to teach, telling the students: "We will close and see what is going on, for you know nothing about the lesson anyhow." It wasn't long before students as well as professors were leaving spontaneously, fleeing to various places of refuge. When one undergraduate, perhaps in jest, told his classmate that they ought to get official permit slips before they left, the latter exclaimed: "Let the faculty go to grass and you come on!"[127]

Union troops were forced eventually to abandon Gettysburg town, retreating to strongholds on the ridges nearby. As they left, Confederate forces took possession of Gettysburg College. They immediately converted it into an emergency hospital to treat their wounded. As the battle raged on, the College was hit several times, but suffered no serious damage. Most of the professors had retreated to homes in town, hiding out in basements and storage rooms. President Baugher refused to leave his house on the college campus, however. The Baugher family took in eighteen wounded Union soldiers during the battle and kept a Union officer in a place of concealment. A faculty member, Professor Stoever, also cared for wounded Union soldiers and hid several officers in his cellar.[128]

By 3 July the battle had reached its climax. With the repulse of Pickett's charge, Lee had no alternative but to retreat to Virginia. Early in the morning of 4 July the Confederate occupiers withdrew from Gettysburg College. Union forces quickly moved in, taking over the

school's principal building and its emergency hospital. Michael Colner, a
senior, returned to the campus a couple of days later; he has left us a
description of what he found:

> On our arrival we found in and around the building . . . seven hundred wounded
> rebels. When I came to my room I saw it afforded ample accommodation for
> three — one on the bed and two on the floor . . . All rooms, halls, and hallways
> were occupied with the poor deluded sons of the South. The moans, prayers,
> and shrieks of the wounded and dying were heard everywhere. Only a heart
> dispossessed of all feeling of humanity could refuse sympathy and help in such a
> time as that . . . Students and citizens combined to act the part of the Good
> Samaritan. And from all to whom we ministered we received a hearty thanks
> and from many a "God bless you."[129]

Gettysburg College announced soon after the conclusion of the fighting
that classes were cancelled for the remainder of the summer. The faculty
also voted to award degrees to members of the Senior class without
further examination and without formal graduation exercises. This was
done, it was stated, "in consequence of the College edifice and all the
other public buildings being occupied with the wounded and the dying."
In September 1863 the College opened its fall term on schedule. Eventually
it collected $625 from the federal government to pay for the wartime
damage to its facilities. A special joint appeal with Gettysburg Seminary
subsequently netted an additional $4,000.[130]

Fear of future Confederate attacks lingered in southern Pennsylvania,
however. In July 1864 news arrived that General Jubal A. Early was
leading a hit-and-run Confederate raid into the state. Early's men did not
stay long enough to disrupt the work of any of Pennsylvania's colleges.
They did, however, burn down the town of Chambersburg and people on
some campuses were genuinely alarmed. Franklin and Marshall College
closed down for five weeks, and at Gettysburg College the student body
petitioned the faculty to suspend classes temporarily. Although this request
was turned down, the College did agree to allow students to return home
if their parents or guardians specifically requested it.[131]

West of the Appalachians, Union forces in July 1863 braced for possible
Confederate attacks. At Pittsburgh, students from the city's University
labored frantically with other volunteers to build emergency defense
works.[132] Farther west, John Morgan led a small force of Confederate
raiders into southern Ohio. Panic spread and college militiamen mobilized
once again on the campuses. Morgan escaped their pursuit, however, and
was only stopped when regular troopers surrounded him many miles to
the east. Meanwhile, there were disturbing alarms in some of the college
towns. At New Concord, Ohio, where Muskingum College was located, a
sentinel, "thinking he saw the Confederates approaching in the distance,

rang the college bell, sending the townspeople into near pandemonium. At noon a mounted and armed company rode north to Otsego in fruitless search of Morgan, who had already surrendered ... The citizens could now go about the retrieval of their hidden and buried valuables."[133]

Reactions to the "Brothers' War": The Northern Campuses

From 1861 to 1865 at least three principal reactions to the ongoing civil conflict surfaced on Northern campuses. They may be described, respectively, as pro-Unionist, anti-Administration, and uncommitted. The first group, perhaps the predominant one at most colleges, was firmly supportive of the war for the Union. The second, usually in the minority on the Northern campuses, blamed the war on Lincoln and the Republicans, felt it was unnecessary, distrusted antislavery policy, and favored a negotiated peace with the Confederacy. The third body of campus opinion, perhaps outnumbered only by the Unionists, was noncommittal and essentially indifferent. Either not personally concerned with the issues of the war or uncertain about the way in which it was being conducted, members of this group felt no urgent call to crusade actively for the Northern cause. These three divisions of college opinion mirrored rather closely the principal subdivisions in Northern public opinion.

Campus impact on public opinion during this period unquestionably played an important role in shaping attitudes towards the events of the day but probably no more so than the press, the churches, the politicians, and the reformers. The colleges do not seem to have been quite as dominant in influencing the resolution of the Civil War crisis as the activists of academe had been in helping to determine the outcome of the American Revolution.

College commencements during the war frequently served as display cases enabling campus Unionists to proclaim their allegiance. Thus at the commencement held by Rensselaer Polytechnic Institute in July 1862 the school's president asked his audience whether it could be possible "that the only result of the labors of Washington and his compeers should be a so-called 'Confederacy,' with human bondage as its cornerstone?" Answering his own question, he exclaimed that humanity was revolted at the idea. The trouble, he declared, was that a few men in the South had worked all this mischief; because "it was a land in which the few did the thinking for the many."[134]

Patriotic militancy was also the dominant note at Princeton's graduation exercises of 1862. Rev. T. L. Cuyler exhorted the young graduates "to give themselves in hearty self-sacrifice for their whole country." The attempt to overthrow the United States government, he said, was "a phantasm of absurdity." Princetonians must "stand by the starry ensign of the Union until its folds wrapped round them as their winding sheet."[135]

College alumni associations played an important role at many of these commencements in whipping up Union sentiment. During the summer of 1862 pro-Union resolutions drawn up by alumni organizations were read to the audiences at the graduation exercises of such schools as Williams College and the University of Vermont. These resolutions usually pledged support for the Union's war effort under any and all circumstances including, if necessary, conscription. College alumni stood ready, it was declared, to endorse any measures that might be required to crush "the slave-holders' great but causeless rebellion."[136]

On some campuses, pro-Union students proclaimed their views in innovative ways. At Amherst College a parade on 4 July 1862 observed "The Funeral of Jeff Davis" complete with an ancient hearse and the burial of the "corpse" in a grove of trees. A solemn salute was fired in honor of the deceased.[137]

At Bucknell, patriotic meetings were held on the campus to rally support for the war effort. "Impassioned appeals for support of the Union" were made again and again and there was much mass singing of patriotic songs.[138]

At Princeton the scene was similar:

> Faculty and students alike talked war outside the classroom, and the campus was not only "the daily arena of exciting political discussion," but the scene of occasional "somewhat exuberant demonstrations," joyous when victory attended the Union armies, sad when reverses were reported.[139]

The "Lit," Princeton's leading student publication, pulled out all stops when President Lincoln made public his Emancipation Proclamation. This document, the periodical declared, "gives to Abraham Lincoln an heirship of Immortality, placing his name side by side with that of Alexander II of Russia, on the brightest pages of history." The editors imagined that they were already hearing "the exultant shouts of victory ... Slavery, thank God, is doomed, whatever be the issues of the struggle in which we are engaged."[140]

In the Middle West, too, fervent Unionism could be found on a number of campuses. At Wabash College, it was reported, students "in their chapel exercises, talked about the war, and prayed about the war, day by day."[141] The students and professors at Muskingum College were similarly zealous in their support of Lincoln, but many of the rural Ohioans in the Muskingum Valley surrounding the college supported Clement Vallandigham, a bitter critic of the Lincoln Administration. Like the Ohio Democrat, the country people yearned for a compromise with the

Confederacy that would make possible an early end to the war. At Muskingum College, "uneasiness at Vallandigham's Copperhead program to take Ohio out of the war turned into wild alarm before the grim summer of 1863 had run its course."[142] To make its sentiments clear to all, the campus community organized a big pro-Union meeting, inviting former and present-day presidents of the school to deliver addresses. In his speech, the current Muskingum chief executive passionately defended the wisdom and constitutionality of Lincoln's controversial wartime measures, including military conscription. When he finished his address, the audience unanimously approved a resolution declaring that: "the destruction of the Southern Confederacy should be the desire of every Christian as well as every lover of freedom in the land."[143]

Other pro-Union Middle Western colleges felt threatened by pro-Confederate partisans alleged to be lurking in the hinterlands. Students at Wabash College received reports that a local Indiana contingent of the pro-Southern "Knights of the Golden Circle" was holding military drills just a few miles from their campus. The students promptly organized a militia unit and appealed to the state government for arms and equipment.[144] Similar fears troubled the strongly Unionist students at Illinois College; they were warned to stay on the alert for hostile moves by Confederate sympathizers in the immediate vicinity. A historian of Illinois College writes that: "Imagination filled the surrounding region with 'Knights of the Golden Circle,' and an organization was formed ... to protect the town (Jacksonville) from a possible rebel invasion."[145]

Pro-Union professors and administrators were just as active as their students in supporting the North's military effort. One of the most vocal of these was Dr. Francis Wayland, former president of Brown University, who contributed a pamphlet to the series of propagandistic tracts distributed to the public by the Loyal Publication Society. Wayland's pamphlet, which appeared in 1864, was entitled *No Failure for the North*. In it, he warned his fellow countrymen to "beware of men who urge peace." Wayland recommended all-out war instead:

> Use every weapon which the God of battles has placed in our hands. Put forth all the power of the nation. Encourage and promote all fighting generals; ... arm, equip, and discipline negroes, not to burn, plunder, and massacre, but to meet their and our enemies in fair and open fight ... Send to the Coventry of universal contempt every lagging and lukewarm official ... To hesitate is worse than folly; to delay is more than madness.[146]

It is clear, then, that solid support for the Union's war effort existed at many colleges and universities in the North. Despite this fact, little pockets of anti-Union sentiment could be found on certain campuses.

Some students and professors disliked specific actions and measures sponsored by the Lincoln Administration while more extreme dissenters sympathized with the grievances of the Southern Confederacy. A few of the latter wished to see the Southerners win their battle for independence. Such extremists, however, remained a tiny minority on Northern campuses.

A small group of Northern schools, justifiably or not, acquired the reputation of being friendly to "Copperheadism." One such college was Trinity, in Hartford, Connecticut.[147] Another was Princeton, where zealous Unionists felt that Dr. John Maclean, the school's president, never properly supported the North's war effort. It is evident that Maclean thoroughly disliked Lincoln's emancipation program, but nonetheless he was careful to walk a fine line, wherever possible, in dealing in public with issues relating to the war.[148]

Princeton had in the past enrolled a large group of students from the South, and even after 1861 there were still a considerable number of students at the school who sympathized with the South. Popular suspicions of Princeton's loyalty were fueled by reports of the activities of pro-Southern students. As late as the summer of 1864, these "rebel sympathizers" met to celebrate the return from exile of the celebrated "Copperhead," Clement Vallandigham. They built a bonfire around one of the cannons on the campus and gave many loud cheers for Vallandigham, Jefferson Davis, and the Southern Confederacy. The affronted Unionist students quickly built an even larger bonfire around "the same old cannon," hung up an effigy of Vallandigham, and cheered mightily for "Honest Old Abe, Our Next President" (the 1864 national election was soon to be held).[149]

Anti-administration sentiment could be found at New England colleges as well. Hostility to Lincoln and antiwar views were freely expressed on the campus of Bowdoin. The trustees of the Maine institution were predominantly anti-administration Democrats. A historical account of Bowdoin notes that they "had not clearly approved the war."[150]

In some Middle Western schools, opposition to Lincoln and the Unionist cause flared up occasionally. This was certainly the case at the University of Michigan. In April 1862, when the antislavery radical, Wendell Phillips, returned to Ann Arbor to make a speech in favor of immediate, un-compensated emancipation, seniors from the College armed with clubs had to post themselves once again around the church where he was speaking and this prevented a mob attack. And the following November, in 1863, a delegation of anti-Lincoln students from the University journeyed to Windsor, Ontario, to pay their respects to Clement Vallandigham.[151]

In Ohio, a student at Hiram College was permitted to deliver an anti-Lincoln oration. His speech on "Once Happy America," so angered Unionist students at the school that they started a near-riot outside the lecture hall. At Ohio Wesleyan, Unionist students collected money to publish resolutions in local newspapers asking President Lincoln to arrest all "enemies of the Republic." Pro-Democrats among the students responded by publishing resolutions of their own attacking military arrests and calling for an end to arbitrary imprisonment. At the College of Miami, pro-Lincoln students complained that some of their classmates were permitted to deliver "disloyal" speeches. In response, the College ruled that henceforth all public addresses by students had to be faculty approved before delivery. Thirty students protested against the new rule as an infringement of free speech, but it remained in effect. The pro-Union activists failed, however, in an attempt to have the president of the school, John W. Hall, fired. Hall marshalled support from the faculty, trustees, and alumni to keep his job. The Unionists, already suspicious of Hall because of his Southern origins, complained that he believed that states' rights were guaranteed by the U.S. Constitution.[152]

Although Hall survived the onslaught against him, Nathan Lord, the longtime president of Dartmouth College, did not. Lord, a theological ultraconservative, believed that slaveholding was justified, since it was mentioned in the Bible and not disapproved there. In 1863 the Merrimac County Conference of Congregational churches in New Hampshire passed a resolution asking Dartmouth to look into the matter. The Dartmouth governing board thereupon sent Lord a statement disapproving his views and asking him to moderate them. Lord, however, regarded the trustees's statement as an unwarranted attempt to censor his political and religious beliefs and declared that he had no alternative but to resign immediately. The Board, seemingly without excessive regrets, accepted his resignation.[153]

Supporters of the Union in academe were understandably disturbed by colleagues and students who sympathized with the other side. Even more obnoxious to them, however, was the much larger group that would not commit itself one way or the other. What factors produced noncommittal attitudes at the colleges? Undoubtedly, considerations of personal safety played a part; a disinclination to interrupt preparation for careers was probably influential as well. Prejudices of various kinds, including a partisan dislike of the incumbent Administration and its policies might also have dampened campus enthusiasm for the war. In addition, there were what might be termed philosophical difficulties bothering some students and professors. The current conflict was no ordinary war; it was a struggle in which Americans were obliged to kill fellow Americans. It was difficult for that reason for some people on the campuses to participate wholeheartedly in the conflict. It was difficult for students and alumni to visualize having to face former classmates on fields of battle.

There were, in addition, troubling considerations of campus security and order that had to be taken into account during these years. On some campuses, such as that of the University of Indiana, student sentiment was almost equally divided between partisans of the Union and the Confederacy. At such schools, the authorities had good reason to fear the outbreak of internal turmoil. To head off such disturbances, college administrators did their best to dampen expressions of views respecting current political developments. Their aim was to avoid divisiveness on the campus and to project an image of quiet studiousness to the general public.

Whatever the reasons, a "cool attitude" toward the war came to prevail at prominent Northern colleges such as Harvard and Yale. "College life went on much as usual," writes Samuel Morison, and there was "scarcely diminished attendance."

> Public opinion in the North did not require students to take up arms, ... and draftees who hired a substitute were not despised. President Lincoln kept his son at Harvard until he graduated in 1864, and then gave him a safe staff appointment. The Harvard-Yale boat race was rowed off Worcester, before a large and enthusiastic crowd, on July 29, 1864, at a time when the Union was desperately in need of men; not one of the twelve oarsmen enlisted.[154]

At Yale, the campus atmosphere was, if anything, even more "cool" than that at Harvard. Students with passionate Unionist loyalties had already volunteered for service early in the war. Among those who remained after 1862, writes Eliot, "the majority [were] either lukewarm or indifferent, remained merely spectators throughout the entire conflict." Alumni who had been at Yale during the early 1860s recalled the quietness of the scene: "No rallies were held at any time to encourage enlistment; neither did the President nor any member of the faculty, in any religious or college exercise, endeavor to promote enlistment for the defense of the Union." On top of this, the repeated defeats suffered by Union troops in Virginia resulted in deep discouragement among the students. Some of them "had lost relatives and intimate friends." Whenever possible, the young men sought to avoid discussion of the war among themselves. This proved difficult to do in 1864 when news arrived of terrible Northern losses during the Wilderness campaign. By this time, student patriotism at Yale had reached its lowest ebb. There was no longer "any reference made by the *Yale Literary Magazine* either to those who had joined the colors or, in fact, to any event of the war."[155]

A number of colleges found it expedient not to pay undue attention to the war or to encourage their students to do so. At Colby College in Maine, the school's historian noted that "one can read the records ... of the trustees from 1861 to 1865 without suspecting that the nation was at war." Colby's faculty minutes for the same period were similarly silent on the subject.[156] At the University of Vermont, the main subject of campus attention in 1862 was the annual football game between the Freshmen and Sophomores. Faculty concerns, at this time, seem to have been focused on a campaign to raise money to complete construction of a new university library and art gallery.[157]

Roman Catholic schools, apparently concerned with avoiding a reputation for controversy, did their best to cultivate an atmosphere of noninvolvement during the war years. Thus, the faculty of St. John's College in New York City (now Fordham University) was principally concerned, after the attack on Fort Sumter, with the difficult question of whether the school should play a baseball game against the Free Academy (now the City College of New York). And in July 1863, "the month of Vicksburg, Gettysburg, and the Draft Riots," the St. John's authorities were preoccupied with planning for "Father Rector's trip to Albany for the Regents' special meeting."[158]

Boston College also strove to be above the battle and to avoid trouble. Its faculty became concerned early in the war because some of the Seminarians studying at the institution were committed Unionists while others had strong prosecessionist opinions. What was to be done? One of the students from that period recalled that the Superiors "would kindly admonish us, in accordance with the rule, to avoid speaking of the war."[159]

Lafayette, a small liberal-arts college in Pennsylvania with a predominantly Protestant orientation, similarly found it expedient to remove its campus community from all current controversy. David Skillman, after reviewing the minutes of the faculty and trustees from 1861 to 1865, writes:

> One would conclude that the little college community was completely oblivious to the great struggle for existence in which the nation was engaged. They lived within their cloistered halls and went on with their consideration of the ancient languages and the abstractions of mathematics.

The faculty's purpose was clear. There were troublesome potential conflicts that might explode at Lafayette if the pro-Union and pro-Southern partisans at the college were permitted to flaunt their loyalties. The school was determined to short-circuit such possibly disruptive disputes before they could get started.[160]

The same type of situation existed at Indiana University, and the solution arrived at by the institution's administration was very similar. Opinion on the Indiana campus was divided fairly equally between pro-Northern and pro-Southern partisans. Anxious to avoid violent confrontations on the school's grounds, the Indiana faculty mandated a campus

policy of total noninvolvement. It purposely went about its business as if
the North-South war was not in fact raging a couple of hundred miles
away. Once again, faculty minutes made little or no reference to the
conflict. "Not even John Hunt Morgan's scare raid north of the Ohio in
July, 1863," writes Thomas Clark, "disturbed the monastic complacency
of the professors, or stirred students to unusual action. Staff and students
alike kept to their daily routine of reciting, misbehaving, cutting classes,
and being censured by the faculty court. Courthouse square brawling was
left to the unwashed masses."[161]

The War's Impact on the Colleges of the South

For most Southern colleges and universities, the Civil War was nothing
less than a catastrophe. The history of Southern higher education during
these years presents a grim picture of privation, dislocation, and disaster.
Schools felt the destructive impact of the conflict no matter where they
were located. It made no difference whether they were in the Deep
South, Upper South, or Border States; all were vulnerable and few
survived completely unscathed.

In Maryland, a key Border State, colleges were in peril because the
area had great strategic importance for the two contending armies. The
unsettled conditions forced institutions of learning to close down or move.
In Annapolis alone, three schools faced serious difficulties. Financial
problems and enrollment shortages caused St. Johns College and the
Female Collegiate Institute to suspend operations in 1861. In that same
year, the United States Naval Academy was ordered, for security reasons,
to leave Annapolis and move to Newport, Rhode Island.[162]

The war caused trouble for other Maryland institutions as well. When
rioting broke out in Baltimore in April 1861, anxious parents withdrew
their children from Mount Washington Female College. The College of
St. James, a small Episcopal school, was repeatedly harassed by the
incursions of armed detachments from the rival armies. It somehow
limped along until 1864, when it finally had to close its doors.[163]

The University of Maryland was able to survive the war in fairly good
shape. Certain of its subdivisions, however, fared better than others. In
the liberal-arts college, for example, enrollment dropped so precipitately
that the school had to be shut down for a while. By way of contrast, the
colleges of pharmacy, dental surgery, and medicine that were affiliated
with the University did fairly well during the war years. The college of
agriculture also managed to survive, attracting an adequate number of
students. According to rumor, however, it was compromised somewhat
when Jubal Early's Confederate raiders arrived on the scene one night in

1864.[164] Reportedly, the rustling of ballgowns and the strains of waltz music were then heard on the campus. Whether or not the "Great Confederate Ball" actually occurred, the Maryland state legislature was later to take the possibility seriously when appropriations for the University were discussed. In addition, Unionist members of the legislature were displeased by the blatant pro-Southern statements that had been made by some University of Maryland faculty members. This situation was most unfortunate for the University because it faced possible bankruptcy by the end of the war, with thousands of dollars of unpaid bills piled up. Its plight was not unique, however. Other Maryland schools — Mt. St. Mary's, St. James, Mount Washington, and St. Johns — also went heavily into debt as a result of the war.[165]

South of the Potomac, the auspices were hardly better for colleges and universities. The proud University of Virginia, Thomas Jefferson's cherished creation, saw its enrollment drop during the Civil War years from 645 to 65 or even less. The size of the teaching staff at the University suffered a comparable decline.[166] Another Virginia school, Randolph-Macon College, lost a major portion of its student body as a result of enlistments in the Confederate army.[167] The cadets of the Virginia Military Institute were too deeply involved in fighting to be able to study. Inevitably, the school became a prime target of the Union military. When General David Hunter's federal forces finally reached Lexington, Virginia in mid-June 1864, they had explicit orders to burn V.M.I. to the ground. These orders were carried out with thoroughness and dispatch; it was not until October 1865 that the Institute, using makeshift classrooms, was able to resume academic work.[168]

Similarly in other parts of the Upper South, colleges battled for survival in the face of severe wartime challenges. In North Carolina, Trinity College saw most of its students leave for the army. By June 1863, a report of its commencement exercises stated: "The Senior Class having been reduced by war, there was but one graduate."[169]

In Tennessee, the situation was no better. Tusculum College, located in a hotly disputed valley, closed down its collegiate department and tried to stay in business by running an elementary school. "There was no little bushwhacking and some guerrilla fighting," a history of the college notes. "Soldiers had camped on the campus and property had suffered from 'private depredations' of other irresponsible parties."[170] Another Tennessee school, Cumberland University, had the misfortune of being located squarely "in the path of the devastating armies." The noted political scientist, John W. Burgess, was one of the students then at Cumberland. He recalled later that "the School of Law had suspended operations, since most of the students in this school had already enlisted in the Confederate Army." The University's Collegiate Department tried to keep going for a while, but one Sunday evening in February, 1862, Burgess reports, the minister of the town's Presbyterian church was just about to conclude his sermon when,

> the clatter of horses' hoofs was heard outside. A moment afterward the rider appeared, spurred and booted, in the aisle of the church, and strode up to the pulpit. He handed the pastor a slip of paper and then retired. With ... trembling lips the pastor read the contents of the message to the waiting and expectant congregation. "Mill Springs is lost. Fort Donelson has fallen ..."

These events meant that the effort to keep Cumberland University going was hopeless. In the months that followed, writes Winsted Bone, "buildings, endowment, libraries, apparatus, and other equipment were all swept away."[171]

As if such difficulties were not enough, colleges in the wartime South had yet another obstacle to overcome. This obstacle, military conscription, was one created by their own government. Faced with a critical shortage of manpower, the Confederate Congress, on 16 April 1862, enacted a comprehensive draft law. This legislation was actually the first such measure in American history, preceding the federal conscription act by nearly one year. The Confederate measure specifically exempted college professors from being drafted but was a threat nevertheless to institutions of higher education because it authorized the conscription of the few remaining students aged eighteen or over.

From the very beginning, heads of Southern colleges sought to blunt the impact of the new legislation and, if possible, gain an exemption from it for their students. Even before the law had been formally approved, Braxton Craven, president of Trinity College, wrote an urgent letter to the governor of his state, protesting against the proposal. "Will students have to stand the draft?" Craven asked. "I hope not," he continued. "It is all that can be done to sustain our colleges at all, and I hope the few who will go to school will be allowed to remain. We have about twenty that would be subject to the draft ... I hope you will allow the students to be exempted, otherwise we shall inevitably be broken, which you do not desire. ..."[172] Governor Clark gave Craven little encouragement. Students would indeed be subject to conscription, he said. "I regret the necessity for any draft, but the necessity of the country, now, can respect neither individuals nor institutions."[173]

While the Trinity College president and his students, like most members of the general public, viewed the conscription system as humiliating and dishonorable, their distaste did not extend to other forms of military service. As already noted, volunteers for the army were highly respected, as were members of what might be termed home-front security units.

Apparently there were a number of opponents of secession in the area of North Carolina where Trinity College was located. A local security force made up of students and commanded by Craven himself was assembled; it was called the Trinity Guard. In 1861 this unit was given the mission of suppressing critics of secession. The college militiamen swept through three North Carolina counties, looking for "traitors." The Trinity Guard's activities call to mind the Yale College volunteers a couple of years later in New Haven. The Trinity College crusaders, however, besides hunting out dissenters, were at one point detailed to guard Union prisoners at Salisbury, North Carolina.[174]

A Trinity College senior, Fletcher Watson, explained in a letter to his father in May 1861 the reasons for the popularity of service in the Trinity Guard.

> This drilling takes away none of my attention from my books ... — it was understood that the company should not be called out unless at an actual invasion of this State by the enemy ... I am endeavoring to study as hard as ever and to make as close application as possible ... I shall certainly hold on and graduate if I can.[175]

Trinity was not the only Southern college to attempt to find loopholes in the much-resented draft law. In July 1862 there were only thirty-nine students left at the University of Georgia. The head of the school, fearing that conscription would take away even these, sent a personal appeal to the President of the Confederacy, Jefferson Davis. His letter implored Davis to allow college and university students under twenty-one to remain at their schools, subject to emergency callup if urgently needed. Davis politely refused this request, explaining that he had no power to alter the provisions of a law passed by Congress. The sequel was predictable: Georgia's student body shrank to a total of twenty in 1863, with only one senior remaining on campus. On 10 March 1863 the faculty of the University recorded in its minutes: "Thos. Grimes, having arrived at the age liable to Conscription, it was resolved to recommend him for a diploma, without examination."[176]

In February 1862 the Executive Council of South Carolina issued an edict that, in effect, forced South Carolina College to close down. The Council warned that beginning in March any shortages of military manpower would be made up by conscripting men between ages eighteen and forty-five. Daniel Hollis notes that for "the high-spirited youths" at South Carolina College "a considerable amount of odium was attached to conscription." As a result, all the remaining students at the College rushed to volunteer. The *Charleston Courier* was appalled by the apparent obtuseness and callousness of the Council. "The fatal order of the Council," it editorialized, "was generally communicated to the students at breakfast on the 8th of March. Before dinner the students had enrolled for military service, and the College was virtually broken up."[177] President Longstreet of South Carolina College issued a report detailing the difficulties he had confronted in trying to keep the school alive. With more than a trace of bitterness, he concluded his review by remarking: "It is not my purpose to arraign the wisdom or policy of the order which proved so disastrous to the college; but I will say that the faculty did all that circumstances would allow to preserve its numbers and continuity." He did concede, however, that "our State authorities only anticipated by a brief interval our Confederate Congress."[178]

Little could be accomplished by open defiance, but one Southern state university used a different tactic; it adopted an ingenious plan to soften the impact of national conscription on its students. This scheme was based on an elaboration of the college militia idea. At the University of Alabama, President Garland announced that his institution had become a pioneer version of an ROTC Corps. No longer a conventional university, the Alabama institution was now a high-level military academy. In addition to pursuing regular academic courses, its students would train to be military cadets. As such, they would supply future officers to the Confederate army. In the meantime, Garland assumed that these students would be immune from conscription by the Confederacy. There was "no necessity for hurrying off," he declared, "when by staying and availing themselves of their opportunities of improvement, they may finally go prepared to serve their country with much greater efficiency."[179]

The Governor of Alabama fully supported Garland's scheme, advising the educator in February 1863 that he was authorized to resist any attempt to interfere with the school's new program by Richmond conscription officials. In 1864, however, Garland learned that the Confederate government was finally formulating plans to draft his student cadets. He immediately wrote to the Governor again, warning him that if such a program were carried out, the Alabama cadet corps "would be dissolved and all study at the University made impossible." Once more, the Governor supported the University, sending an urgent request to the Confederate Secretary of War to cease at once all interference with the Alabama school's program. The upshot was that the government in Richmond decided to leave the University cadets alone.[180]

Garland visualized a dual role for his campus militia unit. First, it would be an officer-training corps. Second, it would be a home guard to defend against Unionist invasion and to suppress disorder fomented by anti-secessionists or slaves. The University of Alabama was located in Tuscaloosa; many of the residents of the surrounding area were known to have opposed the secession of the state. Garland and the Governor felt that such people might still bear watching; should Union troops reach the area, they might commit acts of sabotage against Southern forces.

There was an additional concern: the haunting fear of a massive slave rebellion that might be triggered by news of Union military victories. The University cadets could come to the rescue of local residents in the event of such a dire emergency. With this in mind, Garland informed the Governor:

> While the Cadets should not be needlessly exposed to destruction in an assault against superior numbers of the enemy, yet in the event of insurrectionary movement anywhere in the dense slave population of the middle counties, I shall not hesitate to fly as rapidly as possible to the defense of women and children.[181]

Government demands upon colleges and universities went beyond the conscription of students. Wartime necessities also obliged Confederate authorities to requisition college physical facilities for military use. In 1864 the Confederate army requisitioned buildings of the University of Georgia for use as a quartermaster depot and an ophthalmic hospital. The Confederates also quartered Union prisoners in one of the University buildings in Athens before they were shipped on to the notorious military prison at Andersonville.[182]

Other schools similarly were forced to turn their properties over to the military. After the battle of Shiloh in 1862, the University of Mississippi was told to make its buildings available for use as a hospital for Confederate wounded.[183] In mid-June of the same year, South Carolina College was ordered to make its campus available as an army medical center. For a time, the Confederate government paid rent for these facilities, but as it neared collapse late in 1864 the payments stopped. By the time Lee surrendered, the Confederacy owed the College ninety-nine thousand dollars in unpaid rent. This money was never recovered.[184]

Such unavoidable losses only compounded the financial difficulties that most Southern colleges experienced. These institutions did what they could to avoid total fiscal disaster. Trinity College, for example, sought to retain teachers by prorating salaries on the basis of fees received from students. A Trinity spokesman reported in 1864: "The country was drained of its surplus to feed the soldiers, and Confederate money had so depreciated in value that it had almost lost its power of purchase." Under these circumstances, students had to resort to ingenious methods of paying for board. One Trinity undergraduate, a wounded veteran, paid for "two and a half months board with seven bushels of wheat and two hundred and fifty pounds of salt."[185]

At Cumberland University, the entire endowment of the school of theology was swept away by the war.[186] The University of Georgia sought to survive by cutting professors' salaries 20 percent and by leaving faculty vacancies unfilled.[187] Schools such as Wake Forest, Emory, Oglethorpe, and the University of North Carolina had invested funds in questionable assets — Confederate bonds, securities of individual Southern states, or Southern railway stocks; now most of their endowments became worthless. Out of desperation, institutions began to accept shaky securities or even farm products as payment for tuition. In 1863 Huntsville Female College announced that it would accept donations of cotton, wheat, and bacon as tuition payments. Jefferson College in Mississippi followed a different tack: It gave parents the option of signing promissory notes to pay for the education of their children. These notes would not come due until six months after the war ended.[188]

Despite such heroic efforts, one Southern college after another was forced to close its doors. The University of Georgia, for example, eventually found that it could no longer operate under the conditions that prevailed. In February 1864 its faculty members were given an indefinite leave of absence and the institution closed. The professors had one advantage over other Georgians, however; they were permitted to live in University quarters rent-free.[189] Other schools in the state, such as Oglethorpe and Emory, were forced by similar financial difficulties to suspend operations.[190] In North Carolina, the same wartime financial crunch forced Wake Forest College to shut its doors. The school lost over $56,000 it had invested in state and Confederate securities.[191]

Leaders of Southern higher education resorted to a variety of expedients to try to keep their colleges alive. They were limited somewhat in what they could do, however, by the highly conservative outlook that prevailed in their region. This situation made it difficult to introduce such innovations as coeducation or technical and engineering courses that might have helped some colleges to survive. Most Southerners still preferred to have young women educated in separate women's colleges or "female academies." And many of them still did not consider advanced training in agriculture or engineering appropriate for a traditional college. Such technical education, meanwhile, had been given the full support of the Northern Congress by the Morrill Act of 1862. However, Chancellor Lipscomb of the University of Georgia did not share these local prejudices. He proposed early in the war that a school of engineering be set up at his institution. Nonetheless, the university's board of trustees refused to take the action he recommended.[192]

One enrollment-boosting tactic employed by Southern colleges during the war was to expand their preparatory divisions. As a matter of fact, some small institutions below the Mason-Dixon line that had called themselves "colleges" and "universities" before 1861 were little more than glorified high schools. Therefore, when the Oxford Female College or the East Tennessee Female Institute expanded preparatory departments during the difficult wartime years, it hardly represented a major change.[193] More noteworthy, however, was the fact that larger and better-known schools such as the University of Alabama, the University of Georgia, and South Carolina College were taking similar action. Alabama in 1861 established a special department for boys twelve years of age or older.[194] Georgia in 1863 suspended a regulation that barred boys under fourteen from entering the University and set up a University High School.[195] And the South Carolina College faculty in 1862 also voted to admit younger students.[196]

In addition, Southern colleges, like their Middle Western counterparts, found returning veterans to be a promising source of replacement students. Some schools offered to admit veterans, particularly wounded veterans, free of charge. Mercer College adopted this policy and its president announced that "provision is also made to aid them with books, board, etc." The University of Virginia was not willing to go quite that far, however. Its faculty voted to admit disabled veterans tuition-free but made it clear that such students would still be responsible for board and matriculation fees. A Baptist church in Richmond attempted to do more than this; the church announced that it would try "as far as possible . . . [to] furnish facilities for such men to attend the University of Virginia."[197]

As in Ohio, public funds became available to aid student veterans. Anticipating the GI Bill of 1945, two Southern states passed acts supporting veterans' education. The Virginia legislature enacted a law in 1864 that granted disabled veterans who were citizens of the Commonwealth free tuition at the University of Virginia. As noted, the University's faculty had already taken such action on its own. The legislature, however, also directed that eligible persons not be charged laboratory fees or dormitory rent. To qualify for aid, the veteran was asked to show proof of discharge from the army due to wounds and also to present evidence of financial inability to pay the University's charges.[198]

Soon after the war ended, the state of Georgia took similar action. A bill was approved by the legislature in November 1866 that provided free tuition, books, board, and even clothing to disabled veterans under the age of thirty who were indigent. They could use their grant to attend schools such as the University of Georgia, Mercer University, and Emory University. The applicants had to prove that they were citizens of Georgia and, in return for the state aid received, agree to teach in the schools of the state for as many years as they spent at a university or college under the program. The program lasted three years; besides helping student veterans, it contributed to the successful reopening of the University of Georgia.[199]

In addition to their other troubles, a number of Southern colleges had to face a menace that most Northern schools were able to escape, namely, possible destruction of their campuses by military forces. The University of Alabama was one such victim. Just before the war's end, a Union military detachment reached the campus of the Alabama institution. Four of the University's buildings escaped destruction, but the rest of the school's facilities were burned to the ground. This was no impulsive act; the invaders were carrying out specific orders. As we noted, Alabama University had transformed itself into a military academy and was training officer candidates for the Confederate military forces.[200]

Other Southern schools had their physical properties damaged or destroyed by military units. In 1862, for example, rampaging, insubordinate, and thoroughly drunk Union soldiers "fired and destroyed the principal building recently erected" of William and Mary College. Louisiana State University was luckier; it survived the conflict in better shape. Although Louisiana State was forced by the fighting to shut down temporarily, matters could have been much worse. It probably helped that General William T. Sherman had once been head of the school. In any event, when the Union army occupied Louisiana, it was under specific orders not to harm the University.[201]

The University of Georgia was another Southern institution that was quite fortunate. Sherman's famous march through Georgia bypassed the University's campus at Athens. The University of Mississippi also survived the war fairly well, with most of its buildings escaping serious damage. General Grant's family in Galena, Illinois, were close friends of the family of Professor Quinche, the faculty member who had been appointed as custodian of the deserted University.[202]

In South Carolina, damage to the facilities of the College of Charleston was only minor, despite heavy fighting in Charleston harbor. Shells did hit the school's buildings, however. One of the missiles passed through the roof of the library, but no serious harm was caused since most of the books had already been sent off to the countryside for safekeeping.[203]

Another Southern school, South Carolina College, had a narrow, truly harrowing escape from total destruction toward the end of the war. Sherman's victorious Union army reached Columbia, South Carolina, early in 1865. Most of the buildings in that unfortunate city subsequently perished in a great fire, but the campus of South Carolina College escaped damage. It proved to be extremely fortunate for the institution that it was being used at this time as a military hospital. In addition to the Southern wounded, a number of Union soldiers were being taken care of there.

Perhaps this explains why Sherman gave explicit orders that South Carolina College must be protected at all costs, and sent a special detail of Federal soldiers to guard it. This proved to be advantageous as the general breakdown of law and order in the city grew worse. At that point, a mob of drunken marauders tried to force their way onto the College grounds, but the Union guards drove them off.[204]

The Colleges at the War's End

Out of the darkness and tempest, we are sailing into the quiet harbor of peace ... We celebrate not merely the achievement of our aims for the four years past, but no less the victory of the moral conflict which for a half century preceded and culminated in the conflict of arms.[205]

Thus did one of the professors of Oberlin College sum up for his school's commencement in 1865 the significance, as he saw it, of the end that spring of the bloody civil warfare that had been tormenting Americans ever since 1861.

Three dramatic events marked that turning point in American history, events which, one after another, rocked the college campuses during April 1865. Two of these events, for the North at least, seemed exhilarating and uplifting; the third quieted all feelings of triumph with an unanticipated shock of tragedy and deprivation.

The first of these climactic developments came on 3 April when Richmond, the Confederate capital, fell to advancing Union forces. News of the city's capture, when it reached the North, led to happy, sometimes raucous scenes of celebration at many colleges. At Brown University, for example, if we are to believe the outrageous pun that appeared in the campus newspaper, "... enthusiasm threw down all *defenses* [!] of the college and, unable to let well enough alone, set fire to the ancient curb."[206] At Princeton the reaction was, if anything, even more uproarious: "The bells of Seminary and College pealed out 'good news,' the national colors were run out ... floating from windows and housetops." Professors delivered stirring addresses as large bonfires blazed in back of Nassau Hall. Soon fireworks were set off and faculty and students marched in procession through the main street of Princeton village. Observing the scene, with "flags flying, handkerchiefs waving, windows blazing, torchlights burning, fireworks flying through the air, everyone shouting, horns sounding—who ever beheld such a sight, in usually quiet, serene Princeton?" asked the local paper.[207]

Nor was this all. Sensation was destined to be piled on sensation. On 9 April, faced with inevitable defeat, Lee surrendered his Confederate army to General Grant at Appomattox, setting off even wilder celebrations at the colleges. At Yale, news of what had just happened reached the campus just before midnight on 9 April. Immediately, "an almost crazy delirium of excitement" erupted. The hastily improvised demonstration that followed was, in the opinion of one historian, "much more intense" than the outburst at Yale that greeted the signing of the Armistice in 1918 at the end of World War I. "Great crowds thronged the streets" that night in April 1865. "Throughout the entire city, student and 'townie,' radical Republican and 'Copperhead'—all united in wild paroxysms of joy ... now the cruel war was over."[208]

The end-of-the-war celebration at Brown was no less boisterous. Leading the way, the sophomore class ignited "a mammoth bonfire, to which they generously devoted all the movable combustibles that could be borrowed in the city." A few days later, students from all classes at the University staged a giant campus demonstration to mark the end of the conflict. "Colored lanterns shone in all the windows and hung in festoons from the elms; rockets and Roman candles shot in every direction ... while in the rear of the college, an effigy of Jefferson Davis blazed in the curling flames of several hundred tarred barrels."[209]

The long-awaited news traveled swiftly to Middle Western campuses. By 10 April church bells were ringing without cease in Oxford, Ohio, the seat of the College of Miami. According to the school's historian:

> Candles glimmered in the windows on High Street. A bonfire blazed beside the market house. The following morning students of Old Miami and the towns-people assembled in the chapel. President Hall spoke gravely of the meaning of what had transpired and prayed that the land would never again be darkened nor the college divided by fratricidal strife.[210]

When news of Lee's surrender reached them, "students from Denison College and the Young Ladies' Institute in Granville trooped arm in arm up Sugar Loaf, to the west of the village to watch the bonfires and listen to the bells echoing across the valley." At Ohio Wesleyan, the president announced to his campus community: "All Hail! Lee has surrendered! Let the day be given to rejoicing!" It was declared further that: "There will be no recitations today ... Let God be praised!"[211]

At the colleges of the South, the end of the fighting was greeted with a very different reaction. The response was mixed—gloom at the failure of the South's costly struggle for independence but, at the same time, relief that peace had come at last. The scene at Trinity College epitomized the bittersweet mood of the hour. In early April 1865 large numbers of Confederate soldiers began to congregate on the campus of that North Carolina school. These men, fleeing Sherman's advancing Federal army, became so numerous that they finally forced a total suspension of all classwork. Professor Gannaway, then a faculty member at Trinity, has left us a vivid description of the Confederate encampments at his college:

> General Johnston's army in full retreat ... was moving in this direction, and in a few days the advance division, under General Hardee, arrived at Trinity

College, and General Hardee's tent was pitched within a few yards of the college door. His officers' tents were scattered about among the streets on the north side of the college building, and the soldiers were encamped for six or eight miles along the road leading through Archdale. The presence of the soldiers, the anxiety and consternation of the people, rendered further college exercises useless, if not impossible ... An army of more than 20,000 half-clad and half-fed Confederate soldiers and thousands of perishing horses were quartered in our midst, eating out our substance ... We cheerfully gave them what we had ...

Finally peace negotiations were concluded, and the order came to General Hardee to disband his army. Then a shout of joy resounded throughout the camp, and at once commenced the busy preparation for their departure. Their arms were thrown in piles, their cannon abandoned ... On breaking camp, they formed a line in marching order, which reached for miles through town and country. Their gladdened shouts at the thought of peace, and home, and friends, made the welkin ring ... It was springtime, in the month of May.[212]

The third event that burst shockingly and unexpectedly on the nation's campuses in this pivotal month was the grim anticlimax to the whole epic drama. On 14 April the President of the United States was assassinated in Washington, D.C., by John Wilkes Booth. As the news of the murder of Abraham Lincoln reached the Northern colleges, the prevailing mood of euphoria and rejoicing turned suddenly into shock, incredulity, and despair. "As suddenly as the celebration had erupted [on the campuses], it collapsed into stunned silence."[213] At Princeton, "friends and foes were alike mourners." Flags flew at half-mast; the College building and the Chapel were quickly draped in black. Later, on 24 April, Lincoln's funeral train passed through Princeton junction. The students gathered "in a body to pay their last tribute."[214] At Rutgers, students were excused from their classes but required to attend chapel services and observe "due solemnity and decorum."[215]

News of the assassination reached the Middle Western colleges by Saturday, 15 April. At most of them, "there was barely time to replace the flags and bunting with black cloth before the Sabbath service the next day." All across one Middle Western state, Ohio, "presidents of educational institutions led the tribute to the fallen leader ... Faculty and students mourned side by side with townspeople." And as the funeral train passed by on its sad journey, "students from Oberlin and other schools along the route wept unashamedly."[216]

The American Civil War and the Colleges: An Overview

Colleges during the years 1850 through 1865 were unquestionably affected by the great and burning issues of the day—slavery and freedom, states rights and Union. Not surprisingly, their reactions tended to parallel the dominant attitudes of the section in which they were located. In many cases, college students and professors, graduates and administrators, articulated and publicized the points of view that had become the established political orthodoxy of their particular region.

The college communities were somewhat less influential, however, in shaping opinion and action than they had been eight decades or more earlier, during the American Revolution. Why was this so? The explanation may well be that in the intervening period American society had become so much more complex and diverse that by the 1860s the role played by college-based elites, while still immensely important, had diminished in impact. This is what Edward P. Cheyney, comparing the situation in 1776 with that of 1861, noted: "The stage was larger, those who crowded upon it were more numerous, and distinction was with more difficulty obtained."[217] There certainly was, within both the North and South, less openly voiced opposition on the campuses to the dominant sectional orthodoxy than the limited amount of Tory dissent that had existed at some American colleges in the 1770s. Isolated cases of nonconformity were quickly suppressed. Nathan Lord had to resign his presidency at Dartmouth because of his views on slavery, but there were no other such cases in the North. In the Confederacy, Unionist-minded college presidents simply did not exist. Frederick Barnard at the University of Mississippi and William T. Sherman at Louisiana State had left their executive posts at the beginning of the war because they were unable to go along with the dominant secessionist viewpoint that prevailed in their communities.[218]

There were isolated examples of professors in the North who, while not opposing the Union war effort outright, were highly critical of the way in which the Lincoln administration was conducting it. One of the most outspoken of such critics was a professor at Harvard Law School, Joel Parker. In treatises published in 1862 and 1863, Parker argued that black slavery "need not be destroyed to crush the rebellion." President Lincoln's sweeping assumption of war powers, the professor contended, was not only unconstitutional; it verged on dictatorship.[219]

Lord and Parker were not representative of the vast majority of academics in the North. While there was no mass mobilization of professors to aid the war effort comparable to the flooding of academics in 1917–18 and in 1940–45 to serve the government, many members of college faculties supported the fight to preserve the Union. A number of them offered to make their expertise available to help the Northern cause.

One of the most zealous of the academic activists was Charles Eliot Norton, a professor at Harvard. Norton worked hard throughout the war, distributing propaganda for the New England Loyal Publication Society. In addition to Norton, there were two eminent professors of science who were prominently involved in war work. Oliver Wolcott Gibbs, a chemistry professor at the New York Free Academy and later at Harvard, worked for the United States Sanitary Commission and advised government agencies on specifications for scientific instruments. Joseph Leidy, a professor of anatomy and paleontology at the University of Pennsylvania, set aside his personal research during the war to work in army hospitals.[220]

A colleague of Joel Parker on the faculty of the Harvard Law School, Professor Theophilus Parsons, developed an elaborate legal argument to support the actions of the wartime Administration. In 1863, Parsons published a scholarly work, *Slavery: Its Origin, Influence, and Destiny*, which was designed to prove that there were no discernible limits, under the United States Constitution, to Lincoln's authority to do all that he deemed necessary to preserve the Union.[221]

The most influential of all Northern academics during the war was a distinguished political scientist, Dr. Francis Lieber, a professor at Columbia College in New York, who had come to the United States as a refugee from political repression at the German universities. Lieber, who developed a national reputation for his teaching and his scholarship, was a passionate supporter of the Union cause. He seemed to be an ideal choice to become the head of the Loyal Publication Society, a private organization that functioned during the Civil War period as the principal national agency disseminating pro-Union propaganda throughout the North and throughout the world. In just one year, 1864, Lieber's society distributed more than 470,000 copies of its various imprints to the public.[222]

In addition to his unceasing labors as chief Union war propagandist, the energetic Lieber found time to contribute to administration of the army. His memorandum, *Instructions for the Government of the Armies of the United States*, became the standard legal code used by the Northern forces.[223] His detailed study of guerrilla warfare was extensively employed by Union military authorities. Lieber concluded that the international laws of war as applied to guerrilla fighters had no validity during a civil conflict. In the latter case, he stated, special municipal ordinances would apply to guerrilla activities when they led to "assassination, robbery, and devastation."[224]

There were no academics in the Confederacy with the stature and influence of Francis Lieber, but a number of professors offered their services to their embattled government. Robert Barnwell, a professor at South Carolina College, worked in Confederate army hospitals. He died as a result of typhoid fever while serving at battlefield installations. One of Barnwell's colleagues, Professor John LeConte, took charge of a nitre manufacturing plant for the Confederacy. John's brother, Joseph LeConte, also a professor at South Carolina College, served as chief chemist of the Confederate Nitre and Mining Bureau. The LeContes were successful in discovering new sources of raw materials that could be used by the Southern military authorities for the manufacture of munitions.[225]

There were other Southern college teachers who tried as best they could to contribute to the Confederate war effort. Maximilian La Borde, for example, was the leader in the movement to create a Confederate Relief Association. He also came from the South Carolina College faculty.[226] John W. Mallet, a chemistry professor at the University of Virginia, developed improved techniques for replenishing the Confederacy's dwindling supply of materials necessary to manufacture vitally needed explosives.[227]

It is clear, then, that American academics North and South made important contributions to the governments and armies of their respective sections during the Civil War. There is a parallel question, however. Did the war in any way produce significant changes or advances in American higher education? The answer to that question is somewhat paradoxical. As has been seen, the conflict turned out to be devastating for many colleges and universities in the South. Higher education in that area was seriously set back by it. The reverse was true in the North. Not only did most Northern institutions of learning survive the conflict in good shape; in some cases, they were able to realize important gains. Many of them could say what was stated about Ohio University, namely, that "the end of the war brought prosperity in the form of larger enrollment and increased income."[228]

The booming wartime economy of the North made available significantly increased funding for higher education. More than five million dollars was donated to Northern colleges and universities while the war was still going on. New buildings were erected, additional professorships were endowed, and new departments of instruction were established. Perhaps most impressive was the fact that twelve new colleges were founded in the North during wartime. Among this number were Vassar and the Massachusetts Institute of Technology. At the same time, planning and fund raising was going on that would result, shortly after the end of the war, in the establishment of Cornell, Swarthmore, and Lehigh.[229]

It was also significant that during these war years the opportunities for women in Northern schools to acquire a higher education notably increased. Middle Western institutions were busy expanding their coeducational programs at this time. Northeastern educators were moving in a somewhat different direction, planning separate, high-quality women's colleges with standards that hopefully would rival those of Harvard and Yale. This was clearly the aim of the most notable of the new women's institutions, Vassar College, which was created during the war as the result of a large donation from a wealthy industrialist.[230]

The continuing vitality of wartime higher education in the North was demonstrated also by the notable innovations in college courses of study that were being introduced. Newer schools such as Pennsylvania State were offering a variety of technical and vocationally-oriented courses as well as the traditional liberal arts curriculum. Soon after the termination of the fighting, a number of institutions, including Cornell and MIT, featured this type of broader, more diverse program of studies.[231]

The trend toward liberalization and broadening of the college curriculum received a big boost during the war years from the federal government. Although the nation was fighting a major civil war, the Union Congress was able to find time in 1862 to give its approval to a pioneering law in higher education, the first Morrill Act. This legislation made possible a significant educational experiment by making federal aid available to institutions that would offer new and innovative courses of study. The aid was in the form of federal land grants and would be available only to those existing colleges or newly-created state institutions that agreed to offer courses in agricultural science and in "the mechanic arts" (i.e., engineering). Older schools such as Rutgers and Yale and newer ones such as Cornell and Pennsylvania State were quick to apply for the aid, which enabled them to offer a more diversified and utilitarian curriculum than would otherwise have been possible. Thus schools aided by the Morrill Act were in an excellent position to grow and prosper in the postwar period.[232]

The situation in the states that made up the Confederacy was, as indicated, very different. At the war's end, there was no possibility of a postwar boom in higher education below the Mason and Dixon line. The main task confronting Southern educators in 1865 was the extremely difficult one of trying, with little or no resources, to revive institutions of higher education that were almost moribund.

In spite of the discouraging conditions that confronted them, Southern college presidents and members of their boards of trustees determined to undertake to the best of their abilities the daunting tasks of educational reconstruction. In August 1865, when the last of the demobilized Confederate soldiers left the Trinity College campus, the school's trustees met and discussed plans for the future. They decided that Trinity College should "commence operations as soon as practicable." Braxton Craven, the former president of the institution, was formally reappointed to his post and by January 1866 instruction "of sorts" had been resumed.[233]

The Trinity story was fairly typical of developments on other Southern campuses at the end of the war. Somehow those schools that had not been ruined completely surveyed the physical damage, if any, shook off their bad memories of what had transpired the past few years, and did what was necessary to resume operation. In November 1865, for example, the College of Charleston made energetic preparations to reopen.

Professors were rehired and were promised that they would be paid salaries once again; students were asked to return to the college and enroll for classes.[234]

The University of Georgia made similar ambitious plans to reopen. Within two months of Lee's surrender, the school's board of trustees had held a meeting at which they received a report that the University was "in as good a state of preservation as could be expected." The board was also happy to learn that the Chancellor had succeeded in persuading the Union army authorities to release their control over the school's campus and other facilities. Plans were accordingly made to resume instruction as soon as was practicable. The governing board also approved Chancellor Lipscomb's long-standing plan to establish a school of civil engineering at the University.[235]

Farther south, academic reconstruction rapidly went forward in the state of Mississippi. One of the first official acts of the new Unionist governor of that state, William L. Sharkey, was to convene a meeting of the trustees of the University of Mississippi. At that session, which was held in July 1865, detailed plans were formulated for the earliest possible reopening of the school.[236]

As the war slowly faded into either nightmarish memory or semi-mythological glorification, the final stage of the response of the colleges to the conflict involved the construction of campus war memorials. During the summer of 1865 the alumni associations of various colleges in the North met to discuss plans for such memorials. It was finally decided to erect memorial auditoriums, classroom buildings, or chapels, financed by contributions from interested alumni. It was provided, in this connection, that these memorial structures would list the names of students or graduates from the school who had been killed in the war.[237]

As a result of the postwar alumni fundraising drives, a number of impressive commemorative buildings were erected on American college campuses, including Harvard's Memorial Hall, which paid tribute solely to the University's Union dead, and the memorial chapel at Princeton, which listed the school's fallen sons from both armies.[238] These gestures sought to insure that recollections of these sacrifices by students and other members of academe would not, in future times, "grow obscure with the passing of their generation."[239]

3

The American Campus and the Great War in Europe, 1914–1917

The "Guns of August": Campus Reactions

Wᴉʟʟɪᴀᴍ W. Sweet met a colleague, Professor Longden, on the campus of Indiana-Asbury College the morning of 1 August 1914.

"Have you seen the papers this morning?" Longden asked.

"Not yet," Sweet replied, "but I am on my way to the library to look them over."

As Longden walked away, he remarked, "I fear a European war is inevitable."[1]

In just three or four days, the professor's forebodings proved all too true.

The shocking developments overseas proved difficult for American professors to accept as credible. High in the Colorado mountains, a vacationing history professor from the University of Kansas, Frank Hodder, refused to believe the early reports. "It can't be so," he told his friend, journalist William Allen White. "They aren't telling the truth. Why, there's a treaty between Belgium and Germany that would prevent it!"

White reported that later, when the professor found out that the invasion of Belgium had indeed occurred despite the aforementioned treaty, that academic's "faith in modern civilization completely caved in . . ."[2]

Perhaps the outbreak of World War I came as such a shock to American professors because for nearly fifty years their schools had been mainly turning inward. To be sure, the research orientation and teaching methods of the modern German university had become quite influential in the New World, but fundamentally, American higher education remained focused on domestic problems. There had been no great and transcendent cause that challenged the sensibilities of American professors and students since the Revolution and the Civil War. Forced-draft industrialization had produced significant national growth in numerous material categories. Young college men tended to focus pragmatically on personal business and professional careers. They professed utter disdain for what was happening in distant parts of the world. Campus life was almost obsessively dominated by so-called "extra-curricular" activities—fraternities, inter-collegiate athletics, and campus publications. The rationale for this emphasis was that it helped prepare undergraduates for the intensely competitive, profit-centered world they would encounter upon graduation. "Don't let your studies interfere with your education" was a characteristic watchword of the period.[3]

And then came 1914. News of the shocking events overseas hit America's smug, intensely preoccupied college campuses with devastating impact. What was one to make of this wholly unanticipated catastrophe? How could such a thing happen? American colleges were swept by a strange mixture of incredulity, sympathy for European colleagues, and a somewhat smug feeling of superiority to the overseas "militarists and monarchists."

Eventually regional differences were reflected in the varying campus reactions to the war. At colleges in the Northeast, for example, there was some instinctive pro-Allied sentiment early on. Nevertheless, in August 1914 there were few panicky or angry calls in that area for immediate action by the United States government.

Morris Bishop, reviewing the events of that month, writes that "by and large Cornell dismissed the war, and Cornell was a miniature of America."[4] When Columbia University students returned to their campus for the Fall semester, they found that their school newspaper was mainly concerned with such vital matters as a song contest and the varsity crew's glorious victory at the regatta at Poughkeepsie.[5] Similarly, we are told, "for some months the conflict in Europe seemed of little significance to Amherst."[6] And at Yale, William Howard Taft, the former U.S. President and now a law professor, appealed to university men to be especially careful in expressing sympathies for one belligerent or another lest such statements be taken too seriously by people abroad.[7]

Elsewhere in the country, the early campus responses to the news from overseas were not substantially different. At the University of North Carolina in Chapel Hill, as people went about their daily work, the war did not seem very near. Campus attention was focused instead on the prospects of the football team in the second year of coach Trenchard's regime.[8] In Ohio, the College of Wooster "carried on as usual as if Europe were not soaked in blood. Classes, parties, games, concerts went on. Everyone, to be sure, read the morning papers with distress, hoping against hope that all this carnage would end in victory for the Allies."[9]

At Wheaton, a little denominational college in Illinois, students apparently were greatly "confused about the complex issues" of the war. Seeking to enlighten them, the president of the school explained in the campus paper that the conflict was a divine judgment for "grievous national transgressions." All nations were equally guilty. "Men must turn back to God or be destroyed."[10] From the perspective of the University of South Dakota, the world-wide struggle seemed to be a moral aberration indeed, and a distant one at that. If anything, the students had the feeling "that such Old World rivalries pursued by antiquated, monarchical regimes proved anew the good fortune of living in the United States — and South Dakota."[11]

The Beginnings of Unneutrality

The early campus mood of indifference and occasional moralistic condemnation was not destined to last long. The nation's president, Woodrow Wilson, had asked his countrymen to be neutral in both thought and deed. The march of events, however, made this stance increasingly difficult to maintain. Frank C. Porter, a professor at Yale Divinity School, observed that "the feeling of neutrality appropriate in a neutral land is not easily cultivated." One reason this was so, noted George W. Pierson, was that, as developments unfolded, "the war outraged too much that was part of the fiber of academic idealism."[12]

At Harvard, wrote Samuel E. Morison, "sympathy for the allied cause was unconcealed; not for a moment was the Harvard community neutral in thought or deed." Campus sentiment swung to the Allied side as a result of two developments that occurred early in the war: the bombastic "Manifesto of the German Intellectuals" and the destruction of the University of Louvain in Belgium by the German army.[13]

The launching of unrestricted submarine warfare by the Germans also attracted much unfavorable attention in America. At the University of Michigan, for example, "Germany on the march" was increasingly seen as "a ruthless machine, casually indifferent to the guaranteed neutrality of Belgium, cruel in submarine warfare, and submissive to a kaiser and military hierarchy."[14] Similarly, on the Amherst campus it was the invasion of Belgium and the submarine campaign that turned local opinion toward the Allies.[15] And at Kansas State, pro-Allied sentiment made an appearance when German violations of neutral rights were publicized.[16]

Most informal surveys of faculty opinion in 1915 indicated a decided preference for the Allied side. In August 1915 one J. J. McCook published the results of an analysis of the attitudes of American professors on the war. In twenty-five colleges and universities that he surveyed, more than 95 percent of the faculty were found to be pro-Ally. In nine schools of theology only one professor in seventeen sympathized with Germany; in seven law schools, the ratio was even more definitive — one in forty.[17] As early as October 1914 Albion W. Small, a well-known sociologist at the University of Chicago, asserted that nine out of ten American professors were, like himself, skeptical of Germany's claims that it was the injured party. Germany, he said, was the most thoroughly militarized of any of the belligerent powers and had been preparing for this test of arms for some time.[18] Almost from the beginning of the conflict, contends Carol Gruber, 'the preponderance of opinion on the American campus was hostile to Germany and in favor of the Allies."[19]

College presidents were no less explicit in publicizing pro-Allied sympathies than were the members of their faculties. None were more outspoken than President Dabney of the University of Cincinnati who in December 1914 characterized the Germans as "robbers and murderers." Cincinnati's German-American Alliance worked constantly, but unsuccessfully, to have Dabney removed from his university presidency.[20] Equally vehement in his support for the Allied cause was the president of the University of Rhode Island, Howard Edwards. At one point Edwards told his students that "the good American could not but hope for the defeat of German arms because the United States and Germany were as inherently irreconcilable in their aims and institutions as God and Mammon."[21]

In America's heartland, the president of little Wabash College in Indiana took up the Allied cause early in the war. In his chapel talks, President Mackintosh predicted week after week the imminent victory of the British forces.[22] However, the most influential supporter of the Allies among American college presidents was Dr. Charles W. Eliot, the venerable president-emeritus of Harvard University. In May 1915 Eliot declared in an article written for the *New York Times* that "the sinking of the *Lusitania* ... outraged not only the existing conventions of the civilized world in regard to naval warfare, but the moral feelings of present civilized society." Dr. Eliot asserted that 'the German method of conducting war omits chivalry, mercy, and humanity, and thereby degrades the German nation."[23]

Early in the war, therefore, majority opinion on the campuses, especially in the Northeast, favored the Allies. This meant that, long before America's entrance into the conflict, influential voices in the academic community were presenting a picture of Germany, to quote Gruber once again, that was full of "suspicion and revulsion" and "susceptible to the absolutist, moralistic interpretation of the war as a contest between good and evil."[24]

The Drive for "Preparedness" Reaches the Colleges

College students in 1914 and 1915 were generally not as anxious to ensure Allied victory as were their elders. The earliest reaction to the war on the part of undergraduates was one favoring humanitarian aid wherever possible to victims of the conflict. At Yale, a mass meeting was held in October 1914 to raise money for Red Cross work in the war zones. Money for war relief was also collected at Yale football games. Eventually, enough was raised to purchase twelve ambulances to be sent overseas. As a sign of their impartiality, the Yale contributors shipped three ambulances each to France, Belgium, Austria, and Germany.[25] In mid-January 1915 students at Harvard joined their Yale counterparts and raised money for five additional ambulances. By this time the student-initiated Red Cross Ambulance Fund had collected a total of $436,000.[26]

Early in the war, older members of America's academic community—faculty members, college presidents, and prominent alumni—desired a more active response to the issues raised by the conflict than undergraduates were willing to make. These elders feared that a decisive victory of the Germans over England and France would pave the way for an attack on the Western Hemisphere. To discourage such an onslaught, the pro-Allied partisans in academe called for an all-out campaign to achieve security by means of "preparedness."

Support for "preparedness" came from the business and the social elite of the Northeast, many of whose members were influential alumni of Ivy League universities such as Harvard, Yale, and Princeton. It also came from ambitious politicians in the Republican and Progressive parties, hoping to find an issue that would embarrass the incumbent Democratic administration of Woodrow Wilson. And it came finally from a small group of high-ranking United States Army officers like General Leonard Wood, who wished to revitalize and modernize the American military establishment.[27]

Wealthy pro-Ally individuals in the Northeast such as George Haven Putnam, an Anglophile publisher, and Grenville Clark, an energetic corporation lawyer, organized lobbying groups to bring pressure on government to strengthen miliary preparedness. Working zealously for the same cause was the National Security League, founded in December 1914 by a committee of fifty wealthy and influential New Yorkers. Also active in this campaign was the American Legion, established in New York City by a similar group in March 1915. In addition to the above organizations, such lobbying groups as the National Civic Federation, the American Defense Society, and the Council of National Defense rallied to the cause.[28]

General Leonard Wood, until recently Chief of Staff of the United States Army, encouraged the drive for "preparedness" in every possible way. Wood was convinced, as were many of his army colleagues, that the United States military was antiquated and inefficient, and that it was not prepared to defend the country against an attack by a major power.[29] As Chief of Staff, one of Wood's pet projects had been to expand programs of military training in the nation's colleges and universities.

The Morrill Act of 1862 mandated that all land-grant colleges and universities receiving aid from the federal government must offer military training courses. By 1914 some thirthy thousand American students, about 8 percent of the total college enrollment, were enrolled in military science courses.[30] By that year, the land-grant colleges had sent to the army three times more officers, including fifty generals, than had the United States Military Academy at West Point.[31] Why, then, were Wood and his colleagues so thoroughly dissatisfied? For one thing, they felt that many of the existing campus military programs were too mechanical and inefficient to turn out adequately trained reserve officers. Secondly, they wished to expand the scope of college military training. Many Morrill Act institutions had by this time made their military science courses entirely voluntary. This trend had become particularly marked after student protests flared up during the 1880s. In addition, General Wood was irked that prestigious private universities, particularly in the Northeast, had no provision at all for military training. The Morrill Act did not apply to them. Should Germany achieve total victory, Wood was convinced, America's security needs would require a much larger force of trained reserve officers than the campuses were currently turning out.[32]

Wood found a number of willing allies in academe for his preparedness ideas. President Henry S. Drinker of Lehigh University was induced to serve as the head of an organization known as the National Reserve Corps, which in 1913 and 1914 sponsored summer officer training camps for college students.[33] And in January 1915 Dr. John G. Hibben, President of Princeton University, endorsed the idea of summer training camps for college men in an article in the *Nassau Literary Magazine*, which was later quoted at length in the *New York Times*. Summer officer-training camps, said Hibben, were the best way to strengthen America's military security while avoiding the militarism and the ruinous drain on economic resources that a large standing army would necessitate.[34]

In late January 1915 the *New York Times* published the results of a survey it had made of the reactions of college presidents to Hibben's proposal. The response, it turned out, was overwhelmingly favorable. Student military training, most of the educators declared, could become a highly significant factor in the defense of the nation.[35]

In the weeks and months that followed, a number of university presidents made speeches or published articles endorsing the concept of military training for college men. More or less summing up the gist of these public statements, Andrew Dickson White, the founder and former president of Cornell, remarked in May 1915 that he would like to "have a nation of men who are peaceable, but who are ready for war."[36]

The sinking of the British liner *Lusitania* by a German submarine in the spring of 1915 increased the pressure on many college campuses for "preparedness." That summer, nearly one thousand men, seeking training as reserve officers, enrolled in General Wood's summer-camp program.

Half of this number went to the highly publicized camp at Plattsburg, New York. Prominent Harvard alumni like Grenville Clark and Elihu Root, Jr., with other young business and professional men from New York's "Committee of One Hundred," sweated through the drills at Plattsburg.[37] The key role played by students and alumni of Northeastern "Ivy League" schools in the summer-camp movement was made clear by a report published in September 1916. *School and Society* magazine reported at that time that 15 percent of the Princeton student body had enrolled in the summer camps, more, proportionately, than the contingents from any other large American college. Harvard's student trainees ranked second and those from Yale were third.[38]

Thus, the first phase of the preparedness movement as it affected the colleges was dominated by summer officer-training camps. This phase, which reached its peak in August 1916, resulted in an enrollment of 9,932 college students and alumni in the camps. More than two-thirds of this number came from schools in the Northeast. There were substantial contingents, however, from such large state universities as Virginia and Michigan. And a few enrollees came from smaller institutions all across the land.[39]

In the fall of 1916 the well-organized campaign for preparedness entered a new phase as it began to pursue a much more comprehensive agenda. The change in strategy was largely due to new developments in Washington. President Woodrow Wilson, originally unsympathetic to the demands of the militant "patriots," suddenly experienced a change of heart, and in November 1915 announced his conversion to the national defense cause. Whether this new approach was due to the President's increasingly troubled diplomatic exchanges with Germany or to the potential importance of the preparedness issue in the coming national election, is not entirely clear. The important thing for the colleges was that the presidential decision gave a big boost to the movement for campus military training.

Some organizations wished to go much further than the President. The National Security League, for example, loudly called for universal and compulsory military training. A small group of people in academe such as Professor Edwin Mims of Vanderbilt and, yes, Dr. Eliot of Harvard, endorsed the NSL proposal enthusiastically.[40] The vast majority of professors and university administrators, however, preferred the more moderate plans of President Wilson. They believed that the nation's defenses could best be strengthened by expanding and revitalizing existing military-training programs. Wilson's proposals along this line were debated and amended in Congress, resulting finally in the passage of the National Defense Act on 3 June 1916.

What impact did this legislation have on the colleges? First of all, it authorized a major expansion of campus officer-training programs on a

year-round basis. All institutions of higher education, regardless of whether
they were public or private, were now encouraged to apply for inclusion
in a greatly expanded government officer-training program. The new
system, including amended provisions in June 1920, placed all military
training at the colleges on a more standardized and centralized basis. A
Reserve Officers Training Corps (ROTC) was created and all colleges
were invited to obtain Washington's approval to set up units of the new
Corps on their own campuses. They would then be able to offer courses
of military instruction during the regular academic year. All such courses,
along with the summer training camps, would be carefully supervised by
the War Department. It was still left to the individual institution, as was
the case under the Morrill Act, to decide whether the new ROTC courses
should be elective or compulsory.[41]

Heads of colleges had played an active part in planning the ROTC
program. Presidents of nineteen colleges and universities, including
Harvard and Yale, met in Washington with officials of the War Department
in mid-October 1916 to decide on a list of schools that would begin
operating under the new program.[42]

Two trends soon became apparent as ROTC was introduced in various
colleges. First of all, the fears and passions of the wartime years led the
authorities at certain colleges and universities to make the new military
courses compulsory for all students. Second, a number of schools decided
to award credit toward academic degrees to students who had completed
the ROTC courses. Among the institutions moving in this direction were
Princeton, Harvard, Williams, Minnesota, Bowdoin, and Wesleyan. At
such places, there seems to have been little or no faculty opposition to the
move.[43] At Yale the situation was different, however. There the policy
had to be implemented without the formal blessing of the faculty. The
president of Yale demanded that a meeting of senior faculty approve his
proposal for awarding regular credit for the newly instituted ROTC
courses. Despite his plea, a substantial number of the senior professors
abstained from voting. Some of the abstainers later made public the
reasons for their action, explaining that they refused to equate military
training courses with the university's established academic offerings.[44]

By the end of 1916, in any event, the preparedness movement had
introduced a larger military element than ever before into American
institutions of higher education. Anxieties created by the bloody struggle
in Europe had led colleges in the New World to institute important
changes in their programs. And these changes were just beginning. The
World War would ultimately push American higher education even more
deeply into the military sphere than anyone could have visualized during
the summer of 1914.

Non-Interventionists Make a Stand

As more and more academics hopped onto the preparedness bandwagon, a few professors and college presidents resisted the powerful surge. These members of academe objected to what they saw as the unseemly haste of their colleagues to abandon scholarly objectivity and propagandize in support of the Allies.

Paul Elmer More, a literary critic, complained that professors bore an especially heavy responsibility for stirring up the American people to an irrational hatred of Germany. William M. Sloane and William R. Shepherd, faculty members at Columbia University, agreed with this analysis. Professor Simon Patten of the University of Pennsylvania declared that it was a gross oversimplification of long-standing European rivalries to single out Germany as the only aggressor nation. Franz Boas, a highly regarded anthropologist at Columbia University, maintained that the war was due to many complex causes, such as "German arrogance, French lust for revenge, English envy, and lust for power."[45]

At least one American historian strove at first to be as objective as possible in analyzing the crisis. Albert Bushnell Hart of Harvard published a book late in 1914 which declared that it aimed "to treat the subject fairly and impartially." This volume, *The War in Europe*, reviewed historically the causes of the war. The conflict, Hart concluded, was rooted in deep-seated national animosities and imperialistic rivalries that went back for many years.[46]

Henry M. MacCracken, former Chancellor of New York University, was one of the few university heads to break with the pro-Allied consensus. Since the Allies were equally responsible for the outbreak of the war, he declared, anti-German statements such as those of Dr. Eliot were in his opinion, "extreme" and "extravagant."[47] MacCracken's successor as Chancellor at NYU, Elmer E. Brown, stated in March 1915 that "our universities in the interest of a stable civilization should do all in their power to cultivate the preventives of war."[48] And on the West Coast, President Benjamin I. Wheeler of the University of California outraged pro-Ally academics in 1915 by stating publicly: "It seems terrible to go to war with a nation which does not want to go to war with us, even if some of our ships have become the victims of submarines."[49]

The foregoing individuals were obviously classifiable as advocates of continued neutrality and nonpartisanship. They were not by any stretch of the imagination pro-German. Only one prominent American academic during these years genuinely fits that description, Professor John W. Burgess, the founder of Columbia University's Political Science faculty. In his volume, *The European War of 1914*, Burgess, an ardent admirer of all things German, blamed the war solely on Allied imperialism. British naval power always menaced American interests, he wrote, and it would be helpful for the United States if Germany won the war.[50] Many of Burgess's fellow political scientists were greatly angered by his opinions, calling him a "doddering old idiot" and viewing his book more as evidence of his senility than of his knowledge.[51]

It is apparent that those academics who were against intervention in the European war were a distinct minority on the campuses and had a minimal effect on public opinion. The situation is quite different, however, when early student attitudes are taken into account. Student leaders and student editors were much more vocal and definitive during the first two years of the conflict in expressing opposition to any American military involvement overseas. These concerned undergraduates took pains to make clear that they did not oppose preparedness for national defense per se, but that they rejected its use as a smokescreen to maneuver the country into the European war on the Allied side. They also opposed the use of the preparedness cause to hasten the establishment of compulsory military training with attendant militarization of the nation's colleges.[52]

Student noninvolvement sentiments surfaced early. At Columbia University pro-peace views dominated undergraduate opinion all through the Fall of 1914 and the early months of the following year. A national news magazine, the *Literary Digest*, reported 6 February 1915 that: "Columbia both in its faculty and its student body, seems opposed to military training in colleges beyond what already exists in State institutions."[53] The Dean of Columbia College, Frederick Keppel, sympathized with this anti-war sentiment. Dean Keppel was quoted in a letter sent to Columbia students as stating that any effort to build up American military power now would lead Europe to lose confidence "in our sincerity and disinterestedness."[54]

When Columbia students returned from their Christmas-New Years vacation a big rally was held in Earl Hall at which a committee was set up to send anti-war statements to other universities. In the meantime, a proposal that Columbia establish military drill on its campus and encourage volunteers to attend a summer training camp was immediately rejected by the Student Board of the University.[55]

That the views of Columbia's students were shared by undergraduates elsewhere was made clear in a letter published in the *New York Times* in early March 1915. This communication, purporting to represent the sentiments of a considerable number of students at Princeton, asserted that the majority at "Old Nassau" did not agree with the military preparedness proposals of the school's president, John G. Hibben. Of some sixteen hundred Princeton undergraduates, it was stated, only about five hundred indicated that they approved Hibben's ideas and even these, when informed about the implications of the plan, "had no intention of joining a student military corps if one were organized."[56] Similar coolness to the concept of military training on college campuses appeared on the West Coast. A mistaken report was published in mid-March stating that the Regents of the University of Oregon would soon institute compulsory military training for all male students. When this rumor first appeared, women's peace groups in Portland made so strong a protest that the university hastened to issue a statement disavowing the plan.[57]

Meanwhile, the neutralist and peace sentiment at Columbia only got stronger with the passage of time. A number of prominent speakers were brought to the Columbia campus to promote the noninvolvement cause. On 15 January 1915 Rabbi Stephen S. Wise of the Free Synagogue addressed a student mass meeting in Earl Hall, warning his audience to avoid entanglement in foreign wars. "Militarism means the subordination of civil affairs to military affairs," he said. "It means the death of democracy."[58]

The same Earl Hall assemblage voted to organize a Collegiate Common-Sense League. This new body announced that it would work to limit armaments, secure the discontinuance of summer camps for college men, support an embargo on all arms exports or war loans to belligerents, and seek government ownership of munitions factories.[59] In February and March 1915 more anti-war mass meetings were held at Columbia. Notable peace advocates such as Jane Addams and Hamilton Holt addressed these meetings.[60]

The climax of this peace activity came when yet another anti-war student organization was established, the Collegiate Anti-Militarism League. The League, which soon attracted supporters on a number of other campuses, became the most active organization expressing the anti-involvement mood of American college students. Obviously influenced by the antimilitarist philosophy of the American Socialist party and by prominent pacifists of the day, the League stirred the ire of conservative alumni and nervous trustees anxious that contributions from men of wealth not be discouraged. It probably never represented as powerful a force as its excited opponents feared, but in the days before German aggressions choked off serious debate, the Anti-Militarism League attracted a surprisingly large number of campus sympathizers.[61]

Even before the sinking of the *Lusitania*, the League mailed out letters to eighthy thousand students questioning the value of the summer military camps so dear to the heart of General Wood. These communications solicited student opinion on the various campuses, and later the League announced that sixty-three thousand replies disapproved of military drill for collegians. This widely publicized survey led students at a number of universities to make their own polls of local views on the subject.

At the University of Michigan, a poll showed male students to be fairly evenly divided. At Cornell, there was considerable support for the training camps. At Wesleyan, though, only four students signed up for the 1915 Plattsburg camp.[62]

In any case, the Anti-Militarism League had made its mark. On many campuses, the response to its agitation revealed that in 1915 a number of students were skeptical about General Wood's military-training program. John Dos Passos, who graduated from Harvard in 1916, recalled that:

> We were quite exercised by the advance of militarism — the people I saw had a strong pacifist tinge — and some even viewed Plattsburg and the ROTC with alarm. Of course, all the right thinkers were full of horror and atrocity stories about the Lusitania and Brave Little Belgium.[63]

It was especially ironic that at Princeton University, where the campaign for campus military training was launched, a number of student leaders made their opposition to the program public. In an open letter printed in a pacifist periodical *The Advocate of Peace* in April 1916, young Princetonians argued that the proper way to strengthen the nation's defenses was to enlarge the regular army and navy and set up new military and naval academies. Colleges were not the right places for instruction in military science. It would be more appropriate, in their view, for institutions of higher education to encourage student interest in international affairs and to study the causes of war.[64] Similar antipreparedness views were published by five Seniors in the *Princeton Alumni Weekly*. Military-training advocates were angered by this statement but Norman Thomas, a 1905 Princeton graduate, defended the sincerity of the peace-minded students in the same publication. Given the prevailing state of opinion at Princeton, said Thomas, "it took real courage" for the Seniors to publish their anti-drill views, "a sort of courage which is all too rare in our college and in our civic life."[65]

The Anti-Militarism League was repeatedly criticized by the editors of the *New York Times*. Fearing the potential impact of the League's campaign on campus opinion, that pro-Ally newspaper was thoroughly exasperated with the student peace crusaders.[66] In addition, a group of prominent Columbia alumni, concerned about their university's reputation, issued a statement asserting that the majority of Columbia graduates resented the League and disagreed with its views.[67] And the League's poll of student opinion on summer camps so enraged the pro-preparedness former President, Theodore Roosevelt, that he launched one of his characteristic diatribes at it, blasting the organization as preaching nothing more than cowardice and "emasculated morality." If the members of the anti-war group were "not all poltroons," thundered Roosevelt, "they teach 'Poltroonism' and ... would breed a nation of poltroons."[68]

A handful of college presidents did not agree with the angry responses of the academic establishment to the anti-war students. Indeed, higher education leaders such as Jordan of Stanford, Hutchins of Michigan, Meiklejohn of Amherst, and Day of Syracuse, sympathized with the goals of the campus noninterventionists.[69] In mid-November of 1915 David Starr Jordan told a peace meeting at Cooper Union in New York City that the greatest menace from autocratic Europe lay in its militaristic ideals and methods, which America would do well not to copy.[70] Chancellor Day in the Fall of 1915 publicly scoffed at the growing war hysteria and stated his conviction that the nation was defended adequately and that campus military training was therefore unnecessary.[71]

In 1916, an election year, the debate about preparedness became much more heated both on and off the campus. Antimilitaristic students continued to be active at Columbia. In early 1916 some Barnard college students, together with people from the Columbia School of Journalism, launched an unorthodox college monthly entitled *Challenge*. The first issue of this periodical included an article highly critical of the Plattsburg training camp. Its author, a School of Journalism student named Silas Seadler, asked what character training college men would receive when the town of Plattsburg had some 102 saloons, a large corps of prostitutes, and army medical personnel on hand to "make the path of dissipation easier" by supplying products to recruits "to prevent physical harm coming to the one who dissipates."[72] The Columbia campus newspaper, *The Spectator*, followed up on this theme in March 1916 by publishing statements from eight college athletes and student leaders questioning the value of the kind of military training given at places like Plattsburg. They argued that the purpose of such training camps was not to turn out better soldiers or officers but to generate "propaganda for preparedness."[73]

Early in April the Columbia antimilitarists were at it again. A mass meeting in Earl Hall protested the University's plans to send a contingent of students to Plattsburg. One student speaker asserted that President Henry Drinker of Lehigh was promoting the summer camp movement because he "is president of a college subsidized by the Du Ponts." The head of the Anti-Militarism League told the audience that the real purpose of the summer military camps was to assure profits for those backing "the Army and Navy Co-operating Company."[74]

An even more dramatic student protest against preparedness occurred at the College of the City of New York. General Wood came to that institution in March 1916 in order to explain the educational advantages of courses in military science. Wood made his presentation to an audience of about thirty-five hundred students in the Great Hall of the college. As the General concluded his address, a sophomore pacifist, Leon Samson, called for "those opposed to militarism" to follow him out of the Hall.

Only a handful responded and a scuffle between protesters and student ushers ensued. More fighting erupted outside the building. The City College authorities hardly appreciated the unfavorable publicity that the incident attracted to their institution and Samson was unceremoniously expelled shortly thereafter.[75]

Despite the long campaign carried on by the Student Anti-Militarism League, it was apparent by the later months of 1916 that the tide of opinion on the campuses and in the nation at large was running against the peace advocates. Increasing fear of German intentions made it easy for proponents of military mobilization to win support from the American people. As John Patrick Finnegan puts it: "The major remaining leaders of the peace forces ... could be dismissed as parochial cranks; others were scored off as Socialists, impractical idealists, or worse. It was overwhelmingly clear that the other side had the ... leaders, the newspapers, and the bulk of the financial resources."[76]

Pressures for American Involvement Grow Stronger

In 1916 and early 1917, as we travel from one American university to another, the story is essentially the same. Pressure was steadily mounting on the campuses for all-out United States participation in the world conflict. At the University of Michigan in the Spring of 1916, a history professor, Charles H. Van Tyne, and thirteen of his colleagues published a memorial detailing the various reasons for their strong sympathy for the Allied cause.[77] At the University of Indiana about the same time, a number of faculty members announced their approval of the increasingly strong foreign policy of the Wilson Administration. "There was no mythological midwestern isolationist myopia about their views and expressions."[78] At Princeton, several professors forwarded a statement to General Joffre in April 1916 making clear their deep sympathy for the soldiers of France and the courageous battle they were fighting against the German invaders.[79]

More campus sympathy for the Allies was stirred up when the Germans in 1916 arrested two professors at the University of Ghent in Belgium, imprisoning them because they refused to cooperate with German plans to convert their school into a pro-German university. Ninety-three professors of history at American universities petitioned the Secretary of State to demand the release of the two Belgian historians.[80]

No American academic better personified the pro-Allied partisanship that was sweeping the campuses than did a popular professor of English at Harvard, Charles T. Copeland. J. Donald Adams calls him "one of the most effective recruiting sergeants the country ever had." Former students who had traveled to the war zones were promptly pressed into service by

"Copey" to tell people what they had seen. Pro-Allied propaganda was brought unashamedly into class on any and all occasions, and woe betide the poor students who did not have the good sense to share the professor's uncritical zeal for the Allied war effort.[81]

Late in 1916 and in January 1917 the few remaining advocates of peace and neutrality at American colleges were busy trying to fight a rearguard action. At a subcommittee meeting in the House of Representatives where a bill for universal military conscription was being considered, a group of antiwar students testified against the proposal. Universal military training was unnecessary, they maintained; its supposed benefits were illusory. The concept would suppress the rights of students as individuals. Those who had attended summer military camps, it was asserted, subsequently lost all interest in international relations or world peace. This desperate last-ditch effort was made by Wayne Myers, president of the Anti-Militarism League, Edward M. Earle, head of the Columbia University student assembly, and Robert Dunn, a student at Yale. It failed, however; Congress ultimately approved a bill for universal conscription.[82]

Columbia University in mid-January 1917 was still the main center of the student peace movement. A meeting held there on 15 January sought to mobilize campus sentiment against the proposed universal military training bill. As many as two hundred students showed up, but James R. Harrison, editor of the Columbia *Spectator*, told newspaper correspondents that the "vast majority" of students at Columbia favored the bill. Antiwar faculty members, such as R. L. Hale and Leon Fraser, addressed the Earl Hall protest meeting. Fraser predicted that compulsory military training would encourage the formation of an officer caste, a "snobocracy" of rich young men. Another faculty member, Carleton Hayes of the History department, told the meeting that "universal military training is unAmerican and inhuman. It will lead in time straight to war."[83]

The peace meeting stirred up the pro-intervention students and faculty at Columbia. A few days after the Earl Hall protest was held, a petition to President Wilson was drawn up by hundreds of people on the campus. It declared that Americans would not remain "silent and inactive" in the face of Germany's continually escalating belligerence and depredations. The President of the University, Nicholas Murray Butler, was the first to sign the statement.[84]

During the same crucial weeks in early 1917, dramatic actions by the Imperial German government added further impetus to the mounting war fever in the United States. On 31 January Berlin announced a top-level decision to launch immediately a campaign of unrestricted submarine warfare against all neutral ships as well as those of belligerent powers. The effect of this declaration was all the more devastating because, just a few days before, President Wilson had delivered a "Peace without Victory" speech to the United States Congress, calling on all the warring nations to bring an end to the bloody conflict by diplomatic means. The German resumption of unrestricted submarine warfare, therefore, was a harsh rebuff of Wilson's mediation efforts. In reply, Wilson appeared before Congress on 3 February 1917 to announce the severing of all diplomatic relations with Germany.

A shock wave of disbelief and rage swept the nation and the nation's college campuses when Germany's brusque U-boat announcement was made public. On the Columbia University campus, however, opinion still remained somewhat divided. Several petitions now began to circulate. More than one hundred faculty members signed one of them, a hastily drawn-up request that Wilson do what he was shortly to do anyway, namely, break diplomatic relations with Germany. That same day, 1 February, a counterpetition was formulated, cautioning against any drastic anti-German action. This document was signed by a smaller group of Columbia professors, including Carleton Hayes, John Erskine, and H. W. L. Dana. A group of students, meanwhile, circulated a third petition. This document, whose sponsors claimed that they represented a broad spectrum of campus opinion, asked the president to try to get Germany to follow a more reasonable policy before he resorted to forceful measures.[85]

America's Colleges Opt for War

Reactions to Berlin's submarine campaign may have remained divided at Columbia University, but on other campuses students and faculty responded with anger to what they saw as a gauntlet flung in their country's face. At Princeton, President Hibben announced that his university would organize immediately a student battalion to train army officers.[86] Also, it was learned now that aviation squadrons were being organized at Yale, Harvard, and the University of Pennsylvania.[87] At New York University, Dean Marshall Brown took special pains to pledge the loyalty of his institution to the nation. In so doing, Dean Brown told his students that if a war broke out because "America has to fight for neutral rights," it would indeed be a terrible calamity, "But there are worse things."[88]

At the City College of New York, a mass meeting was convened to demonstrate the willingness "of all students ... to prepare themselves to serve the nation in the present crisis."[89] A group of professors at Harvard decided to form their own drill unit.[90] President Wheeler of the University of California recommended that students and faculty at Berkeley be placed entirely at the disposal of the War Department in the event of the outbreak of war.[91]

The administration of Columbia was particularly anxious to show that, newspaper accounts notwithstanding, campus opinion was solidly behind Wilson's diplomatic break with Germany. On 6 February 1917 four thousand students showed up for a mass meeting to hear several patriotic speeches. President Butler contributed a speech of his own on this occasion, comparing the developing confrontation with Germany to the crisis at Concord Bridge and the firing on Fort Sumter. At the end of the meeting Butler telegraphed a special message from the University to Wilson, pledging its "earnest and enthusiastic support ... to the services of the nation whenever the call shall come."[92]

Even this late in the day, however, a stubborn minority on some campuses continued to campaign desperately against American entry into the European conflict. The alumni association of Holy Cross College, for example, sent an urgent letter to President Wilson urging him "to lead the warring nations to peace rather than to join them in war."[93] In the Middle West, a small group at Oberlin College opposed American involvement in the overseas war. Dave Allen, a Socialist activist, led the group and also published a pacifist paper on the campus.[94] At the University of Michigan, it was reported that anti-interventionist sentiment still had some support.[95] And at the University of Southern California as late as March 1917 a large number of students polled were reported as being opposed to entering the war against Germany.[96]

Such sentiments, though, began now to run into forceful, if not openly violent, opposition. As war hysteria mounted, it became clear that academic freedom would be one of the first casualties. Attacks on alleged pro-German academics began as early as 1915. Harvard alumni tried at that time to force their Alma Mater to dismiss Hugo Munsterberg, a professor of psychology, from the faculty. The German-born psychologist had indeed issued statements seeking to explain the point of view of his native land to the American public. Many of his colleagues responded by ostracizing him and pro-British zealots charged that the professor was working for the German secret service. His daughter, after all, kept pigeons in the Munsterberg back yard! President Lowell and the Harvard Corporation refused to fire Munsterberg, however, and the Harvard president devoted an important part of his 1916–17 Annual Report to a defense of academic freedom.[97]

In the fearful, semi-hysterical atmosphere of February and March 1917 the level of tolerance for peace-minded dissenters on many campuses began to approach the vanishing point. When a couple of pacifist-minded students attempted to explain their point of view at a "patriotic" rally at Columbia on 8 February, they were roughed up. The would-be speakers were advised to "Go out and play with the Barnard girls!" A flying wedge of students formed to deny them access to the rostrum and to throw them out of the building. The chief speaker of the occasion explained that the aim of the gathering was to show that "Columbia is a patriotic, red-blooded institution and has no pacifist yellow streak."[98] The "red-blooded" students may have been encouraged in their new-found zeal by pro-Allied faculty members such as Franklin Giddings, a professor of sociology. Giddings was quoted in the papers as calling pacifists "indecent" and a mob of "morally obtuse women and their consorts."[99]

At the City College of New York, the administration boasted in mid-February that "the pacifist element which was numerous and active last spring, apparently has vanished."[100] To make sure that these unwanted agitators did not recover a measure of influence, President Mezes suspended the editor of *The Mercury*, the principal student magazine at City College. That young man was forbidden to appear within the College grounds at any time before 1 May. His crime seems to have been that he had written an editorial praising pacifism.[101] Nor was this all. In mid-March, the CCNY authorities ordered that two editors of the campus newspaper be removed from their posts. This was done because they revealed that the administration had ordered them not to publish the results of a poll of City College students on the highly-controversial question of military training. When the big newspapers in New York City got wind of this action, they all ran stories claiming that City College wanted the poll suppressed because its results would have shown that the school was a "hotbed of pacifism."[102]

At Harvard, just before the official declaration of war by Congress, the *Crimson* ran an editorial condemning neutralists and pacifists and declaring that: "The time has now come when such nonsense should stop." The *Crimson*, it was announced, "will print no more communications of a pacifistic nature."[103]

At Yale, a furor arose when William Lyon Phelps, a popular professor of English, continued a personal antiwar campaign by making an emotional speech in which he proclaimed: "If a foreigner should spit on our flag, that would not disgrace us so much as if we dyed our flag with American blood to avenge the insult." Widely reported in the press, the statement put President Hadley under great pressure to discharge Phelps. The President stubbornly refused to do so, however.[104]

A similar incident occurred at Columbia, where David S. Muzzey, a history professor, spoke out against Wilson's policy. Muzzey declared that America should go to war only in the event of a hostile invasion, and for no other reason. In a public statement, Muzzey asked: "Before going to war, would I wait until they had sunk seven ships?" His answer: "Yes, I would wait until they had sunk seven times seventy ships, and then I wouldn't go to war." A prominent New York businessman who was a Columbia alumnus demanded that President Butler dismiss Muzzey at once. Butler would not do so, however, explaining that: "In his capacity as a citizen and as an academic officer, he is of course at liberty to hold and to express whatever views on current topics his conscience may dictate. Those of us who hold different views ... if we believe our views to be sounder and wiser than his ... must use every effort to convince our fellow citizens of the fact."[105] But when the United States actually entered the war, Butler no longer felt bound by his previous concepts of academic freedom; at that point he approved the dismissal of Professors Cattell, Dana and Fraser because of their continuing antiwar activities.[106]

At this time, the most highly publicized antiwar campaign by a university figure was that carried on by David Starr Jordan, Chancellor of Stanford University. Invited to Princeton on 26 March by two peace-minded students, Jordan was refused the right to speak in any University building by the pro-intervention president of the school, John Hibben. The visitor had to deliver his plea for peace off campus in the First Presbyterian Church. There, a group of students listened quietly until Jordan specifically attacked President Wilson's policies. At that point, the boos and whistles grew so loud that they disrupted the remainder of Jordan's address.[107]

A couple of days later, the Stanford Chancellor carried his anti-war campaign to Yale. At the invitation of Professor Phelps, he spoke in a large lecture room on the university campus. Every seat was taken, and the audience, unlike that at Princeton, listened respectfully to Jordan's views. However, when he finished, a procession of fifteen hundred Yale students formed outside the lecture hall. Led by a brass band, they paraded noisily through downtown New Haven, aiming to show their loyalty to their country's policies.[108]

In Baltimore, conditions were very different. Jordan was denied the right to speak in any of the institutions of higher education in the city. At last, it was arranged that he deliver his anti-war message at the local Academy of Music. On the night of his address, however, an angry mob converged on the hall, broke through a police cordon, and pressed forward to attack the speaker. Jordan barely escaped with his life.[109]

The desperate, last-ditch campaign by peace-minded academics like Jordan to avert an all-out conflict with Germany came to an unsuccessful end in early April 1917. German submarines by this time were sinking neutral American ships without the slightest warning, even in supposedly secure "safety zones." Wilson, seeing no alternative, prepared a request to Congress to issue a formal declaration of war. He delivered his war message on 2 April and by 6 April both houses of Congress had responded by voting for immediate hostilities against the German Empire.[110]

The nation's colleges and universities now moved swiftly to mobilize their resources for all-out war. Plans to expand military training on the campuses were speeded up. The brain power and expertise of key members of academic staffs were offered to the government to help serve its wartime needs. A number of colleges decided it was expedient to waive traditional graduation requirements for Seniors who had left school in order to enlist in the armed forces.[111] Harvard sought to accommodate such students by giving them special final examinations in April and May 1917. The Cambridge institution also established a new kind of emergency degree, called the "war degree," which was to be conferred on departing undergraduates who had completed twelve full courses. Previously Harvard had required no less than sixteen such courses for graduation.[112]

Unhappily, some of the immediate campus responses to the declaration of war against Germany took the form of ugly, highly emotional outbursts of anti-German hysteria. These reactions, in turn, led to frantic efforts to crack down on local "disloyal" elements, especially pacifists and "slackers" who were not sufficiently enthusiastic about the war. The reputation of colleges as purveyors of wisdom and judicious guidance was not especially enhanced by the thoughtless fervor and incredible irrationality that now swept through some of them.

On the night that Congress declared war, President Grose of Asbury — De Pauw University told a noisy, boisterous throng that opponents of the war should be "put up against a brick wall and fed bullets."[113] Later that year Chancellor Kirkland of Vanderbilt University made it clear that no professor who had the slightest doubt about the wisdom of America's "great crusade" for democracy could expect to retain a teaching post at his school.[114] Chancellor Day of Syracuse expressed very similar sentiments. "If there is any man on the faculty," he warned, "who goes around the campus chattering about Germany, let him go where he can fight for Germany."[115]

Encouraged by inflammatory statements such as these from men of influence in academe, mobs in college towns began to hunt for "disloyal" professors. A Swedish-born pacifist on the Cornell faculty was sent messages threatening his life, and one night his house was smeared with yellow paint. Alumni from Cornell's class of 1873, angered by the controversial campaign for peace carried out by their fellow-graduate, David Starr Jordan, petitioned the University authorities to rescind his degrees. Jordan, they declared, was "soiled, smutted, bespattered, bedaubed, stained, and stinking with un-Americanism."[116] At the University of Akron, those students who joined the Akron Home Guard and received uniforms and real guns were expected, according to a contemporary source, not only to patrol the dam at Lake Rockwell, which provided the city's water supply, but to be on the lookout for "disloyal elements" and "be prepared to quell riots or disorders."[117]

Retrospect: The Colleges and "The Great Crusade"

What impact did colleges and universities have on the national debate respecting the proper American response to the Great War? University faculty and students certainly played an important part in contributing to the national soul-searching that preceded America's entry into the war. But was this role a decisive one? *New Republic* magazine felt that indeed it was. In April 1917 the *New Republic* editors wrote that contemporaneous contributions by people on the college campuses rivaled in historical significance the part played by professors and students during the American Revolution. They added that idealistic intellectuals, especially college professors, had induced America to enter upon a "thinking man's war," a crusade on behalf of ideas, not crude economic interests. "College professors, headed by a President who had himself been a college professor," continued the article, "contributed more effectively to the decision in favor of war than did the farmers, businessmen, or the politicians."[118]

In retrospect, the *New Republic*'s version of history seems somewhat too simplistic and exaggerated. Many complex factors — strategic, diplomatic, political, economic, military, propagandistic, and yes, ideological — combined to impel the United States to enter the war against Germany. During the crucial years in which this decision was being formulated, the campus communities without question were involved, but their involvement tended to be reactive rather than determinative. To be sure, at a few prominent institutions there was a real debate over the wisdom of military mobilization and the necessity of direct intervention in the conflict. Undoubtedly, the fact that the bulk of the academic establishment, especially in prestigious Eastern universities, was strongly pro-Ally, was one of the important factors influencing public opinion. At the same time, the very considerable effort made by the student antiwar and antipreparedness movement also had a certain impact. In the end, though, the student peace crusaders and their faculty allies were unable to overcome the built-in advantages possessed by the pro-Allied establishment.

Ultimately, the rush of events in 1916 and 1917 submerged all possibility of further dialogue on war issues at American colleges and universities. The German decision early in 1917 to launch unrestricted submarine warfare against all ships, including neutral American ones, was the final straw. Academic seekers for truth and defenders of rational discourse were now transformed, without any evidence of serious qualms, into highly emotional crusaders for righteousness against inveterate evil. As George Pierson noted: "Afire for the cause of freedom and justice for mankind, not a few (professors and academics) had been in advance of the public authorities. Now, patriotic and detesting militarism, they encouraged the Government and helped the military to take over."[119]

And once they had enlisted in Wilson's "Great Crusade," writes the historian of Iowa State, the nation's colleges and universities "demonstrated their effectiveness in providing officers, training soldiers, and supplying the resources for carrying on the war. Their instructional, research, and extension functions now found the fullest justification."[120]

It was truly ironic, however, that at the very moment of academe's enthusiastic participation in what it saw as a great and idealistic cause, the ensuing crusade was marred by actions that abrogated its guiding principles of objectivity, critical judgment, and freedom. War hysteria for a time effectively submerged the special values that had always set higher learning apart from other forces in society. What William Summerscales wrote about Columbia during the years of the "Great Crusade" could very easily have been applied to a number of other institutions of higher education at that time:

> The standard set in the war years by Butler and the University was conditioned by a headlong patriotism that abrogated democratic principles and denied scientists and scholars not only security and dignity but also basic civil rights . . . Not only was there no shelter for the ideals of free speech, social justice, and international sympathy, but also there was an absence of critical insight and judgment concerning the atavistic emotions the war released.[121]

4

The Second World War: From Peace Strikes to Pearl Harbor

Peace Advocates on the Campuses, 1919—1939

IRONICALLY, the collegiate antiwar movement of 1914 through 1917 had its greatest influence during the post-World War I years. While the 1920s were reputed to be a time of materialism and hedonism on college campuses, a number of concerned students campaigned strenuously against militarism during those very same years. One of their main targets was compulsory military training on college campuses. Drives against required ROTC programs surfaced at such schools as Ohio State, the University of Wisconsin, Boston University, the University of Colorado, and the University of Washington.[1] These campaigns achieved significant gains; by the end of the decade, only 197 of the 382 American colleges that the War Department listed as offering Military Science courses still mandated that students take them in order to graduate.[2]

The College of the City of New York was one of the most highly publicized centers of anti-ROTC sentiment. The campus newspaper at CCNY was ordered in 1925 to refrain from printing editorials criticizing the Military Science requirement. Not in the least intimidated by this policy, the Student Council two years later renewed the call for abolition of compulsory ROTC. Its campaign achieved a partial victory when the faculty in 1928 made military training an elective. The course still retained a favored position in the curriculum, however. Students who chose to avoid the two-year ROTC program were now obliged to take a *three*-year Hygiene course in place of it![3]

With the arrival of the 1930s, the antimilitarism campaign at the colleges began to heat up considerably. The era was a tumultuous one in the history of American student activism, a time perhaps matched in passion and intensity only by what was called "The Movement" during the '60s. The Great Depression was ravaging the economy, unsettling the outlook of many college students. Some turned to political radicalism as a panacea, calling for fundamental reconstruction of what they saw as a failing social order. The antimilitarism crusade was an offshoot of this growing campus unrest.[4]

The campus enemies of militarism found renewed strength and inspiration in dramatic developments that were going forward at European

123

universities. In February 1933 a group of students at Oxford University assembled to take an oath that under no circumstances would they take up arms "to fight for king and country." This highly controversial "Oxford Oath" was soon appropriated by American peace activists, although the wording was rephrased to accommodate the situation in the United States. American students were asked to subscribe to a revised "Oxford Oath," which stated that they would not "support the United States government in any war it may conduct."[5]

About this time, the *Daily Herald*, a campus newspaper at Brown University, launched a nationwide campaign against military training. The *Herald* sent invitations to student representatives at some 145 colleges asking them to sponsor campus demonstrations for peace. It was proposed that undergraduates from coast to coast take one of two possible actions: either subscribe to the uncompromising oath that had originated at Oxford or support a more moderate pledge repudiating overseas military adventures but conceding that defense of one's own homeland against an invader was justified.[6]

In New York City, peace demonstrations in 1933 began to assume a nonpacifistic aspect. When a student anti-war committee at City College threw a cordon of pickets around Lewisohn Stadium protesting a Memorial Day ROTC review, scuffles broke out with the police. Twenty undergraduate demonstrators were subsequently expelled for participating in the protests.[7]

In the spring of 1934, campus peace agitation entered a new phase as a national "Student Strike Against War" occurred. More than twenty-five thousand demonstrators turned out for this first coast-to-coast student mobilization against war. While hardly involving a majority of the country's collegians, the 1934 strike did attract a certain amount of public attention to the anti-war cause. In addition, the demonstration revived the campaigns that were already under way on college campuses for termination of compulsory military training.[8]

The 1934 strike had planted a seed; a year later the college anti-war campaign began to bear some fruit. In the Spring of 1935, a much bigger student "Strike for Peace" swept the colleges of the land. Over 175,000 anti-war demonstrators assembled at large institutions and small ones, at public colleges and private ones, at denominational schools and secular colleges, at colleges for men and at colleges for women. They waved placards reading "Abolish ROTC"; "Scholarship, not Battleships"; "Jesus, not Mars"; "Fight Imperialist War." At some of the rallies, large numbers of students subscribed to the "Oxford Oath."[9] Reactions were varied. In some instances, veterans' groups and anti-radical vigilantes invaded campuses in an effort to disrupt the demonstrations. In other cases, faculty and college administrators helped make arrangements for the peace rallies and even participated in them. At some schools, however, administrators expressed disapproval of the strike and sought to ban it. For their part, the strike organizers, perhaps over-optimistically, pronounced the national student demonstration a huge success.[10]

The largest number of peace demonstrators came from colleges in the Northeast. There were, however, substantial numbers of protestors in the West and South as well. At the University of Kansas, seven hundred students met on the college lawn to show the American people that college students were "declaratively against war and all the agents of war." In Tennessee, students from Scarritt College and Vanderbilt University marched through the streets of Nashville to show their support for the strike. These local peace strikers were a small part of the total student population at Vanderbilt, however. At the University of California, when President Sproul refused to allow the peace strikers to assemble in the Hearst Greek Theatre, two thousand of them held a "calm and orderly" rally on city property just outside the university's Sather Gate.[11]

The demonstrations of 1934 and 1935 were just a tune-up for a more grandiose student strike in 1936. On 22 April 1936 half a million college students participated in the largest "Strike for Peace" of the decade. The strike organizers, mostly members of left-wing organizations such as the American Student Union, were able to mobilize a large contingent of student protestors. Many of these did not subscribe to the radical ideology of the leaders, but they were nonetheless eager to demonstrate their opposition to compulsory ROTC and their aversion to entanglement in foreign wars. Polls of sentiment on college campuses at this time reveal a vast, not-so-silent, student majority that was adamantly anti-war and anti-interventionist.[12]

Anti-war students eventually found unusual and whimsical ways to express their viewpoint. In the spring of 1936, two undergraduates at Princeton decided to establish a campus chapter of an organization they called "Veterans of Future Wars" or "VFW." The idea caught on instantly at one college campus after another, and soon chapters of the unique organization were springing up everywhere.[13] At Drew University, the "Post Commander" of the Veterans of Future Wars demanded that the government pay an immediate bonus to all students because, he said, "many will be killed or wounded in the next war and the most deserving will not get the full benefit of their country's gratitude." His chapter also voted to request that part of the university grounds be set aside as a cemetery "for the war dead of the future" and that a monument be erected on the Drew campus to the "unborn, unknown soldier."[14] At Rice University in Texas, similar demands were made for the government to pay future-war bonuses to students, making veterans' groups like the American Legion livid with rage. The college dean, however, refused all demands that the school take immediate action against the local "VFW" chapter. It was merely a harmless student prank, he told the irate protestors.[15] Meanwhile, coeds from coast to coast rushed to get into the act, forming an organization of their own—"Gold Star Mothers of the Future." One of their ingenious leaders proposed that all college girls be given free trips to Europe so that they could visit the as-yet unexcavated graves of their unborn soldier sons.[16]

The Veterans of Future Wars movement spread like wildfire. Within a few months, there were 415 collegiate chapters of the new group with upwards of thirty-five thousand student members. As the idea gained momentum, a number of related organizations were formed. These included such interesting associations as Future Chaplains of Future Wars and Future War Profiteers of America.[17]

Majority sentiment on the college campuses of the Thirties was certainly in step with dominant sentiment in the country at large. Critics of the student peace movement may have been offended by some of the outrageous methods used by the collegians, but in its basic anti-involvement attitude the campus was not radically alienated from the nation. Public disillusionment with the results of Wilson's crusade to "make the world safe for democracy" was reaching its peak. From 1934 through 1936, Senator Gerald Nye conducted a highly publicized Congressional probe into the role of munitions makers and international bankers in propelling the United States into World War I. Isolationist sentiment in Congress was very strong, and President Roosevelt began to deliver anti-foreign-entanglement, "I Hate War"-type speeches. Furthermore, neutrality acts approved during this period prohibited bank loans or arms shipments to warring powers abroad.

This was the setting then, in which the student peace crusaders of 1936 assembled with their placards and banners. They gathered in small schools and large ones, in rural institutions and urban ones. At Wooster College in northern Ohio, bugles and drums summoned the students to gather around "The Rock" to hear fervent anti-ROTC and anti-war speeches. The Wooster campus had been plastered with placards bearing slogans such as "Future Gold Star Mothers Demand Their Bonus" and "Buy Your Own Wreath Now."[18] In a more urban setting, more than one thousand students with banners and flags turned out for the protest demonstration at Wayne State University in Detroit. The president of the American Student Union chapter read the "Oxford Oath" to the throng and they subscribed to it unanimously. There was, however, some "heckling—with firecrackers."[19]

Back east at Syracuse University, the administration offered help to the organizers of the April demonstration. Orders were given to dismiss classes between 11 A.M. and noon on strike day. At that time, at least fifteen hundred students joined by some of the faculty listened to a series of speeches for peace.[20]

The campus peace movement thus reached the apogee of its influence in 1936 and 1937. Appearances were somewhat deceiving, however. Behind the facade of unity and dedication, troublesome disagreements and divisions began to develop. The very slogan used by student peace strikers — "Against War and Fascism" — was self-contradictory, containing within itself the seeds of dissension. How could idealistic students defeat militaristic Fascism without, as a last resort, waging war against it?

A turning point in the movement came during the Summer of 1936, when General Franco's fascist army, supplied by Mussolini and Hitler, rebelled against the elected government of the Spanish Republic. Liberals and radicals the world over called for aid to the Spanish Republicans; conservatives and pro-Fascists favored General Franco. The Spanish Civil War thus became a rehearsal for World War II.

On American college campuses, the conflict in Spain produced significant repercussions. Liberals and radicals in the American Student Union began to advocate strong collective security measures against Franco, Hitler, and the "Axis" powers. Some student leaders were ready to jettison the "Oxford Oath," hitherto the cornerstone of the campus peace movement.

The dramatic events overseas induced a faction of the American student leadership to support President Roosevelt's foreign policy, which was now abandoning isolationism in favor of international sanctions against aggressor powers. The President's new orientation was made clear when he delivered his "Quarantine the Aggressors" speech in October 1937.

Campus pacifists and Socialists remained unreconciled to the new direction, however. These groups wished to retain the "Oxford Oath" at all costs. They insisted that students continue to resist the buildup of the country's armed forces and oppose without equivocation any resort to war, no matter what the alleged provocation.

The collective security issue was hotly debated at the December 1937 convention of the American Student Union. At that meeting an uneasy coalition of Communists and liberal internationalists won a dramatic victory when, by a two-to-one vote, the "Oxford Oath" was discarded. The stated policy of the ASU was now coming closer to that of the Roosevelt Administration.[21]

These developments had important consequences for the campus peace movement. Attempts to stage anti-war demonstrations were vitiated by the factional squabbling. At schools such as Columbia, where peace sentiment had been strong, there was a notable falling off of student support for the anti-war demonstrations. And, meanwhile, events overseas continued to make it difficult for advocates of the "Oxford Oath" to rally support on the campuses. Japan had invaded mainland China and Hitler's legions were gobbling up Austria and Czechoslovakia.[22]

A new anti-fascist militancy began to appear on a number of campuses. At Wayne State University, for example, volunteers were leaving for Spain to fight for that country's Republic as members of the "Abraham Lincoln Brigade." Coeds on the same campus were sponsoring a boycott of Japanese silk stockings.[23] Undergraduates at Marquette made no effort to hide their sympathies for the underdog Chinese.[24] At the University of Michigan, local American Student Union leaders stirred up the students to deplore the sacrifice of Czechoslovakia and to condemn the appeasement of Hitler by British Prime Minister Neville Chamberlain.[25] The *Princetonian* managed at one and the same time to caution against American "meddling" in Europe while sharply condemning the policies of Hitler and Mussolini.[26] The campus newspaper at the University of Rochester summed up the growing student sentiment on the eve of World War II with a simple two-word headline — "Stop Hitler!"[27]

Thus, as world catastrophe approached nearer and nearer, campus opinion, much like that in the nation at large, remained confused and ambivalent. A considerable majority of students were adamantly opposed to any American military buildup and to involvement in overseas war. These same students called, however, for worldwide resistance to Fascist aggression. The American Student Union's platform for 1938, reflecting this ambivalence, called for the United States to take the lead in sending aid to the Chinese and to the Spanish anti-fascists. A coalition of nations, it declared, must band together to stop Fascist aggression. At the same time, the platform opposed large military budgets, compulsory ROTC, and plans for industrial mobilization. The net result, wrote one commentator, was that ASU members "were in fact taking steps toward war without adequately preparing for it, or admitting the consequences of their actions to themselves or to the public."[28]

Reactions to the "Phony War"

When all-out war came once again to Europe, it arrived in such a surprising way that it further confused and divided the peace movement at American colleges. On 23 August 1939 the world was astounded to learn that Hitler and Stalin had concluded a totally unexpected non-aggression pact. This agreement, in turn, served as a go-ahead signal for the Nazis on 1 September to attack Poland. The German "Blitzkrieg" soon overran Poland, and in late September that unhappy country was divided up between the new Nazi-Soviet partners. To protect Russian security along its borders, the Soviet military then annexed Roumanian Bessarabia and demanded military bases and territorial guarantees from Finland. When Finland resisted these demands, the USSR invaded it. In the meantime, Britain and France decided to honor the pledge they had previously given to defend Polish sovereignty, and consequently declared war on Germany on the first of September 1939. At last, the long-feared World War II had begun; the "long Armistice" was over.

These events created great anxieties on the college campuses of the United States. They had a particularly important effect on the tenuous coalition of student peace activists in the American Student Union and the American Youth Congress, which to this point had been moving cautiously toward advocacy of some kind of collective security. That coalition was now shattered. Communists and their left-wing allies in the student leadership faithfully echoed the Soviet line, proclaiming once again: "We-must-stay-out-of-the-war." The leftists also now demanded that America follow a strict "hands-off" policy toward the Russo-Finnish War.

Liberals and pro-democrats in the ASU and AYC were bewildered and angered by the flip-flop of their Communist fellow students. The liberals wished to condemn Soviet as well as Nazi aggression. The poorly organized liberals found themselves consistently outvoted at most student conventions. In December 1939, at the American Student Union convention in Madison, Wisconsin, the Communist leaders came well prepared. They arranged to have the meeting hall packed with delegates who supported their position.[29] In addition, they achieved tight control over another important national student organization, the American Youth Congress. This group convened in Washington, D.C., in February 1940 to define its position on the war. Like the ASU, the Youth Congress had previously endorsed the principle of collective security. Under left-wing pressure, the AYC proceeded to reverse itself, contending that the earlier policy would involve the United States in war. In addition, a motion to condemn the Soviet invasion of Finland was decisively rejected.

Mrs. Eleanor Roosevelt had persuaded her husband, the president, to make an appearance at the convention in order to rally the young people to support his policies of aiding the Western Allies wherever possible. But when the chief executive dared to criticize the AYC leadership for not condemning the Soviet invasion of Finland, he was roundly booed by some of the young Youth Congress members.[30]

The rigid ideological line espoused by the Communist bloc in these two student organizations does not, of course, give an accurate picture of rank-and-file undergraduate sentiment. All indications point to the probability that there was much more sympathy for "Poor little Finland" among American college students than the pro-Soviet activists wished to acknowledge. At the same time, collective security proponents in the early months of 1940 were forced to recognize the hard fact that the vast majority of students, noncommunist as well as communist, remained unshakably opposed to United States involvement in the overseas war. For most of them, 1917 must not be allowed to happen again.[31]

Even before the Second World War had broken out in Europe, a University of Kansas publication articulated the dominant view. Why should the Roosevelt Administration "fan the flame of preparedness?" it asked. "How long will it take us," the periodical continued, "to understand that militarism is the denial of democracy? How long before we realize that war is the antithesis of Christianity?"[32] Neutralist sentiment was strong, too, among students at Rutgers University. Most young people on that campus felt that the conflict in Europe was "remote from American concerns."[33] At Drew University, a campus poll disclosed that more than half the enrolled students in the fall of 1939 intended to become conscientious objectors should the war spread to the United States. A columnist in the Drew campus paper warned his classmates not to develop excessive sympathy for England and France. "Think what you are saying," he wrote. "It is you and I who are going to fight — it is you and I who are going to die, or if we live through the hell that we would bring upon ourselves, we can but emerge as the living dead."[34] At Princeton, a student poll revealed an almost unanimous campus opinion that the United States had no business getting involved in the European war.[35] A few months later, an Elmo Roper poll reported that 64 percent of the students at New York University preferred that the United States stay out of the war in Europe regardless of the fate of the Western Allies. The NYU students declared that they would be willing to fight in a war only if the United States proper were invaded.[36]

In other sections of the country, similar sentiments were being expressed. Ten percent of the students polled at the College Park campus of the University of Maryland in December 1939 displayed an odd sense of humor, if that is what they intended, when they recorded themselves as hoping that Nazi Germany would win the war.[37] In the Middle West, most students at Northern Illinois University reportedly believed that Europe was so far from the United States that any conflict there need not involve America.[38] Similarly, two-thirds of the students at the University of Michigan told local pollsters that America must not intervene in the European war even if England and France appeared to be losing it.[39]

Undergraduate opinion in the Far West was not substantially different. Pollsters in the fall of 1939 found that 95 percent of the students at Santa Clara University in California wanted to stay out of the conflict overseas.[40] And undergraduates on the Berkeley campus of the University of California held very similar views.[41]

Interesting parallels to the pre-World War I campus peace movement emerged. In October 1939 students from Princeton, Harvard, and MIT came together to form the "American Independence League." Like the Collegiate League against Militarism of 1915 and 1916, the new association announced that it intended to bring the "stay-out-of-the-war" message to campuses across the land. By November its leaders claimed that they had established at least twenty college chapters. In the Middle West, students with similar noninvolvement views formed a body called "The Collegiate Front for Peace," with headquarters at Northwestern University. In the Far West, students at UCLA established a similar group, the "Youth Rally for Peace." These various student organizations shared a common desire: they wished to expose what they called "insidious" propaganda allegedly being disseminated to induce the United States to enter the European war.[42]

Left-wing activists in the ASU and AYC joined students from the anti-interventionist organizations to hold demonstrations against involvement in the war on Armistice Day 1939. The numbers turning out for these protests, however, did not match the huge student assemblages of the midthirties.[43] A second wave of campus anti-war rallies took place in April 1940. The demonstrators loudly proclaimed: "The Yanks are *NOT* coming!" But once again the number of participants was not huge, apparently because of the growing ideological differences within the peace movement at the colleges.[44]

Meanwhile, in Washington, President Roosevelt was moving precisely in the opposite direction from the majority of students. After a bitter struggle, the President succeeded in getting Congress to revise American neutrality legislation. The export of arms to belligerent powers was now permitted, though only on a strict "cash-and-carry" basis.

Anti-intervention student leaders bitterly denounced Roosevelt's policy as meddlesome and unneutral. The University of Michigan *Daily* typified this campus response when it complained that the neutrality act should never have been modified. Instead, it editorialized, the United States should embargo all trade with belligerents, develop a self-sufficient economy, and give up the relatively small percentage of national income that derived from foreign trade.[45] On other campuses, however, there were differences of opinion with respect to this question. A survey of students at Syracuse revealed that half of those polled approved the modifications of the arms embargo.[46]

The conflict in Europe had meanwhile settled down into a wary, nervous stalemate. During the winter of 1939–40, the Nazis, entrenched behind their Siegfried Line, and the British and French, protected by their supposedly impregnable Maginot Line, eyed each other anxiously but made no major move. Newspaper columnists began to speak of a "Phony War."

As the wearisome weeks wore on, new differences of opinion surfaced on American college campuses. These differences were not primarily between opponents and proponents of intervention in Europe, but between students and faculty. It became increasingly clear that a generation gap existed on the question of the proper response America should make to the war in Europe. Many college professors had come to believe that the United States could not afford to stand idly by and allow the Nazis to crush Great Britain and France. Western civilization, they feared, would not survive such an outcome. The bulk of the students at their colleges, however, strongly disagreed.

A pro-Allied orientation was apparent in the speeches delivered by college presidents at the formal opening of the Fall 1939 semester. President Sills of Bowdoin, for example, told his students that to concentrate only on keeping Americans safe was "shortsighted and selfish." President Wilkins of Oberlin warned: "In Europe, democracy is truly at bay; our own democracy ... must stand on guard." President Cowley of Hamilton College observed: "In democratic countries the voters have well-established privileges and responsibilities which are denied the people of the totalitarian states. In the last analysis, the war ... is being fought to protect these precious bulwarks of civilization."[47]

At Syracuse University, Professor W. Freeman Galpin challenged the keep-out-of-war sentiments of his students in an article published in the Spring of 1940 by the campus newspaper. "A totalitarian victory marks the disappearance of the European democracies," he pointed out. "We must join with those who seek to rid the world of our enemy ... STOP, LOOK, AND LISTEN, before it is TOO LATE."[48] At the University of Michigan, another history professor, Preston Slosson, sent a series of letters to his campus newspaper to protest its isolationist editorial position. In one of these, he argued that an embargo on American foreign trade would only serve to aid Hitler.[49]

President Wilkins of Oberlin returned to the attack in January 1940 and contributed a long article to *School and Society*. "The fact remains," Wilkins argued, "that in this still stupid and self-seeking world, war may be ineluctable, peace suicidal." As the "Phony War" ground on, Wilkins warned, the citizens of academe might someday be forced to confront an alternative most of them had long dreaded. "Let us assume," he speculated, "that war is forced upon us by an invasive enemy, under circumstances which leave us no rational opposition save to fight."[50]

The Nazi Blitz Shakes Up America's Campuses

The "Phony War" came to an abrupt end in the Spring of 1940. Nazi columns swarmed over Denmark and Norway and then, breaking through

Allied defenses, rolled through Holland, Belgium, and Northern France. By July Paris was in their grasp, and soon thereafter, the French government agreed to an ignominious surrender. All that remained in Western Europe to defy Hitler were the British and a faction of Free French which refused to accept defeat. The "softening-up" bombing of Britain had begun, preparing the way for a probable landing of German troops.

Faced with the imminent possibility of a Nazi-dominated Europe, a sudden panic swept America. President Roosevelt picked up bipartisan support for sending increased aid short of actual war to the forces that were still fighting Hitler. To bolster America's defenses, Congress authorized huge increases in military appropriations. Somewhat more controversial was a proposal for universal peacetime conscription, the first in the nation's history; that bitterly disputed measure also received legislative approval. In addition, the President, dropping all pretensions of "neutrality," took the risky course of shipping arms, ammunition, and airplanes from America's dangerously depleted arsenals to the embattled British and Free French. In September he made another dangerous gamble, sending fifty older United States destroyers to the British to help them defend their shores. This was part of a deal—destroyers in exchange for ninety-nine-year leases of British bases in the Western Hemisphere.

These actions triggered a major national debate, with internationalists in both political parties supporting Roosevelt and an angry isolationist opposition, also bi-partisan, proclaiming it a major disaster. William Allen White's Committee to Defend America by Aiding the Allies emerged as the principal organization seeking to arouse the American public against the Nazi danger. On the other side, the America First Committee sought to convince the people that they must stay out of the European conflict and arm themselves only to defend America itself.

The great debate agitated the college campuses as it did the nation at large. Without question, the Nazi Blitz increased student support for sending aid to the beleaguered European democracies, although stay-out-of-war sentiments remained strong among many undergraduates. As before, professors were mostly pro-Ally. Epitomizing faculty response to the events of the spring, Professor William Lyon Phelps of Yale, who had been a strong opponent of America's involvement in World War I, now scathingly denounced a peace petition approved by fourteen hundred Yale undergraduates. America would achieve such splendid isolation if Hitler won, Phelps asserted, that it would not have a friend left in the world. "I would prefer to lose the war on the side of the Allies," declared the professor, "rather than win it with Hitler. The Allies stand for everything in which I believe."[51]

Phelps had plenty of company in academe. In late May 1940, fifty members of the Northwestern University faculty sent telegrams to

Congressmen urging that money and military equipment be sent immediately to Britain and France.[52] About the same time, the majority of the faculty of Hobart and William Smith colleges in upstate New York issued a statement asking that the United States give the Allies "at once and free of charge, airplanes, *matériel*, and funds as they are needed."[53] President James B. Conant of Harvard wished to go even further. In addition to immediate American supplies and money for the Allies, Conant urged that compulsory military service be introduced in the United States. His proposals were endorsed by President Corson of Dickinson College and his faculty. The faculty of Lehigh wired President Roosevelt urging that he use his powers as Commander-in-Chief to aid the Western democracies.[54] And at Princeton University, seventeen prominent faculty members, including Albert Einstein, telegraphed the President on 19 May, warning him that totalitarian aggression placed America's security in danger and suggesting that "our best national defense consists in assistance to those forces which are now opposing this aggression."[55]

Blitz or no Blitz, a number of undergraduates during that troubled summer still feared that sending aid to the European democracies would involve the country directly in the European conflict. Nevertheless, Hitler's unbroken series of triumphs began to have a significant impact on the campus atmosphere. A growing body of student opinion, alarmed by the events overseas, was coming reluctantly to the conclusion that forceful American measures might indeed be needed. The historian of one Western institution, Colorado College, reports: "Student attitudes toward the war changed as England, standing alone, underwent heavy daily bombing attacks by the Nazis."[56] At Marquette, a Roman Catholic college in Milwaukee, there was a dramatic change at this time, writes Raphael Hamilton, "from complete pacifism to war fury."[57] At Syracuse University, the Blitz emboldened student internationalists on campus to organize openly once again and launch a campaign for aid to Britain and France.[58]

In the Northeast, one of the principal ideological battlegrounds among the colleges could be found at Yale University. As previously noted, some fourteen hundred "Yalies" signed an appeal in late May 1940 asking that the United States stay out of the European war. A week later, six hundred pro-Ally Yale undergraduates forwarded a petition to President Roosevelt and Congress urging that massive aid be sent to the anti-Hitler forces in Europe. President Charles Seymour and several of the deans at the University signed this petition.[59] In mid-June, a special rally was held, attended by several hundred undergraduates and a number of professors and prominent Yale alumni. Henry L. Stimson addressed the meeting, along with President Seymour. Resolutions were approved declaring universal military training to be essential to protect "the safety and free institutions of the United States." The meeting was called at the request of the Yale branch of the Military Training Campus Association. The latter organization apparently represented an attempt to revive the "Plattsburg Idea" of World War I days. It claimed that it had attracted strong support at various campuses for its proposal to require military training for all civilians.[60]

About this time, too, a number of nationally prominent student leaders — people like James Wechsler, Joseph Lash, Eric Sevareid, and Molly Yard — who had been active in the anti-war demonstrations of the thirties, became firm supporters of all-out aid for the Allies.[61] These people worked in close partnership with the collegiate chapters of William Allen White's Committee to Defend America by Aiding the Allies. Members of these chapters now called themselves "Student Defenders of Democracy." The White Committee also sought to organize faculty members and university administrators to campaign for aid to Britain and France. Committees of academics in various disciplines were set up at all major universities and at many smaller institutions as well. These units directed their appeal to historians, economists, political scientists, natural scientists, and other specialists.[62]

The anti-involvement forces were equally determined to do all they could to sway opinion at the colleges and universities. Indeed, America First, which was the isolationist counterpart of the White Committee, made its formal debut on a university campus. In 1940 the stay-out-of-war movement drew its strength from three curiously disparate sources — party-line Communists, secular and religious pacifists, and conservative isolationists with ties to big business. An offshoot of this third component undertook during the summer of 1940 to organize an anti-involvement group at Yale. The principal organizer, R. Douglas Stuart, Jr., was a student at the Yale Law School. His father was a vice president of the Quaker Oats Company, and this connection proved to be extremely useful for the fledgling organization. Through family contacts, Stuart was able to induce retired General Robert E. Wood, Board Chairman of Sears, Roebuck, to become the titular head of a new national anti-involvement organization that would become known as America First. The organization campaigned against any involvement in the European war and strenuously opposed Franklin Roosevelt's policy of aiding the Allies. It also called for a quick buildup of an impregnable defense structure for America and the whole Western Hemisphere.[63]

At Yale, two of Stuart's most active isolationist colleagues were Kingman Brewster, Jr., editor of the *Yale Daily News*, and Richard Bissell, an assistant professor of economics. Other faculty members who sympathized with the cause were A. Whitney Griswold and Edwin Borchard. Two of the original founders of America First, A. Whitney Griswold and Kingman Brewster, later became presidents of Yale University.[64]

The America First movement attracted considerable attention on college campuses. It obtained the warm endorsement of such prominent anti-interventionist academics as the historian Charles A. Beard. One of its most famous speakers from outside the academy was the legendary aviator Colonel Charles A. Lindbergh, who in 1940 launched a national tour to promote the movement with an impassioned address in Yale's Woosley Hall.[65] America First established a special College Division in its Chicago headquarters. Besides Yale, the University of Chicago, Harvard, and many other schools had their own local America First Chapters. A manual, *Colleges for America First*, was distributed to help students start up new chapters.[66]

As the great debate continued, anti-involvement sentiment among college students seemed to increase in intensity during the summer and fall of 1940. Influential campus newspapers such as the *Harvard Crimson* and the *Yale Daily News* set forth impassioned arguments for keeping out of Europe's troubles.[67] University of Missouri students indicated their sentiments by holding signs aloft that proclaimed: "The Yanks are *NOT* coming!" At Columbia University, a campus Peace Committee asserted that four-fifths of that school's students opposed shipping armaments to any of the belligerents. Seven hundred students at Amherst College endorsed a not-too-serious resolution stating that, if the United States were to be invaded, the East Coast should be abandoned immediately, since it was too decadent to be worth fighting for.[68]

At Harvard, a "Committee for the Recognition of Classroom Generals" was established that forwarded tin soldiers and special citations to five faculty members known to be very outspoken in propagating pro-intervention views. Harvard undergraduates picketed in gas masks outside the classroom of one history professor viewed as being particularly aggressive in arguing in favor of entering the war.[69] At Colorado College, the campus newspaper in its 24 May issue displayed a death mask on its front page with the caption: "Enlist NOW — Travel, Adventure, Experience." The paper's editor added, "You're just a young punk, Mr. Collegian. You may not be old enough to vote, but you are old enough to die."[70]

At Cornell, the American Student Union made its views known in an original way. It constructed a six-foot-high military tank of grey cardboard and forwarded it to the White House with this message printed on its side: "Dear President Roosevelt — Keep America out of war."[71] Also in late May 1940, one Harper Poulson, who listed himself as chairman of the "United Student Peace Committee," announced that a giant student postcard campaign would be launched immediately to protest "the clear intent of our government in Washington to disregard the will of 95 percent of the people and involve us in the war."[72] When the graduation season of 1940 arrived, writes Geoffrey Perrett, the attendant ceremonies frequently witnessed "fervent pleas by professors and alumni for an end to the Third Reich, which were greeted by a stony silence or irreverent catcalls from the assembled undergraduates."[73]

In the Fall of 1940, the editors of the *Atlantic Monthly* took due note of the almost total alienation of many college students from the pro-Allied views of their professors. The magazine published an appeal for the anti-Hitler cause written by a pro-interventionist professor, Arnold Whitridge. Along with this, it printed a number of angry student replies rejecting his plea.[74]

Student attitudes were shaped by a number of considerations. Many undergraduates felt that the older men of America who did not have to risk their lives were engaged in a conspiracy to drag younger people into a war in which the latter would surely be killed. The University of Kansas newspaper articulated their suspicions quite bluntly when it declared: "We should remember that it would be the students' lives that would be at stake if war comes, not the professors'."[75]

President Charles Seymour of Yale noted another factor. In the past, the teachings of these very same interventionist professors had helped develop a deep suspicion in students of involvement in overseas war. "These boys," wrote Seymour, "were born and brought up in a period in which it was fashionable to assert that we had been inveigled into military intervention in Europe in order to snatch British and French chestnuts out of the fire and to swell the incomes of munitions makers ... They have constantly been warned against a propaganda which might trick them into another [war]."[76] The same line of reasoning was pursued by William H. Attwood, editor of the *Daily Princetonian*. In an article written for *NEA Service*, Attwood said that his Class of '41 had been "gypped out of its future." They had

> taken enough courses in the social sciences to develop a fairly hard-boiled attitude toward war ... So it has not been easy for college men to acquiesce in the idea of another war to save democracy. They have been taught to be skeptics, and their skepticism was fortified by the realization that their own postgraduate plans would be wiped out in the bargain.[77]

More difficulties were in store for the college students who returned to their campuses to begin the Fall 1940 semester. They confronted a new and unwelcome situation. Roosevelt had gotten Congress in mid-September to give its approval to the Burke-Wadsworth Selective Service Act. All American males from twenty-one through thirty-five were now eligible for compulsory military service.[78]

Most students greeted the first peacetime draft in American history with resignation but also, predictably, with a good deal of resentment. They did not know "whether or not they could finish the semester's work; employment prospects dimmed when potential employers learned that the student might soon be drafted, courtships were disrupted, and life suddenly was filled with uncertainties," wrote a Middle Western educator.[79] The big question for Marquette students enrolling for the Fall term, as for many others, was: "What happens to our tuition, if we are called to service?"[80] With considerable bitterness, the campus newspaper at Carleton College notified all students over twenty-one that they were obliged to go to Leighton Hall on registration day, 16 October, to "sign away our American democracy."[81] At the University of Michigan, students did more than complain. Petitions were circulated protesting against the conscription bill as "a major step toward preparation for an involvement in war." A thousand students signed these petitions.[82]

College presidents took immediate steps to inform their students that, even if drafted, they were permitted by law to remain in school until the end of the college year. When President Dodds of Princeton advised his undergraduates to take advantage of this exemption, the *Princetonian* remarked: "President Dodds might have added that any man who chooses to ditch a chance to an education just to learn to kill people six months sooner is a damn fool."[83]

Many college administrators, like Dodds, advised the students at their schools to take full advantage of their rights under the draft law. Thus, President Simmons of the University of Akron urged the young men on his campus to stay in school until such time as they might be called up. A letter from President Roosevelt advocating this course of action was read to all freshmen. And the Akron Trustees, seeking to calm student fears, announced that tuition fees would be refunded to any undergraduate who might be conscripted.[84] Many other universities, such as Columbia, pledged similar refunds to draftees. Some institutions took specific action to ensure that their students would receive the exemptions to which they might be entitled. Marquette University, for example, set up a Committee on Draft Deferment. During its first year of operation, that body secured deferments for no less than 550 Marquette students.[85]

While the overall student response to conscription was problematical at best, university administrators and faculty were generally favorable to it. It was seen as a necessity to defend America from totalitarian aggression. Even while the Burke-Wadsworth Act was still being debated in Congress, a group of state university presidents from the Middle West, drawing on their experience with Morrill Act military training, gave conscription their warm endorsement.[86] In Cambridge, Massachusetts, a university organization calling itself "The Harvard Group," announced that it had made a survey of faculty opinion on the draft. The results revealed a nearly unanimous sentiment in favor of universal training.[87] A notable exception to this unanimity occurred at the College of the City of New York, where left-wing faculty members opposed the draft. A statement issued on 5 August by sixty-six City College summer-session teachers opposed the Burke-Wadsworth Act because they said it might speed America's involvement in the war.[88]

The Association of American Colleges went on record as favoring conscription, but earnestly requested that it not apply to students under the age of twenty-one. The Association's executive director, Guy Snavely, pointed out that if the younger age groups were drafted, college enrollments would be decimated. The Association's argument prevailed; age limits beginning at twenty-one were written into the final version of the draft bill.[89]

One response at the colleges to conscription was a renewed interest in the previously much-criticized ROTC programs. University administrators liked courses that might enable their students to receive military training without having to leave the campus. They worked hard to get programs of this nature accepted by the military authorities as fulfilling the obligations mandated by Selective Service.[90] Columbia University was one of the most active schools introducing such courses. In September 1940 Columbia mailed out a series of bulletins to the six thousand students who were beginning the fall semester, telling them about the availability of flight training, Marine Corps Reserve training, and courses in military surveying, all of them on campus.[91]

In addition to endorsing compulsory military training, those university leaders who favored Roosevelt's pro-Allied policy threw their wholehearted support behind his efforts to bolster America's national defenses. They rallied their institutions to contribute to the nation's defense mobilization. At Columbia University, for example, a campus committee on national defense was set up in early July to coordinate all of the university's efforts in that area.[92] A similar committee to manage defense-related projects was established at Harvard with Professor Ralph Barton Perry as chairman. The faculty members who worked with Perry's committee called themselves "American Defense, Harvard Group." They promised that their special skills would be available at any time to meet the nation's security needs.[93]

Princeton University, too, was quick to join the parade of schools offering help to the defense drive. At its opening exercises in the fall, President Dodds pledged that his institution would offer "full cooperation with our government" and declared that "its whole organization, men, facilities, and equipment are again at its disposal as it may require them."[94] Nor were the Ivy League schools the only ones to plunge wholeheartedly into defense mobilization. Colleges from coast to coast took similar action, offering a variety of defense-related courses. The University of Texas added such offerings as advanced engineering and aeronautics to its curriculum; Columbia introduced advanced studies in international relations; Marquette established courses in pilot training; the University of Maryland offered studies in explosives, aircraft design, and fire control; and the University of Virginia set up programs in materials testing, production supervision, and principles of radio communication.[95] American academic institutions during the latter months of 1940 were rapidly transforming themselves into national defense centers.

Many of the new courses and defense-related research projects were financed by funds granted by the federal government. A close relationship developed between Washington and institutions of higher education, a relationship destined to become even closer in 1941 and the years following. The universities became increasingly dependent on federal grants for substantial portions of their budgets.[96] As a result, universities were pressured to concentrate their research efforts on areas that would be of maximum value for national defense. And those faculty specialists who did not remain on their home campuses were frequently given leaves of absence to work on government defense programs in Washington and elsewhere. As America's gigantic defense efforts lurched into high gear, the academic world gave the government its fullest possible support.

Intervention vs. Non-Involvement: The Continuing Debate

During the first eight months of 1941, the debate centering on America's proper response to the European war reached new levels of intensity. Hundreds of schools hastily beefed up their engineering, aeronautical, and pilot-training programs. Meanwhile, the undergraduate campaigners for involvement in Europe and their stay-out-of-war opponents turned up their arguments several decibels.[97]

The life-and-death struggle in Europe and Asia was now reaching a new and more critical stage. The Roosevelt Administration, for its part, moved toward increasingly open support of all anti-Axis forces. Having been reelected to an unprecedented third term, the President felt that he was in a stronger position to implement short-of-war shipments to the Allies. Pro-interventionists on the campuses gave their full support to Roosevelt's forceful measures. At the same time, opponents of involvement at the colleges redoubled their attacks on the government's pro-Allied actions.[98]

Grassroots sentiment among the students in post-secondary institutions became more and more pro-Ally during these months. Polls revealed increasing campus support for all possible aid to the anti-Axis coalition. Nevertheless, the great majority of students polled remained opposed to the United States entering the war as an active participant.[99]

Students favoring drastic anti-Hitler measures now felt freer to announce their interventionist views. For example, 350 students from various liberal arts colleges wired a petition to their Congressmen on 25 February 1941 asking for "full American support to the forces fighting Nazism."[100] Students with this viewpoint organized "The Student Roll-Call for Aid to the Allies," a campus organization sponsored by several national interventionist groups. In mid-May, Mrs. Roosevelt addressed the Student Roll-Callers, praising their commitment to the defense of democracy. America, she said, needed the conviction that "beyond material things, there are things worth living for, and, if need be, worth dying for."[101]

Members of college faculties were, if anything, more actively pro-intervention than ever. In early December 1940 three Harvard professors proposed that drastic measures be implemented immediately, such as turning over U.S. warships and cargo vessels to the British and using the American navy to convoy freighter shipments to Allied ports.[102] A month later, eighty professors at the University of Wisconsin petitioned the Administration to implement a policy of "all-out aid to Britain not necessarily short of force."[103] About this time, too, thirty-four research scientists and scholars at Princeton urged President Roosevelt to declare a state of emergency and accelerate the country's mobilization for effective defense.[104] As 1940 drew to a close, the White House was deluged with appeals from leading figures in academe asking for a more active pro-Allied policy. When twenty-nine prominent educators sent a telegram to the President in late December urging "general, immediate, and effective aid to England," the list of signers was very much like a Who's Who of American scholars.[105]

The poet Archibald Macleish added his voice to those who were seeking to alert the country. In a commencement address at Union College in June 1941, Macleish declared that America's young people should join with their professors in giving their wholehearted support to the crusade against Hitler. They must do this, he said, because "in this war it is not possible for any man, no matter how anonymous, no matter how indifferent, no matter how small, to be passed by; ... the outcome of this war will affect every man whatever his wishes."[106]

As if in response to such passionate appeals, student supporters of all-out aid to Britain redoubled their efforts to win converts. One of the principal organizations working for this goal on the college campuses was the Student Defenders of Democracy, an offshoot of the White Committee.[107] A like-minded undergraduate group was International Student Service, which had been established originally to help European students who were victims of Hitler. Mrs. Roosevelt, having severed her connections with left-wing groups such as the American Youth Congress, found the ISS to be much more sympathetic to her ideas, and often appeared before it as a speaker.[108]

Although the pro-intervention cause was obviously making considerable headway at American colleges during the first few months of 1941, it was not helpful that eleven different student organizations were competing against each other to secure aid for the Allies. It wasn't until November 1941 that the various pro-Allied societies were ready to merge into one. At that time, they combined to form a new student association, American Youth for Freedom.[109]

The dedicated groups of students and professors who were working tirelessly for aid to the Allied powers were joined from time to time by a number of nationally-prominent university presidents. Robert G. Sproul, the head of the University of California, addressed a chapter of the Fight for Freedom Committee in August 1941. He told the group that he shared their view that the United States should enter the war against Hitler as soon as possible. How could Americans "stand idle," asked Sproul, "while the catastrophe we can prevent occurs before our eyes?"[110]

James B. Conant, the president of Harvard University, came to this conclusion earlier than Sproul. On 4 May, Conant told a nationwide radio audience that the hour for action had arrived and that America "should fight now."[111] Headquarters of the Fight for Freedom organization, in June 1941, released to the public a list of notables who now favored entering the European war. The list included the names of a sizeable group of college and university presidents.[112]

As pro-Allied activists stirred up students to accept the prospect of an early entry into the overseas struggle, campus opponents of intervention redoubled their efforts to prevent such an outcome. Some of the America First zealots in academe interpreted internationalism and collective security as being something akin to welfare-state liberalism or even Marxism. Their isolationism was strongly tinged with political conservatism and racism.[113] At the other end of the non-involvement spectrum, however, leftist students like those in the American Youth Congress echoed the Communist line that the war was purely an imperialist conflict that could only further subjugate the workers and students of the world.[114]

America First searched diligently for well-known personalities who would be willing to endorse its movement. At Harvard University, America Firsters were able to recruit Joseph P. Kennedy, Jr. This young man was the brother of future United States President John F. Kennedy and the son of the strongly isolationist American ambassador to Great Britain. Joseph, Jr., played an active part in establishing at Harvard a "Committee Against Military Intervention in Europe."[115] America First also assembled its own list of influential college presidents who were willing to make their non-involvement views public. Included in this group were President Hutchins of the University of Chicago; the ex-president of Stanford, Ray Lyman Wilbur; Henry N. MacCracken, president of Vassar College; and Alan Valentine, president of the University of Rochester.[116]

America First's national headquarters also funded a poll of student sentiments that was published by the strongly isolationist *Yale Daily News*. The poll, not surprisingly, found campus opinion to be substantially what its sponsors wished it to be. Sixty-one percent of the students interviewed at colleges in the Northeast opposed American entry into the European war.[117] At Princeton, twenty students in the Theological Seminary with very similar views sent a letter to President Roosevelt in late December 1940 opposing involvement in the war or "any program of full industrial, military, and naval mobilization."[118]

Opponents of intervention staged anti-war "strikes" on a number of campuses on 23 April 1941. Some of these were sponsored by the American Youth Congress; others were organized by a dissident non-Communist peace group, the Youth Committee Against War. The turnout was relatively small, in no way approaching the numbers participating in the peace strikes of the 1930s. At a number of colleges, local units of the Student Defenders of Democracy held counter-demonstrations, handing out pamphlets in favor of all-out aid to Britain.[119]

The battle of words between student interventionists and student isolationists tended ultimately to focus on two key issues during the first half of 1941 — Lend-Lease and convoys. President Roosevelt made a public announcement of his Lend-Lease proposal on 16 December 1940. Americans would lend vitally needed military equipment to the nations fighting Hitler, which they would pay for later. After a bitter debate in Congress, Lend-Lease was approved on 11 March 1941. Students and professors were actively involved in the debate, with college faculty predominantly on the President's side and students somewhat more evenly divided on the question.

At the University of Michigan, for example, 214 faculty members signed a petition to Congress in February 1941 urging enactment of the Lend-Lease bill.[120] But not all professors supported the proposal. Sixty-eight Harvard faculty telegraphed Roosevelt, opposing Lend-Lease on the grounds that it undermined democratic government in America.[121]

On the undergraduate level, the Student Defenders of Democracy distributed pro-Lend-Lease petitions and sponsored lectures on and off the campus dealing with the issue. Prominent youth leaders such as Joseph Lash and Herbert Bayard Swope, Jr., participated in their campaign. One of the special programs arranged by the Student Defenders was a two-way international radio broadcast carried both by BBC and the Columbia Broadcasting System. The broadcast's main theme was: "The world cannot remain half-free and half- fascist."[122]

Other student groups worked to drum up support for Lend-Lease, such as the National Student Federation, which had recently seceded from the American Youth Congress, and the International Student Service, whose efforts were aided by the First Lady, Eleanor Roosevelt.[123] Opposing these groups was the left wing American Youth Congress. Still adamantly hostile to the policies of the Roosevelt Administration, the AYC sponsored a Town Meeting in Washington in February 1941 whose main purpose was "to fight the passage of Lend-Lease." Jack McMichael, Executive Secretary of AYC, launched a bitter attack on Roosevelt for his pro-British policies and warned the President: "You can't pull a Wilson on us." Both sides in the European conflict were depicted as ruthless "imperialists."[124]

The campus debate eventually had reverberations in the halls of Congress. On 3 March Senator Austin of Vermont, arguing for the enactment of the Lend-Lease measure, put on the record a telegram he had received from one hundred faculty members at the University of Illinois urging immediate passage of the bill. Senator Wheeler of Montana, a passionate opponent of the proposal, promptly asked Austin whether he had "any wires from college students who would be sent to war under the bill" while "decrepit presidents who want them to go" stayed at home. Wheeler added that a lot of the college professors who had been brought to Washington by the New Deal might know something about teaching but "couldn't be elected dogcatcher in their towns because they have no knowledge of practical political affairs." The Senate Majority Leader, Senator Barkley, immediately reproached Wheeler for his attack on professors, defending their right to express themselves on any public issue.[125]

The following day, as the debate continued, additional references were made to the colleges. A prominent opponent of Lend-Lease, Senator Brooks of Illinois, quoted from an editorial that had appeared in the *Daily Illini*, the campus newspaper of the University of Illinois. The Senator pointed out that the student editorial was "an eloquent and moving protest against participation in war by the United States based on the premise that the United States had made a colossal mistake to take part in the last World War."[126]

Although Lend-Lease had been approved as official United States policy, the contemplated war supplies would be of little help to Hitler's opponents if they could not be delivered safely to Allied ports. Nazi submarines were sinking millions of tons of Allied shipping. In response to this perilous situation, American supporters of the anti-Hitler coalition proposed that Lend-Lease shipments be sent in convoys that would be guarded by warships of the United States navy. Roosevelt personally favored this idea, but at first hesitated to take such a drastic, brink-of-war step. As the convoy option was being considered by the government, the issue stirred up more heated debate on college campuses.[127]

A few days after Congress approved Lend-Lease, Student Defenders of Democracy sent representatives to set up tables in front of the New York Public Library. The SDD representatives asked passers-by to sign petitions calling for navy convoying of goods to Britain. Similar petitions were distributed on college campuses all over the nation. The goal of the campaign was to collect one million signatures.[128] The SDD effort was paralleled by appeals from faculty groups. In April, for instance, 240 members of the Harvard faculty, plus a number of deans and trustees, sent an urgent appeal to President Roosevelt. They warned him that the purpose of Lend-Lease was being nullified by German U-boats and that he must therefore take immediate action to ensure that American aid to the Allies was effective.[129]

On 23 April peace strikes and antiwar rallies were held on many college campuses. On that occasion, supporters and opponents of the convoy proposal held rival demonstrations. The rallies staged by the American Youth Congress announced total "opposition to convoys and to an A.E.F." The Youth Committee Against War sent a telegram to Roosevelt that declared: "Mr. President, we hold you to your pledge against involvement. Convoys mean shooting war. We oppose convoys." At Lewisohn Stadium, some twenty-five hundred CCNY students assembled and approved resolutions opposing convoys. A somewhat smaller rally in Columbia University's McMillan Theatre adopted similar resolutions. Meanwhile, demonstrators representing the Student Defenders of Democracy mobilized on many of the same campuses and collected signatures to petitions that urged immediate U.S. convoying of supplies to the British. SDD leaders declared that the success of their petition campaign constituted "an answer to those who think that young Americans are indifferent to the issues in this war."[130]

The battle of rival statements and petitions on the campuses continued into May. On 9 May, a thirty-foot scroll was presented to Acting Navy Secretary Ralph Baird. It had been signed by 992 Princeton students and urged the Administration "to use the United States Navy for convoying merchant ships against enemy attack."[131] In early May, too, the *Columbia Spectator* published the results of its own poll of faculty sentiment. The poll reported that 65 percent of the faculty at Columbia College favored American convoys to get Lend-Lease supplies to Britain but still opposed an outright declaration of war on the Axis.[132] About this time, too, a newly established organization at the University of Michigan, the American Student Defense League, announced that it had collected eleven hundred signatures to a petition favoring convoys.[133]

Opponents of the convoy proposal were not ready to give up, however. At Princeton, an organization calling itself College Men for Defense First, set about collecting signatures for an anti-convoy petition. Eventually one thousand students, it claimed, signed its document, which explicitly opposed all convoys or "any use of the United States Army or Navy for the defense of the British Empire."[134] At the New York Public Library, where representatives of Student Defenders of Democracy were still collecting signatures for their pro-convoy petitions, rival tables were set up by spokesmen for the Youth Committee against War. The Youth Committee representatives sought to match the SDD by collecting hundreds of signatures to a petition opposing both convoys and war.[135]

In mid-September 1941 the Roosevelt Administration finally adopted a "shoot-on-sight" policy with respect to Nazi submarine attacks, also authorizing at that time United States naval convoys of Lend-Lease shipments to Allied ports. By then, it was apparent to the entire world that America was waging an undeclared naval war against Germany in the North Atlantic.

During the preceding months, campus partisans of strong action against the Axis and their anti-involvement opponents had hotly debated the issues and had kept the Lend-Lease and convoy questions vividly before the American public. It may be an exaggeration to say that anti-Axis activists on college campuses singlehandedly forced the American Administration to institute convoys and risk an undeclared war with the Nazis. It is clearly apparent, however, that academe's role in mobilizing public opinion for strong anti-Hitler measures was immensely significant.

The Colleges Prepare for War:
The Last Weeks Before Pearl Harbor

Beginning with the spring of 1941, the Roosevelt Administration moved cautiously but nonetheless steadily in the direction of American participation in the European war. In pursuing this goal, the President found it essential to secure a Congressional modification of the 1939 Neutrality Act. When this was accomplished on 17 November 1941, United States merchant ships could be armed and were now authorized to travel through combat zones, if necessary, and to deliver cargoes directly to Allied ports.

As these fateful decisions were being made, majority opinion on the college campuses was shifting decisively in favor of American intervention in the war. The rapid unfolding of events, both at home and abroad, was obviously having a marked effect on student sentiment. On 27 May, the *Princetonian*, a student periodical that in the past had opposed United States involvement in the overseas war, changed its policy and endorsed Roosevelt's proclamation of an "Unlimited Emergency." The paper told Princeton students that "the debate is now over" and that they should loyally support the government's decision.[136]

An even more startling reversal of form occurred after 22 June 1941. On that date Hitler launched a massive surprise attack on his erstwhile ally, the Soviet Union. On American college campuses, left-wing organizations such as the American Student Union and the American Youth Congress were dumbfounded. The left-wing students now had to quickly change their slogans. "The Yanks are NOT coming" was now unceremoniously dropped in favor of "All-Out Aid for the Allies."[137]

By the time the fall term of 1941 began, the hard-core isolationists and noninterventionists among college students were in full retreat. At Princeton this was painfully evident on 28 October, when the local America First chapter assembled to hear Senator Nye, a prominent isolationist. Nye was heckled and booed by a portion of the audience and his speech was bitterly attacked the next day in the *Princetonian*.[138]

Student Defenders of Democracy, buoyed up by the trend in campus sentiment, launched a campaign toward the end of October for repeal of the 1939 Neutrality Act. They claimed that 1,131 students at the University of Michigan had signed a petition calling for this action; on Armistice Day, SDD sponsored a rally at the Ann Arbor campus with the slogan: "Win the War—Win the Peace."[139] A poll taken about this time by the *Nassau Sovereign*, a Princeton student publication, reported that 85 percent of the undergraduates who responded now felt that it was more important to crush Nazism than to stay out of war.[140]

Similar sentiments were expressed on other campuses. A poll in early November by an undergraduate newspaper at Wesleyan reported that 25 percent of the students in seven Northeastern colleges were in favor of an immediate declaration of war on Germany. And more than 50 percent of them felt that American democracy could not survive a Hitler victory.[141] On 26 November, a big anti-Hitler rally at New York University called for all-out aid to Russia and Britain. The author, Rex Stout, drew loud applause when he called for an immediate declaration of war on the Nazis. Mrs. Roosevelt was there, too, and declared: "This nation is going to defend itself and that defense means preparation to see to it that the Nazis do not win."[142] Again, the students applauded enthusiastically.

Pro-intervention statements by faculty members and university administrators significantly increased in number. At the University of Chicago, 131 members of the faculty signed a statement in mid-August calling for "immediate action by our Navy to destroy all enemy vessels and aircraft which threaten our sea lanes."[143] And when Princeton began its fall term, President Dodds appealed for all-out American participation in the war.[144] Similar appeals came from seventy-five professors at Wayne State University and a larger group of faculty at the University of Michigan.[145]

In October there were more faculty appeals for immediate American belligerency. At Stanford, the faculty by a six-to-one margin favored whatever "strong" measures might be necessary to defeat the Axis.[146] Syracuse deans and professors went on record as favoring an immediate war declaration, as did 107 Cornell faculty.[147]

Two days before Pearl Harbor, President George N. Shuster of Hunter College told a meeting of his school's American Student Union chapter that war might be unavoidable. There are times such as the present, said Shuster, when the only way to protect the American Bill of Rights is by the use of armed force.[148]

7 December 1941

When Japanese forces attacked the American naval base at Pearl Harbor, Hawaii, on 7 December 1941, college students joined their fellow citizens in strong support of Congress's swift declaration of war on the Axis. College newspapers reflected the shocked and indignant campus mood and called for an all-out effort to defeat Hitler and the Japanese. The immediate reaction in academe following Pearl Harbor was epitomized by an editorial in *The Kansan*, a student newspaper at the University of Kansas. This previously isolationist publication asked:

> Do you realize, Mr. Hirohito, just what you have done? You have deliberately provoked war with the most powerful nation in the world. You have pitted your people and your scrawny resources against a nation with the greatest natural resources in the world, and the greatest determination in the world that this shall be a bitter fight to the finish. And that finish will not come until America is victorious. You can paste that in your hat, Mr. Hirohito.[149]

All across the land, campus isolationists and campus interventionists closed ranks. In New York City, classes at the municipal colleges were suspended so that students could hear the broadcast of President Roosevelt's message to Congress requesting a declaration of war.[150] At Rutgers, "whatever divisions of opinion there were ... disappeared on December 7."[151] At the University of Akron, the events of 7 December "ended any ambivalence the campus may have had about the draft and war preparations."[152] At Syracuse University, the student newspaper ran a banner headline proclaiming: "It's Our Fight Now."[153] And at the University of Cincinnati, the campus paper noted that "the decision has been made" and declared that it would henceforth deny space "to any expressions which might be deemed contrary to the successful prosecution of the war."[154]

The dramatic about-face of America's left-wing students was nowhere demonstrated more vividly than at the annual convention of the American Student Union. After warning that "we cannot permit any group to take advantage of this crisis for America ... for the sake of private gain," the delegates went on record as unequivocally supporting the war against fascism. The ASU, they declared, placed itself at the service of the country "to secure the destruction of Hitler and his partners, Japan and Italy."[155]

What effect did college students and faculty have on the course of events during the critical weeks and months preceding Pearl Harbor? It is obvious that colleges and universities did not control events during that troubled period. The campuses articulated various responses to these events, however. In a real sense, the colleges were sounding boards for the American nation, reflecting the particular ambiguities of the country's reaction to overseas challenges.

The powerful campus anti-war movement before Pearl Harbor had produced a college generation that was less naive and much better informed about the forces that led to war than any of their counterparts in earlier crises. This political education of the World War II generation may very well have laid the foundations for the campus uprising against the Vietnam War that occurred twenty years later. In any event, the student and faculty activists of the 1940s were important in their own right for the part they played in shaping the events of their perilous time. They helped alert their fellow countrymen to the immense threat to civilization that was posed by Hitler and his Axis allies. The policy statements and petitions that issued from the American campuses were taken seriously in Congress and at the White House. The campus activists analyzed and publicized the contending viewpoints and ideologies that were battling for the nation's soul. This was a critical time in world history when democracy, fascism, and communism fought for supremacy. It was also a time when America's very national survival hung in the balance. Each of the contending ideologies had attracted devotees on the American campuses. In the end, however, colleges and universities were driven inexorably by events to achieve a workable consensus. This, in turn, enabled them to make constructive contributions to public policy and to play a helpful role in influencing the nation's ultimate decisions.

5

The Vietnam Era

Post-War Campus Moods: Inertia Gives Way to Militancy

FOLLOWING World War II, political activism at American colleges declined dramatically. It was an era of a rapidly escalating "Cold War" with Soviet Russia on the international scene and witch hunts against alleged pro-Communists at home. The prevailing atmosphere was unfriendly to dissidents on campus or off. In 1955 a faculty committee at Amherst College found that most contemporary undergraduates were unwilling to take a stand on controversial issues, preferring, as they put it, to "stay loose."[1]

The national mood was hardened by the Korean War. Liberal dissent of any kind increasingly was seen as pro-"Red." The largest student organization of the 1950s, the National Student Association, was secretly subsidized by the CIA.[2] Faculty members were forced from jobs because of past or present political views; Senator Joseph McCarthy and like-minded Congressional "Red hunters" instituted a veritable reign of terror on college campuses. Legislators and university administrators cooperated with inquisitors by instituting loyalty oaths for teachers.[3]

Many observers saw the college students of these years as a "silent generation," unwilling to face the great questions of their time. As it turned out, appearances could not have been more deceiving. The seeming somnolence of the fifties was only the calm before one of the stormiest eras in the history of American higher education. The decade of the 1960s was destined to produce "the most portentous upheaval in the whole history of American student life."[4] And two critical issues helped make it so. These were, first, the crusade for civil rights and, second, the protest against United States involvement in the Vietnam war.

It was the revitalized civil rights movement that ignited the reappearance of student militancy and political activism. The collegiate phase of the crusade for human rights commenced in early 1960 when small groups of black students staged "sit-in" demonstrations against racial segregation in Southern lunchrooms. It was not long before Northern collegians were joining them and were picketing local branches of chain stores whose Southern outlets still enforced racial discrimination.[5]

The civil rights "sit-ins" of 1960 stimulated students to agitate and demonstrate for other causes as well. Some demonstrators traveled to San Quentin to protest the execution of Caryl Chessman, while others picketed against hearings held in San Francisco by the House Un-American Activities Committee. Many young people paraded to show their opposition to America's nuclear arms policy. "The decades of non-involvement were over," observed Frederick W. Obear. He added that the election of John F. Kennedy in 1960 "brought fresh youth and vigor to the Presidency, and much of his rhetoric and some of his actions seemed to reflect the new mood."[6]

There were other signs that the student mood was changing. Radical political organizations made an appearance on college campuses from Michigan to California. Students for a Democratic Society (SDS), the William B. Du Bois Clubs, and the Student Nonviolent Coordinating Committee were all newly active. Newspapers and magazines with a radical orientation appeared at a number of colleges and universities.[7]

It would only be a matter of time before the new ferment sweeping academe would lead student activists to demand radical changes on their own campuses. This inevitable development finally came to pass in the Fall of 1964 at the University of California in Berkeley. It was there that student protest reached a new level of intensity with the Free Speech Movement (FSM). The FSM demonstrators brought to a major university campus the techniques that already had been tested and perfected during the civil rights protests.[8]

In September 1964 the University of California issued a directive banning the collection of funds for off-campus political causes on a twenty-six foot strip of the school's property in Berkeley. From this perhaps not-well-considered decision by the Dean of Students arose what Calvin Lee called "the first massive student revolution in America."[9]

Student activists suspected that the new regulations were instituted to appease conservatives who disliked leftist political activity at the University of California. Student groups set up tables in the proscribed area in defiance of the ban. Tensions increased when campus police arrested Jack Weinberg, one of the leading protesters. Weinberg, a graduate student who was an activist in the Congress of Racial Equality, was later to gain a measure of immortality with his oft-quoted statement: "You can't trust anyone over thirty." When he was arrested, hundreds of students surrounded the police car that had arrived to take him away and, after an impasse lasting all night, the University administrators agreed to release him.[10]

At this time, the most influential student leader in Berkeley was Mario Savio, earlier a committed volunteer in the civil rights movement. Savio saw an explicit connection between that earlier crusade and what was becoming the Free Speech Movement at the University of California. He insisted that "the same rights are at stake in both places [Berkeley and Mississippi] — the right to participate as citizens in a democratic society."[11]

Contemporary observers noted that other goals besides free speech emerged at Berkeley as the controversy escalated.[12] Radicals in the student free-speech coalition hoped to establish a beachhead to politicize and radicalize the Berkeley campus. They drew considerable support from rank-and-file students who were beginning to see themselves as helpless victims of an unfeeling, mechanistic institution. The president, Clark Kerr, had recently published a book, *The Uses of the University*, which lent credence to these resentments. Kerr discussed at length the extreme complexity and diversity of schools such as Berkeley. He even suggested a name to describe the phenomenon — "the multiversity." Students were becoming all too aware of the shortcomings of such a school — its impersonality, its huge lecture sections evaluated by multiple-choice examinations that were graded by machines, its preoccupation with lucrative contracts for "practical" research projects, and, above all, its lack of concern for students as individual human beings. Mario Savio said that students were sick of being "numbered, sorted on punch cards, and moved around on IBM machines."[13] Campus radicals wholeheartedly agreed with this view. They saw the "multiversity" as existing primarily to meet the needs of what Dwight Eisenhower had called "The Military-Industrial Complex." They charged that students were being turned into docile technicians, dispatched overseas by the corporate structure and the military authorities to make this the "American Century."[14]

Civil disobedience had turned out to be a surprisingly successful protest technique in the South during the civil-rights campaign there. The Free Speech leaders in Berkeley decided to introduce it into their campaign, at the same time adding various other types of "direct action" that were just short of outright violence. Their confrontations with the authorities included sit-ins, blockades of streets, occupation of university buildings, and verbal harassment of opponents or nonparticipants. Ordinary academic life at the University of California was disrupted for three months.[15] Critics of the FSM complained that the grievances of the students were not serious enough to justify the almost total disablement of a major center of higher learning or the decision "to attack legal authority indiscriminately as a means of blackmailing the community and then to whine when one is arrested."[16] These same arguments were to recur again and again during the Vietnam War.

The biggest student sit-in occurred on 2 December 1964. First, Mario Savio stirred up a crowd of demonstrators, telling them: "You've got to indicate to the people who run it, to the people who own it, that unless you're free, the machines will be prevented from working at all." When Joan Baez sang "We Shall Overcome," the students, joining in, marched en masse into Sproul Hall, the university's administrative headquarters. After several hours, the student "occupation" of the building was ended by a police "bust." The limp demonstrators were hauled, "none too gently," out the door. The crackdown, in turn, led to a university-wide protest strike by students and some of the faculty. Classes came to a virtual halt.[17]

The attempt by the University of California to demonstrate its authority had led only to a disastrous impasse. After a few days of this, President Kerr and his administration agreed to a settlement with the Free Speech Movement. The authorities agreed that henceforth there would be total freedom of political activity, not just on the hotly contested twenty-six-foot strip, but anywhere on the Berkeley campus. One day later, on 8 December, the Academic Senate made the FSM victory official when it resolved that: "The content of speech or advocacy should not be restricted by the University. Off campus student political activities shall not be subject to University regulation." The Senate furthermore dropped all pending disciplinary measures against FSM activists.[18]

The California Regents later tried to water down the December resolutions, but it was obvious that the students had won. This was immensely significant, coming as it did on the eve of Lyndon Johnson's decision to expand America's role in Southeast Asia.[19] A contemporary observer thought that FSM had demonstrated "the intriguing possibilities of a radical New Left constituency composed exclusively of students." Such a force could radically transform the country; it might ultimately transform the world.[20]

Involvement in Southeast Asia: The Early Reactions in Academe

College students and professors were slow at first to react to the step-by-step involvement of the United States in the fighting in Vietnam between Communist and anti-Communist forces. Many academics took for granted that the issue had been settled by the victory of Lyndon Johnson over the "Hawkish" Senator Barry Goldwater in the 1964 presidential election. Most campus activists were still preoccupied with the civil-rights battle and the Free Speech Movement in Berkeley. There were other matters, too, of particular concern to young people — urban renewal, Vista, and the Peace Corps.[21]

A series of traumatic events during the years 1963 to 1965 shook the campuses and led students to become more vocal in their criticism of the government. In November 1963 President Kennedy had been assassinated. During the summer of 1964, bloodshed occurred in Mississippi as young civil-rights workers encountered violent opposition from segregationalists. A year later, the Los Angeles black ghetto of Watts gave vent to its resentments in a big urban riot. Meanwhile, black extremists had gained control of the Student Nonviolent Coordinating Committee (SNCC), the principal organ of the civil-rights crusade in the South. The militant black separatism espoused by the new head of SNCC, Stokely Carmichael, and by the newly formed Black Panther party, decided to throw their white liberal allies out of the civil-rights movement. It did not matter to these "Black Power" proponents that the original goal of the campaign launched by Martin Luther King, Jr., and others had been all-inclusive and broadly integrationist. Carmichael and the Panthers rejected Dr. King's approach.[22] The idealistic white students who had gone South and risked their lives for the civil-rights crusade now found themselves ignored and unwanted. They hoped to find some great new cause for which to fight. At that very moment, President Lyndon Johnson, determined to involve America more deeply in the battle to stop the advancing Communists in Vietnam, handed the activist students the cause they had been seeking.[23]

There had been a few early signs of campus interest in the Southeast Asia situation. During the fall of 1963, for example, when Madame Ngo Dinh Nhu, sister-in-law of the ruling dictator in South Vietnam, toured America on behalf of that country's regime, she was picketed by student demonstrators. In 1964 Haverford College students collected medical supplies for the Vietcong, the revolutionists who were fighting the South Vietnamese government. In that year, too, a small group of Yale students organized "the May Second Movement" to protest American policy in Vietnam. In August of 1964 a group of graduate students and faculty in Berkeley, California, placed an advertisement in the newspapers protesting the Tonkin Gulf resolution. A few weeks later, seventy faculty members and two hundred students at the University of Pennsylvania published a letter urging the United States government to pursue a policy of negotiations rather than war as the most promising way of resolving the situation in Southeast Asia.[24]

In spite of these sporadic protests, at the end of 1964 the Vietnam issue did not yet command the close attention of the majority of student activists. This situation changed radically on 7 February 1965. On that day President Johnson dramatically escalated the Southeast Asia war by ordering the U.S. Air Force to bomb military targets in Communist North Vietnam. At the same time, Johnson announced that American ground forces in Southeast Asia would be considerably increased. If necessary, these added troops would be raised by Selective Service.[25]

Johnson's actions triggered nationwide campus demonstrations. At many colleges, spontaneous protests were organized hastily the day following the President's announcement. The national left-wing student organization, SDS, called for a protest march on Washington in April. Undergraduate demonstrators were arrested in New York City for blocking the entrance

to the United States Mission to the United Nations. A
undertook a two-day fast to dramatize their opp
decision. A typical SDS public statement asserted'
Vietnam is being waged on behalf of a successic
Vietnamese dictatorships, not on behalf of freedom.

A highly vocal segment of college faculty joined then
protesting the Vietnam venture. Such academics felt personally beu.,
by Lyndon Johnson. They had enthusiastically campaigned for him in
1964, seeing him as a welcome alternative to Barry Goldwater, who was
advocating all-out bombing of Communist North Vietnam. Now, they
felt, Johnson, having been safely elected, had reversed himself and was
putting Goldwater's program into effect.[27]

On 1 March 1965 hundreds of disaffected and resentful members of
college faculties in the Northeast and New England published "An Open
Letter to President Johnson" in the *New York Times*. They specifically
asked the President: "Would it not be both prudent and just to take the
initiative towards peace in Vietnam?"[28] To reinforce their appeal for
negotiations, the professors established a University Committee on the
Problems of War and Peace.[29] This new organization soon announced
that meetings would be held at more than forty colleges and universities
to persuade the public to support a negotiated Vietnam settlement.[30]
Meetings of professional and scholarly organizations added their endorsement of a peaceful solution to those that had already been announced. As
an example, the Association for Asian Studies voted in early April to
petition the President, stating: "We believe that an open declaration of
America's determination for peace in Eastern Asia would increase the
chances of a favorable response from the other side."[31] President Johnson's
Southeast Asia decision had obviously made an impression on American
academic circles, but not quite the one he had anticipated.

The Teach-Ins

It is worthy of note that the first major domestic protest against American
intervention in Vietnam originated in the halls of academe. And to make
their case against the Vietnam imbroglio, the anti-intervention academics
created an ingenious and innovative technique — the Teach-In. With this
intriguing device, professors opposed to Johnson's Vietnam directives
were able to make American foreign policy the subject of open campus
debate for the first time since the peace strikes and demonstrations of the
late 1930s and early '40s.

The Teach-In movement originated almost fortuitously at the University
of Michigan. There, anti-war students staged a protest sit-in at the offices

of the local draft board. When some of the protesters were arrested, anti-war professors announced that they would go on strike. The university administration made it clear that no such interruption of classes would be tolerated. The anti-war faculty group then changed its strategy and announced that it was substituting the country's first Teach-In on Vietnam for the contemplated strike.[32]

On 24−25 March 1965 the night-long Teach-In went off as scheduled at four University of Michigan auditoriums. Participating in these sessions were more than three hundred faculty members and at least two thousand students. The designers of the event were somewhat divided in their concepts of the proper format to employ. Some wished the gatherings to be true debates, with experts presenting data both favoring and opposing Administration policy in Vietnam. A much larger number saw the Teach-Ins as a dignified, non-violent forum for expressing the deep campus dissatisfaction with current Vietnam decisions. The pioneer Michigan gathering followed the latter path, and was primarily critical and adversarial. Most of the subsequent Teach-Ins similarly emphasized an anti-Administration point of view.[33]

The Teach-In formula at Michigan and elsewhere featured expert speakers who analyzed various aspects of the Vietnam issue. At the Ann Arbor gathering, Professor Robert S. Browne, a former State Department advisor on Vietnam, gave a lecture based on his experiences. The students in attendance listened intently to the lecturer, asked questions, probed the arguments put out by the guest speakers, and pursued the issues further in small discussion groups. As a result of widespread media coverage, the Michigan Teach-In captured the attention of the students and faculty on many other campuses. Soon the idea was spreading like wildfire. The Michigan critics of Johnson did their best to ensure this success by getting in touch with like-minded colleagues at other colleges and universities and encouraging them to set up Teach-Ins.[34]

The Teach-Ins became popular campus "happenings" that generated a great excitement and assumed what one observer called "a carnival-like atmosphere."[35] They usually began in the evening and continued into the early hours of the following morning. Pro-war students picketed the proceedings, held banners and signs aloft castigating Johnson's critics and shouted obscenities at Teach-In participants. Sometimes fistfights broke out between adherents of the rival points of view.[36]

Perhaps the most important development was that, for many students, the Teach-Ins turned out to be an exhilarating learning experience. An honors student at the University of Michigan told one of the participating professors that the meeting "was her first educational experience provided by the university during four years' attendance."[37] Students were caught up in the excitement, the feeling of grappling with important, life-and-

death issues, the sense that major portions of the academic con
were at last coming together to confront a great cause. And
participating faculty the Teach-In was equally challenging. They felt obliged
to take time out from their career pursuits and stay up all night to speak
out on issues that they viewed as immensely important. The cause temporarily took precedence over customary academic pursuits.[38]

On 15 May the Teach-In movement went national. The event, planned
by an "Inter-University Committee for a Public Hearing on Vietnam,"
took place at the Sheraton Park Hotel in Washington, D.C. The National
Teach-In, characterized by *Newsweek* as "part bull session, part debating
match, part filibuster," went on for more than fifteen hours. Its sponsors
somewhat ambitiously called it "perhaps the most significant political
gathering of American intellectuals since the Constitutional Convention."
A distinguished audience of some five thousand persons assembled to
hear debates and presentation of views pro and con on Vietnam. The
format aimed at an even-handed exchange of views rather than solely
the voicing of opposition to government policies. Three-and-a-half hours
of the Washington sessions were relayed by radio and television to more
than 100,000 people assembled at some 110 college campuses in thirty-five
states. One educational TV channel carried the program in its entirety.[39]

The Washington proceedings were dampened somewhat when the projected main star of the show failed to show up. McGeorge Bundy,
Johnson's National Security Advisor, had agreed originally to present a
defense of current Vietnam policy. He begged off, however, when the
President advised him that he had much more pressing business elsewhere.[40]
All in all, though, the sponsors of the National Teach-In expressed
satisfaction with what it had achieved. In their view, the well-publicized
gathering had advertised the growing dissent with the Vietnam involvement
on the college campuses. The professors hoped that the Washington
Teach-In had helped the general public understand better the reasons for
the dissenting position of academe.[41]

Petition and Argument Give Way to Direct Action

The National Teach-In constituted a turning point in the development of
campus protests against the Vietnam intervention. There were divided
counsels within academe as to what the next move should be. A moderate
faction wished to continue the Washington approach and function as a
kind of "Loyal Opposition," using petitions, lectures, and debates to
sketch out an alternative foreign policy to that of the Administration. As
time went on, however, the moderates were pushed aside by hard-liners,
who pointed out that the Teach-Ins had not changed any of Johnson's

Vietnam policies. The hard-liners called for drastic, even violent, student demonstrations to force the President to reverse himself.[42]

The hand of the hard-liners was strengthened immensely by the obvious fact that President Johnson, ignoring all campus entreaties, petitions, and Teach-Ins, was moving relentlessly to expand the military's involvement in Vietnam. On 28 July 1965 the President announced a massive buildup of United States troops in support of the South Vietnamese government. Monthly draft quotas would be doubled. In effect, Johnson was throwing down the gauntlet to his academic critics.[43]

Voices of sweet reason at the colleges were now drowned out, and one of the most violent periods in the history of American campus protest ensued. Campus activists were coming to accept the unwelcome reality that Christopher Lasch, a historian at the University of Iowa, had noted in October 1965: "No amount of persuasion will change the central fact of American politics — the fact that there is no opposition party, no political opposition at all to the rhetorical but enormously effective demand that we stand up to the Communists, resist 'aggression,' and avoid another 'Munich.'"[44]

Militants became increasingly influential in the campus anti-Vietnam War leadership. Their point of view predominated in such college protest groups as the Vietnam Day Committee at the Berkeley campus in California. Denouncing old-style "milk-and-water" liberals as ineffective and useless, the Berkeley hard-liners called for all-out opposition to the government, even at the risk of physical confrontation and violent conflict. "We are rife with shame and anger that this bloodbath is made in our name," the Berkeley Committee declared.[45]

Militant academics began to hold "read-ins" in the Fall of 1965 at which they heard bitter anti-Administration presentations such as Susan Sontag's "We are Choking with Shame and Anger."[46] In addition, opponents of Johnson's Vietnam enterprise began protest marches on Washington. On 15 and 16 October, fifty thousand college students and other young people from all parts of the country gathered in the nation's capital to protest United States intervention in Vietnam. A month later, on 27 November, more than twenty-five thousand marchers, most of them college students, assembled in Washington for "The March for Peace in Vietnam." The demonstrators marched around the White House again and again carrying signs reading "Stop the Bombing" and "Supervised Cease-Fire." Another peace march took place in the nation's capital in December. This one was organized by Sane, a national peace organization; it attracted some forty thousand participants, most of them students.[47]

By this time, protest marches were taking place on campuses all across America. The mass demonstrations had become international as well. Left-wing protests against American military ventures and foreign policy erupted in such disparate locations as London, Dublin, Toronto, Stockholm, and Brussels. In the United States, the more strident student marchers began to carry North Vietnamese flags and to chant: "Hey, Hey, LBJ, how many kids did you kill today?" They carried signs displaying messages that read "War on Poverty, Not on People."[48]

On the West Coast, anti-war militancy became more extreme and student protest turned violent. In August the Vietnam Day Committee in Berkeley discovered that the army authorities were sending troops destined for Vietnam on chartered trains through their community and on to the Oakland military base nearby. The VDC decided to dispatch groups of student demonstrators to block the troop trains and prevent them from reaching the Oakland Terminal. These efforts proved unsuccessful. The trains smashed through the protesters' barricades, ripping up their banners and spraying hot steam on the students. Police pulled the demonstrators off the tracks. The only immediate success for the protest came when one troop train temporarily halted and VDC representatives were able to hand out anti-war leaflets to the soldiers on board. In any event, the student protesters succeeded in attracting the attention of the media. One of the students, however, summed up the reasons for the VDC protests as follows: "We won't end the war. Bobby Kennedy or someone like that, will have to end it. But we've got to do something."[49]

In mid-October, the Berkeleyites aimed another blow at the Oakland Army Terminal, which had by this time become the largest base in the country for sending men and supplies to Vietnam. Thousands of VDC marchers left the Berkeley campus and headed for the Oakland base. At the city line, however, three hundred helmeted Oakland police were waiting for them, forcing the demonstrators to halt. The confrontation reminded some students of the police suppressing the civil rights marchers in Selma, Alabama, earlier that year. The situation became dangerous when motorcycle hoodlums known as "Hell's Angels" were permitted by the police to slip through their lines and tear up the protesters' signs. In the ensuing melee a Berkeley policeman was injured and one of the "Hell's Angels" was knocked unconscious. There were no further casualties, however. After this incident, leftist extremists in the VDC distributed a pamphlet advising that in future demonstrations anti-war students should use their picket-sign poles as weapons, if that became necessary, to ward off attackers. When this strategy was publicized in the newspapers, the VDC quickly announced that it was strictly against this policy.[50]

Extreme measures of opposition to the government's Vietnam policy, it turned out, could be launched by lone individuals as well as mass organizations. In mid-October, David J. Miller, a religious pacifist, burned his draft card outside the Whitehall Street Army Induction Center in

New York City. Miller was sent to jail for violating the law, but his symbolic act of defiance began a new phase of militant anti-Vietnam War protest. Miller's action caught the attention of thousands of college students throughout the country. In the years that followed, a number of them would ceremoniously burn their draft cards. The vast majority, however, preferred to employ other ways of making sure that they would not have to serve in a war that they abhorred. A two-page mimeographed statement, for example, was distributed that fall of 1965 on the Berkeley campus, suggesting no less than twelve methods of "Beating and Defeating the Draft."[51]

The Administration Strikes Back

Convinced that Congress, the most important media sources, and the majority of the American public supported his Vietnam policy, Lyndon Johnson had no intention of modifying or reversing it to satisfy critics in academe. However, within the Administration there was the same division between moderate and hard-liners that had surfaced during the spring and summer of 1965 in the campus anti-war coalition. In the Administration, too, as with the anti-war academics and students, it was the hard-liners who ultimately won out.

Administration moderates argued that, without surrendering any basic policy positions, the government should make a vigorous effort to explain the reasons for its actions to the academic community and win support for its decisions among students and professors. The President was skeptical that such an approach would work, but reluctantly agreed to let the State Department send a "Truth Team" of experts and army officers to visit several campuses to explain the Administration viewpoint.[52]

From the beginning, the "Truth Team" mission went badly. At the University of Iowa, the four-man mission was loudly booed. The Team had hoped to make a pro-Administration presentation to sixty key members of the faculty, but was interrupted by "an explosion of protests from the professors."[53] At the University of Wisconsin, the government spokesmen were shouted down when they tried to deliver an explanation. A planned get-acquainted reception and tea was invaded by anti-war students, who showered the chief State Department representative with hostile questions. Squatting on the floor or standing in a ring around the visitors, snapping their fingers for attention, the students harassed the "Truth Team" spokesmen. Later, when a question-and-answer session was held in a larger hall, hundreds of students wearing black armbands as a protest against "the killing in Vietnam" invaded the auditorium, held aloft anti-war signs, and effectively made it impossible to give the pro-government presentations.[54]

Shortly after this, the Administration terminated the "Truth Team" experiment; there were no later attempts to repeat it. Hard-liners within the government were strengthened by the inglorious results of the State Department's experiment in bridge-building. This deepened their conviction that the only way to deal with campus critics was to crack down on them. Such was the approach of the Senate's Subcommittee on Internal Security. Spokesmen for the Subcommittee charged that the Teach-Ins and the whole phenomenon of campus dissidence was simply a plot by subversive Communist professors to brainwash students into espousing anti-American attitudes. The Subcommittee demanded that a government investigation be launched to unmask such traitors.[55]

J. Edgar Hoover, head of the Federal Bureau of Investigation, was eager to launch such an inquisition. The Communists, he declared, were playing a leading role in organizing Teach-Ins at the colleges and staging student anti-war demonstrations in Washington. Other government bodies joined Hoover in seeking to paint the whole campus anti-war movement red. The House Committee on Un-American Activities demanded by subpoena that college and university administrators hand over to it the membership lists of all campus organizations that publicly opposed American policies in Vietnam. Later, Senator John McClellan's Permanent Sub-Committee on Investigations joined in this effort to intimidate the anti-war movement at the colleges by demanding student documents and records, membership lists of campus organizations, and all other data on undergraduate anti-war activity that was available.[56]

College faculties and civil-liberties groups denounced these efforts to silence campus dissidence. In December 1966 more than seven hundred members of the faculty of the University of Michigan went on record as denouncing the willingness of their school's administration to turn over to the House Un-American Activities investigators the membership lists of three radical anti-war organizations on the Ann Arbor campus.[57] And on 13 November 1966 the American Civil Liberties Union published a formal request to all college and university presidents to refuse to make membership lists of student organizations available to government investigators. Such probing could not possibly have been displeasing to President Johnson himself. On 18 June 1965 he told his cabinet: "I will see a line from Peking, Hanoi, and Moscow ... about a month ahead of the time I see it here."[58]

There was one other way in which Administration hard-liners sought to strike back at campus critics. This involved using the Selective Service system as a punitive device, reclassifying campus anti-war activists for immediate induction into the army. In October 1965 Michigan's Director of Selective Service ordered a review of the draft files of twenty-six student demonstrators who had staged a sit-in strike at the draft board office in Ann Arbor. The implication was that these protesters would be reclassified 1-A for immediate induction. The *Washington Post* character-ized this action as "a naked use of the Selective Service law to repress and punish political opinion."[59]

A couple of years later, General Lewis B. Hershey, head of the Selective Service system, sent a letter to all 4,081 draft boards in the land directing that "misguided registrants" found to have taken part in "illegal demon-strations" against the draft or to have interfered with recruiting for the military services should be immediately reclassified 1-A and inducted. Hershey's letter provoked a storm of criticism. The *New York Times* denounced it and the presidents of "Ivy League" universities sent a letter to President Johnson requesting him to make it "crystal clear" that induction would not be used as a punishment for dissenting opinions. The Justice Department had already issued an advisory opinion stating that efforts by Selective Service officials to use the draft to punish dissent were illegal. All in all, the attempt by overly zealous Administration supporters to employ Selective Service as a club to intimidate anti-war critics may be said to have fizzled.[60]

There was, finally, one other tactic employed by the Johnson Adminis-tration to strike back at its critics. This was more subtle than direct repression. It involved cultivating possible sympathizers in the academic world who would be willing to endorse Johnson's Vietnam policy publicly. The Administration was willing to pay such professors generously to encourage them to express favorable views. Subventions would also be paid to student leaders and campus organizers if these, too, would come out in favor of current Southeast Asia policy. The idea was to demonstrate to the general public that campus communities were not as unanimously opposed to the Vietnam intervention as the anti-war activists claimed. For maximum effect, however, the Administration preferred that all such subsidies and subventions be paid in strictest secrecy.[61]

In March 1967 *Ramparts* magazine published evidence, later reported in the *New York Times*, that the Central Intelligence Agency in Washington had helped for a number of years to finance the National Student Associ-ation, using dummy foundations and corporations as intermediaries. The NSA, a middle-of-the-road campus organization, had been openly supportive of America's main overseas ventures, including the Vietnam War. *Ramparts* also maintained that the CIA had provided covert support to other key organizations in American society, including the National Council of Churches, the American Newspaper Guild, the Congress of Cultural Freedom, and the American Friends Service Committee. There was no direct evidence that government subsidies were helping to float such propagandistic groups as the "Support Our Servicemen Committee," which ran full-page advertisements in the newspapers in favor of the war, but the investigation raised suspicions about the source of their financing.[62]

The main academic organization that the Administration counted on to develop support for its policies was the "American Friends of Vietnam," a group headed by Professor Wesley Fishel of Michigan State University. Michigan State during the Vietnam War received millions of dollars in grants from Washington. At this time, Professor Fishel and his colleagues pursued a number of projects in South Vietnam.[63]

The White House employed the services of a friendly financier, Sidney Weinberg, to raise money that could be sent to American Friends of Vietnam so that the latter organization could set up a speakers' bureau and publish a newsletter. Fishel's group arranged a pro-war rally at Michigan State, which was addressed by Vice President Humphrey. It sent out hundreds of speakers to various campuses to give addresses in favor of American foreign policy. It sponsored pro-war letters to newspapers by academics who favored the war. It paid for tours of American college campuses by a group of five South Vietnamese college students who were in favor of the existing anti-Communist regime in Saigon. Professor Fishel also was the author of a public statement endorsing the Administration's Southeast Asia policy and warning that "a Vietcong victory will spell disaster for millions of South Vietnamese and other millions in Southeast Asia." Fishel induced 190 professors, predominantly political scientists, to sign the statement, which was made public on 9 December 1965.[64]

All of this activity went on without the Administration being officially involved. Chester Cooper, a National Security Council official, reported: "While we have been careful to keep our hand fairly hidden, we have ... spent a lot of time on it and have been able to find them some money."[65]

On 14 April 1966 *Ramparts* exploded a second bombshell. A detailed investigation of the American Friends of Vietnam revealed, it asserted, numerous undercover links between the Johnson Administration and Professor Fishel. The Fishel organization was portrayed as a front for Administration policy in academe. Many prominent professors and scholars were not convinced by the rejoinder that the American Friends of Vietnam made to the *Ramparts'* charges. A number of them hastened to resign from the Vietnam association's national committee. One of the most eminent of these disillusioned academics was James Bryant Conant, the former president of Harvard University, who had been a long-time supporter of American foreign policy.[66]

Nature and Scope of Anti-Vietnam War Protest on the Campuses

As student demonstrations against the Vietnam war multiplied and became more extreme, observers began to raise basic questions about these protests. Did they represent a spontaneous outpouring of campus sentiment? Were the majority of students and professors on the nation's campuses really so thoroughly alienated from their country's foreign policy because of this particular overseas entanglement? These questions were tricky ones, indeed, and difficult to address objectively in the midst of such a controversial, emotion-laden military enterprise.

On the matter of spontaneity, one investigator, Gordon Hall, asserted that SDS and other "New Left" student groups played a prominent role in organizing protest demonstrations at the colleges. These events, said Hall, snowballed and captured the attention of thousands of previously uncommitted students.[67] William McGill, who served as a university president during the Vietnam years, also argued that the protests against the war were not spontaneous. Rather they were, he said, "the result of a highly creative and opportunistic process of leadership applied to an excitable and sympathetic crowd."[68] Hill and McGill were substantially correct in delineating the crucial part played by "New Left" leaders in launching the protest demonstrations. It is also important to note, however, that the vast majority of students who decided to demonstrate against the war were not party-liners, but rank-and-filers.

The next question is this: How representative of dominant opinion on college campuses were the anti-war activists? During the early years of the anti-war movement, the committed students who marched and demonstrated were apparently a distinct minority of the total college population. Furthermore, the number of campuses where these anti-war militants were most active was only a small fraction of the total.[69] Contemporary analysts found that, on the whole, most students tended to support the Vietnam War at first. The Harris Poll found that only 24 percent of a national sample of college students in 1965 favored withdrawal from Vietnam. The Gallup Poll reported a year later that much the same division of student sentiment existed. In 1966, also, pollster Samuel Lubbell reported that two-thirds of students interviewed continued to support Vietnam policy.[70]

Many of the students favorable to the war came from two-year community colleges or junior colleges. Others with such views came from small institutions in Middle America, the South, or the Far West, some denominational, some not. Many from such institutions were either commuter students or people enrolled in vocational programs rather than liberal arts. They were, as one analyst notes, "like generations before them," going to post-secondary schools in the hope of someday entering middle-class ranks; consequently, they "paid no attention to protest."[71] Still others were going to technological and professional schools in order to acquire advanced training in a specialized field. These were the nation's "future engineers and technicians" who "imitated their conservative professors and eschewed politics or took cautious positions."[72]

The anti-war minority in 1965 and 1966 tended to be, as Calvin Lee aptly described it, "the best students at the best institutions," an elite, a "prophetic minority."[73] Ultimately, as the war dragged on without a successful conclusion, this activist minority attained an influence over the mass of their increasingly disaffected fellow students all out of proportion to their numbers.

That, however, would not happen until later—1968, 1969, and 1970. In the first two or three years of the war, many college students still felt that they should rally to the support of their country. Conservatives generally, and pro-Administration leaders, were able to show that there was substantial support for Johnson's policies at many colleges. Campus drives were launched to donate blood for United States servicemen overseas. Pro-war rallies and patriotic parades were staged. Meetings and "Teach-Ins" were held *supporting* the war. Sometimes pro- and anti-war students met in angry confrontations. Occasionally, these clashes led to violence, as at Manhattan College in New York in October, 1965.[74]

As the military involvement in Vietnam mounted from year to year, seemingly without visible prospect of victory, as draft calls increased in size, and as the number of American casualties became larger, majority opinion on the campuses began to shift. At that point, the small but deeply involved group of anti-Vietnam crusaders from the nation's most influential and prestigious colleges began to sell their appeal for withdrawal with more success to the mass of students. Many now felt that a war that, for whatever reasons, had gone sour, was seriously threatening their chance for an education, their career plans, even their lives.[75] Polls reflected this new orientation. A Gallup poll in the Spring of 1968 reported that at least 50 percent of America's college students felt that the United States had made a big mistake in going into Vietnam.[76] In April 1968 student leaders from more than five hundred colleges signed a statement published in the *New York Times* that condemned the war. The war was "immoral and unjust," declared the student spokesmen; young people at the colleges "should not be forced to fight."[77] Two analysts of opinion trends during this era, Helen Lefkowitz-Horowitz and David Caute, concur in seeing 1968 as the turning point; by that time, the majority of American students had turned against the Vietnam war.[78]

New complications were arising, however. Just as the campus anti-war campaign swelled in size and influence, it had to face the ironic possibility that its preeminence as a cause would be challenged, not by conservatives, but by fellow students. By the late '60s and early '70s, campus rebels were finding many other issues to attract their attention besides the continuing war in Vietnam. The big question was, would this splintering of the student rebellion divert student attention from the anti-war crusade and weaken its impact? The rival causes included such movements as Feminism, Environmentalism, Consumer Activism, Civil Rights for Blacks, Aid to the Poverty-Stricken, and help for minority groups such as Native Americans, Chicanos, and Asians. Nor did these causes by any means exhaust the possibilities for campus action and commitment. Rebels increasingly turned their attention to conditions at their own universities. Here they found much to protest.

Activists began to demand reform of such things as dormitory regulations, particularly in loco parentis rules. They denounced poor teaching of undergraduates by disinterested faculty members. They complained about the impersonality of bureaucratic, soulless universities and their lack of concern for individual students. They called for a prominent role in college government for student representatives, giving them a voice in the appointment of faculty and the approval of courses of study. In short, Obear observes, the campus activists presented nothing less than "a non-negotiable demand for student power."[79]

The leaders of the collegiate peace crusade were also perplexed by the contemporaneous emergence of what came to be called "the counterculture." Loud advocates of "The Great un-Proletarian Cultural Revolution," sometimes dropouts from previous schools, were confused in the public mind with opposition to United States military involvement in Southeast Asia. "Hippies" or "Beatniks" were presented in the newspapers and magazines as bearded and unkempt characters, repudiating the adult establishment, using drugs, showing alienation from conventional culture by using obscene language, displaying uncouth gestures and affecting eccentric dress and hair-styles.[80] The anti-Vietnam protestors wished to reform society and achieve peace. Many of the counterculturists wished to do so too. But in their experimentation with drugs and sex to "emancipate sensibility," they also seemed to be aiming to drop out of society altogether. As Timothy Leary, a former Harvard professor, put it: "Let's all drop out and change the American consciousness as quickly as possible."[81]

Some campus opponents of the Vietnam War feared that "the Movement" as they called it, was becoming too deeply entangled with what the media called "the generation gap" to be effective with the general public. They wondered if counterculture "flower children" were really an asset for the anti-war campaign. For some devotees of the youth cult, participation in an anti-Vietnam War "happening" seems to have been motivated more by a search for excitement and a desire to defy adult authority than by a wish to make a political statement. One student protester declared: "Don't get me wrong. I picket *seriously*; just the same, it's a place to see the girls and sometimes we have a great time. It's our way of living."[82]

The American Professoriate and the Vietnam War

As protests mounted on the campuses against President Johnson's increasingly frantic Vietnam venture, a key element in the equation came to be the professoriate. Disaffected college faculty were obviously the most active and vocal group of professional people in the country in open revolt against the Administration. But a nagging question persists. Were these zealous Vietnam War opponents truly representative of the majority of the faculty? And, representative or not, were these dissident professors really influential in having an impact on the Southeast Asia conflict?

Available data indicate that overtly anti-war professors did not at first constitute a clear majority. In 1965 and 1966 there remained many teachers and scholars who still believed that there was justification for Johnson's actions in Vietnam. Among these were some academics with national, even international, reputations, notably Professor Henry Kissinger of Harvard.

Studies have been made of academic proponents and opponents of the Vietnam War, breaking down the data by rank, field of specialization, and institutional affiliation. One investigation, by Everett C. Ladd, reviewed 18,500 faculty signatures subscribed to eight anti-war petitions addressed to President Johnson and published in the *New York Times*. The overwhelming majority (66 percent) came from colleges in the Northeast. Only a tiny minority (2.5 percent) were from the South. Ladd also found that privately endowed universities had proportionately greater numbers of anti-Vietnam faculty petitioners than publicly controlled ones. Roman Catholic colleges and universities, however, had few anti-war faculty listed, accounting for only 331 signatures.[83]

Twenty schools led the country in anti-war petition signers: The top institutions were Harvard, with 974 anti-war petitioners; New York University, with 676; Massachusetts Institute of Technology, 600; Columbia University, 524; University of California at Berkeley, 516; Brooklyn College, 450; and City College of New York, 409.[84]

Critics of the anti-Vietnam War petitions pointed out that a disproportionate number of the protesters were untenured faculty or graduate assistants.[85] Ladd insisted that this assumption was incorrect. He found that 32 percent of the petitioners were tenured full professors and another 25 percent were associate professors. William F. Buckley, Jr., a supporter of the Vietnam intervention, advanced another criticism of the faculty petitions. He maintained that the listed professors came predominantly from fields such as the humanities and natural sciences, while social scientists, such as specialists in international affairs and Southeast Asia, were not among those denouncing government policy.[86] Ladd flatly rejected this assertion. He admitted that natural scientists did indeed form a significant group of petition signers, some 34 percent. But he noted that professors in the social sciences also constituted a significant group for his study, amounting to 24 percent of the petitioners. And he reported further that a number of political scientists had joined the signers; they were the second largest contingent of social scientists. On the other hand, Ladd showed unmistakably that in certain fields faculty played an absolutely minimal role in anti-war protest. Thus, professors of business amounted to only 0.4 percent of the petitioners; agriculture (0.2 percent); education (3.1 percent); and engineering (4.6 percent).[87] A possible reason for these variations, Seymour Lipset theorized, was that college faculty who were identified with "intellectual" disciplines were on the whole more "activist and leftist" than those "oriented more toward the professional or scientific world."[88]

Ladd's analysis, which appeared in 1969, was followed by various revisionist studies. One of the most useful of these, by Robert A. McCaughey, appeared in 1976. McCaughey agreed with Ladd's general conclusions, but found that the latter's statistical samples needed some correction.[89]

Among other things, McCaughey concluded that the most active anti-war signatories did indeed tend to be junior rather than senior members of college staffs. Furthermore, he declared, "the signatories were more likely to be in the physical sciences or the humanities than the social sciences." Finally, McCaughey felt that it was remarkable that senior academics from large, research-oriented universities whose field of specialization was Asia were not subscribers to the anti-war petitions.[90]

The last point was also noted by contemporary analysts in 1965 and 1966. Various explanations were given. Senator William Fulbright, author of the Overseas Fellowships Act and a strong opponent of the Vietnam entanglement, saw the situation this way: "Among the baneful effects of the government-university contract system, the most damaging and corrupting is the impact on the education of ... students." Under this system, said Fulbright, the government was paying for the service of scholars, "especially those in the social sciences, who ought to be acting as responsible and independent critics of their Government's policies." Instead, a situation had developed where "academic honesty is no less marketable than a box of detergents on the grocery shelf." The result, Fulbright pointed out, is a subtle one. No one had to issue direct commands or threats to these "service intellectuals." Instead, it was simply understood "that lucrative contracts are awarded not to those who question their Government's policies but to those who provide the Government with the tools and techniques it desires."[91]

Similar conclusions were reached by other observers. In 1968 a special report issued by the Advisory Commission on International Education warned that research-oriented universities were in danger of becoming appendages of the national government, ending up concerned "with techniques rather than purposes, with expedients rather than ideals, and with conventional orthodoxy rather than new ideas."[92] This was also a principal concern of Robert Nisbet, who carefully explored the situation in 1970 in a penetrating study entitled *The Degradation of the Academic Dogma*.[93]

Robert McCaughey did not deny that eminent nonsigning Southeast Asia specialists in academe were financially dependent on Washington. He suggests, however, that there could have been other non-venal reasons for their nonparticipation. They might have had a distaste for the violent methods of the campus anti-war protesters while wishing to preserve a reputation for scholarly objectivity. Their personal judgment of Vietnam realities might have coincided with that of the government. McCaughey agrees, however, that, since World War II, the better-known international relations "experts" had been receiving much larger government grants than their less fortunate colleagues in the humanities departments or their counterparts in smaller, less prestigious colleges. And he concedes that the sources of these generous research grants were very often such key government agencies as the CIA, the Department of Defense, and the State Department.[94]

The situation inevitably calls to mind an ancient adage: "Don't bite the hand that feeds you." Summing up the realities confronting academics in modern America, Seymour Lipset remarks: "In many ways the 'non-expert' American intellectual, similar to the French, has high status but little power and views himself as alienated from the power structure, while the American academic 'expert,' like the English, has considerable status and power and is more likely to identify with the political decision-makers."[95]

By 1968 a new and somewhat different mood emerged as dominant in academe. Disenchanted as many were by this time with the endless, seemingly futile war, McCaughey observes that "even the most vociferous supporters of the war conceded that the 'teach-ins' and anti-war declarations emanated from many of the leading institutions of the country and had the support of some of the most distinguished scholars."[96] Accordingly, professors who had been active earlier in defending the intervention in Vietnam now either retreated to complete silence or joined the anti-war forces.[97] Indeed, by 1968 and 1969, criticism of the Vietnam War had become *the* "establishment" position in the most prestigious centers of the American academic world. Thus, on 11 October 1969 the presidents of the leading Ivy League universities and the heads of more than seventy high-quality colleges forwarded an urgent appeal to President Nixon, urging him to implement "a stepped-up timetable for withdrawal from Vietnam." The university presidents said this action was necessary because the Vietnam War was wounding America badly and stood "as a denial of so much that is best in our society."[98]

Many other appeals of this kind now issued from the most highly respected circles in academe. The Faculty Senate of Columbia University put itself on record as urging the Nixon Administration to institute a total withdrawal from Vietnam.[99] The Faculty of Arts and Sciences at Harvard University passed a similar resolution on 7 October 1969. Brushing aside objections that the action would jeopardize Harvard's traditional apolitical stance and invite attacks by reactionaries, the majority declared that the Vietnam problems "profoundly related" to the regular business of the University because the war "had a poisonous effect on U.S. life in general and University life in particular."[100]

National associations of scholars, for their part, continued to record their opposition to the war at their annual meetings. The American Philosophical Association at its 1966 convention declared that the Vietnam War was a catastrophe on moral grounds and that it was "endangering civilization." The American Historical Association in the same year heard Professor John K. Fairbank of Harvard, an Asian specialist, predict that the United States would never be able to bomb North Vietnam and its Vietcong allies into submission.[101]

Opposition to the Vietnam War obviously had become the consensus position of the American professoriate. But how much influence did this attitude have on campus sentiment? Lipset made an effort to determine the importance of faculty input by investigating patterns of anti-war demonstrations at 181 institutions of higher education during the 1967–68 academic year. He found that professors were actively involved in planning student demonstrations in more than half of these schools. Furthermore, anti-war faculty openly endorsed the actions of student protesters in two-thirds of the colleges surveyed.[102]

Another example of faculty involvement occurred in late September 1969. At that time, twenty-four nationally prominent professors signed a public statement endorsing a nationwide student boycott of classes for 15 October as a condemnation of the war. Among the signatories were Kenneth Galbraith of Harvard, Noam Chomsky of MIT, and Hans Morgenthau of the University of Chicago.[103]

One thing should be noted, however, about anti-Vietnam War faculty. It did not follow that such professors were automatically willing to endorse all campus demonstrations. Many senior faculty opposed violent student demonstrations that got out of control, disrupting classes. Contemporary opinion polls show that faculty opposition was almost unanimous when the goal of campus demonstrations shifted from "Anti-War" to "Student Power" or aimed to weaken professorial authority. A poll taken in 1969 showed that a large majority of professors were disturbed by efforts of student militants to seize university buildings or to prevent classes from being held. Seventy-seven percent of the faculty surveyed by the Gallup Poll said that they favored expulsion of "students who disrupt the functioning of a college."[104] Clark Kerr, former head of the University of California, was not surprised by such findings. "Few institutions are so conservative," he wrote, "as the universities about their own affairs."[105] Thus, in American academe, mindless disruptive behavior was unacceptable while principled intellectual dissent was welcomed.

College Students and the Vietnam-Era Draft

Among all the issues that affected America's campuses during the troubled years of the Vietnam War, the one that stands out most prominently is the military draft. This became the central question for college students, faculties, and administrations. It was the key issue, going to the heart of the Vietnam commitment, its legitimacy and its visibility. Johnson depended on the draft to raise the troops he needed to succeed in his Vietnam venture: his campus opponents believed that any way that they could discredit and undermine the draft would, ultimately, discredit and undermine the war itself.

College students, whatever their political ideology, were forced to react to the draft on an intensely personal basis. As draft calls expanded, many who had been apathetic to the war at first, were shocked by the possibility of imminent induction: they reacted with hostility to the conscription system that was menacing them directly. Their career plans, their hopes for the future, were at stake. More than any other single factor, the draft was forcing college men to adopt an anti-Vietnam War position.[106]

Bashkir and Straus put it this way: "Among this generation, fighting for one's country was not a source of pride: it was a misfortune. Going to Vietnam was the penalty for those who lacked the wherewithal to avoid it." In 1971 the Harris Poll found that most Americans believed that those who went to Vietnam were "suckers, having to risk their lives in the wrong war, in the wrong place, at the wrong time."[107]

As Johnson's need for manpower escalated, the draft tightened up considerably. On 24 March 1966 Selective Service announced that henceforth college men would be deferred only if they were *full-time* students who ranked in the upper half of their class (as first-year students), even higher if upper classmen. The new regulations meant that dropping even one course would make a student vulnerable to the draft. Leaving school even temporarily would have the same effect, as would having a grade point average below the required level. The government expected colleges to supply draft authorities with lists of class ranking for all students.

There was an alternative, however. Students could take a government-sponsored College Qualification Test. Undergraduates must score at least 70 on this examination, while graduate students had to attain a mark of 80 or higher.[108]

Predictably, angry protests were voiced against the new policy from many quarters. The American Association of Junior Colleges charged that it was "especially discriminatory against students from lower-income and middle-income families, those from disadvantaged urban and rural areas, and members of minority groups." Junior and community college students were enrolled only in two-year programs, and many of them were obliged by economic circumstances to attend only on a part-time basis.[109]

Students in four-year institutions, too, were angered by the revised draft. Those at a highly competitive school like Michigan or Harvard had to consider transferring to a college where easier standards might ensure that they would attain the required high class ranking. Students obliged to work outside school to pay for tuition had to face the fact that taking anything less than a full program would get them drafted. Professors were placed in a quandary, also. Could they in good conscience give male students "C" or "D" grades, in effect giving them "a ticket to Vietnam," or must they hand out gift "A's" and "B's"?[110]

Students on many campuses erupted in loud demonstrations against the new regulations. The principal target of these protests were those university administrations that had agreed to hand over to draft boards information regarding class rank. To do so, it was charged, would be equivalent to a violation of academic solidarity and would constitute cowardly collaboration with the war-makers.[111]

The protesters won a dramatic victory at Columbia University on the question of releasing class rank information. The students voted 1,333 to 563 against releasing such data. The faculty of the college made a similar recommendation to the University administration and Columbia's SDS chapter threatened a strike if Columbia did not go along with the recommendation. To resolve the matter, President Grayson Kirk called a special meeting of the University Council, which voted two-to-one to withhold class rank data from draft boards.[112]

In spite of such resistance the draft kept growing. In August 1966 the Administration announced the highest monthly draft call since the Korean War—46,200 men. Draft boards were ordered to conscript men in categories that had previously been considered deferred. Childless married men under the age of twenty-six, for example, could no longer claim exemption.[113]

In the summer of 1967, Congress took further steps to make the draft stricter: once again, the changes struck at institutions of higher education.

All draft deferments for the 650,000 graduate students in the land were summarily revoked, the only exceptions being medical and dental students.[114] In addition, in early 1968, following the Vietcong's Tet Offensive, President Johnson announced the cancellation of a number of occupational deferments.[115]

As the rapidly expanding draft closed in, panic swept many university campuses. Steven Kelman, a student at Harvard, saw his school during the fall semester of 1967 seized by what he called a "burning frenzy." Draft cards by the score were turned in or burned in symbolic protest. Kelman observed "a peaceful campus, only marginally concerned with Vietnam, suddenly become desperate. We felt boxed in."[116] At the University of Illinois, students were similarly confused and alarmed. An Illinois graduate student summed up his reaction this way: "Look, I have money problems. I need to drop out of school and work awhile so I can make enough money to stay in. Can't do it. The draft ...."[117]

University administrators feared a serious disruption of their teaching programs. If the draft caused a mass exodus of young teaching assistants who were taking care of lower-level undergraduate sections, who would replace them and at what cost? And as graduate programs shrank, where would the classes and seminars be found for senior professors to teach? In addition, where would the nation get the Ph.D.'s needed in the future to staff technical, professional, and scholarly institutions? One observer speculated that graduate schools would be "comprised entirely of women, the physically disabled, and men over twenty-five." This prediction was not realized in its entirety only because the National Security Council issued a directive, superseding Selective Service regulations, that continued deferments for graduate students in engineering, mathematics, and the natural Sciences.[118]

Campus draft opponents gravitated to one of two main groups. The great majority during the 1960s and 1970s may best be described as "draft evaders." A somewhat smaller group can most accurately be labeled "draft resisters." The first group was prepared to use whatever legal expedients were at hand to avoid being drafted or, if necessary, to induce an induction center to reject them for service.

The war resisters, whatever their motives, were ready to go beyond legal evasions and openly defy the government and its laws. In so doing, they risked arrest and imprisonment. The dramatic acts of the draft resisters were featured in the media, while the much more widespread draft evasion was mostly ignored by the general public.[119]

A large group of student draft resisters chose not to surrender their deferments but to take a stand only if ordered to be inducted. At that point, the majority in this category chose exile from their native land rather than serve in a war they detested. As many as 150,000 young

Americans, most of them college students, emigrated to foreign countries during the period of the Vietnam War. Most of these opponents of the conflict went to Canada because they were informed that they might acquire citizenship in that kindred land if they lived there for five out of eight years. Others settled in Sweden, France, or Switzerland. The resisters preferred life in these countries to other possible places of exile and were given to understand that they would be relatively safe from extradition proceedings in such locations. There had been no comparable mass exodus of disaffected Americans during a war since the Loyalist flight during the American Revolution, and at that time the bulk of the emigres had not been college students. The public image of the anti-Vietnam War exiles was that they were mostly "white, educated, well-to-do." In this case the truth seems to have fairly well matched the popular stereotype.[120]

Much more extreme in their resistance to conscription, almost seeming to be seeking martyrdom, were those who preferred to stay at home and burn their draft cards. The card burners hoped that their movement would spread throughout the land, until the war effort was disrupted. Resistance leaders like William Sloane Coffin, chaplain of Yale University, and Dr. Benjamin Spock, world-famous pediatrician and anti-war activist, theorized that if as many as a hundred thousand anti-draft students could be induced to abandon their college deferments and burn their cards, there would not be enough jails to hold them. This, in turn, would paralyze the Johnson Administration's Vietnam program.[121]

The card-burning movement started slowly. In March 1966 three young men in New York and one in Boston destroyed their draft cards. In April 1967 as anti-war demonstrators marched in New York City, shouting "Hell, No! We Won't Go," one hundred seventy-five young men in Central Park took the slogan literally and participated in a mass draft card burning.[122] Later that year, in October, a big "burn-in" was staged in Boston at the Arlington Street Church. Dr. Coffin preached an anti-war sermon, after which two hundred fifty young men slated for induction turned in their draft cards to the church's ministers. Another fifty draftees burned their cards.[123]

However even among left-wing SDS activists, there was no great enthusiasm for this extreme strategy. By mid-1968, only a few thousand draft resisters had chosen to fight to the bitter end against being sent to Vietnam. Official government estimates during that time were that during all the Vietnam years not more than ten thousand persons had actually burned their draft cards or turned them back to Selective Service. In 1965 the United States Congress, angered by the anti-draft movement, had enacted a law making destruction of a draft card punishable by five years in prison and a five thousand dollar fine. The draft resisters claimed in their defense that the Nuremberg Tribunal after World War II had condemned as a crime the violation of international treaties and the launching of an aggressive war. This, they maintained, was what the Unites States was doing in Vietnam. Their argument carried little weight, however, because the Nuremberg Tribunal had been set up by the victorious nations at the conclusion of a war, and these nations had carefully refrained from making permanent such a war-crimes tribunal before which they themselves might be arraigned some day. As a result, the only recourse draft-card burners had was to the United States Supreme Court. That hope proved unavailing when the high court upheld the convictions of draft card burners.[124]

By and large, though, many draft opponents during the Vietnam era found the law to be relatively lenient, more so, for example, than it had been during World War I. Perhaps the growing unpopularity of the Vietnam conflict explained this difference. Early in the war, the Johnson Administration had set up a special unit in the Justice Department with the publicly announced mission of prosecuting violators of the Selective Service laws. The number of such prosecutions did, in fact, increase steadily from 1965 through 1970. However, war resisters found the federal courts to be less severe than draft authorities intended. A whole class of lawyers emerged that specialized in draft-resistance and draft-evasion cases. One draft attorney's office had on file upwards of four hundred defense arguments that had been used in court successfully. As thousands of draft-violation cases were docketed for trial, the courts became clogged and proceedings dragged on and on. During the Vietnam years, half-a-million persons were classified as violators of the draft laws and could have been sent to prison. Of this total, federal prosecutors reviewed for possible indictment less than half of the cases and only twenty-five thousand were ever indicted. In turn, fewer than nine thousand of those indicted were convicted. Then, as a result of appeals and court reviews, only 3,250 of the draft violators ended up with a prison sentence. By 1971, the government found it was almost impossible to enforce Selective Service.[125]

Anti-war activists at the colleges who were not prepared to risk jail by destroying their draft cards or fleeing to foreign shores sought other means to express their disapproval of the Vietnam involvement. At the University of Michigan, for example, students staged a "Walk-In" in March 1966 aiming to disrupt the work of a local draft board.[126] At Princeton, sixty-six students in April 1967 paid for an advertisement in the *Daily Princetonian*, denouncing the war. They would keep their draft cards and their deferments, they stated, but if called up they pledged that they would refuse to serve in Vietnam.[127]

One technique that became popular on same campuses was the so-called "Vietnam Commencement." A series of these were held in 1968 and 1969. The movement began in Berkeley in May 1968 when a substantial number of that year's graduates made a public pledge that they would refuse induction if called up. Hundreds more in the California graduating class recited a pledge promising that all those resisting the draft would have their support.[128]

The "Vietnam Commencement" concept appealed to students on other campuses. At the Yale commencement on 10 June, the Reverend Paul Moore, Jr., a Trustee of the University, offered a special prayer for William Sloane Coffin, the school's chaplain, who was on trial in Boston for encouraging draft resistance. Also, a petition was published in which three hundred and twelve of the Yale graduates stated their "opposition to our nation's unjust and destructive policies in Vietnam." In addition, the president of the University, Kingman Brewster, presented an honorary degree to the poet, Robert Lowell, who had been jailed during World War II for resisting the draft. The Yale citation read: "You have followed conscience, even when it led to prison."[129]

Similar demonstrations were organized at Harvard that year. More than one hundred of the Harvard graduating class announced in advance that they would refuse to serve in the Vietnam War if inducted. When Radcliffe College held its commencement on 12 June, the graduates wore white armbands to show support for their male fellow students who opposed the draft.[130]

The anti-Vietnam tone of Dartmouth's 1968 commencement drew varied responses from the audience. James Newton, the class valedictorian, asked his fellow graduates to refuse to be drafted but, if they were, to refuse to fight in Vietnam. If no other course was open to them, he advised them to go to Canada. Newton's message provoked loud boos and hisses from many parents and older alumni and enthusiastic applause and shouts of approval from the graduating seniors. A poll had revealed earlier that few 1968 Dartmouth graduates were actually ready to burn draft cards or flee to Canada, but that an overwhelming majority were opposed to the war itself. They believed that no one should have to fight in what they perceived to be an unjust conflict if a legal way could be found to avoid service.[131]

The anti-war commencements continued in 1969. Again Yale took a leading role in the movement. At its 9 June 1969 exercises, students held up two large signs that read "We Won't Go." William Thompson, Jr., a student speaker, told the commencement audience that 77 percent of the graduating class had signed a petition opposing the Vietnam War and that 143 graduates had pledged that, if drafted, they would refuse induction. The class of 1969 had set up a legal defense fund, he announced, to help fellow graduates if they were prosecuted for draft evasion.[132]

The participants in Hunter College's June 1969 commencement made it clear that they too opposed the military involvement in Vietnam. A number of faculty members joined the majority of the graduating seniors in wearing special armbands to proclaim their opposition to the war and the draft. The commencement speaker, Professor Henri Peyre of Yale, told the audience that the American people had never been so divided over an issue of public policy since the Civil War as they now were over Vietnam.[133]

By far the largest group of anti-war college students neither fled to Canada nor burned their draft cards. Instead, this considerable segment of the student population employed a variety of ingenious techniques to evade the draft. The draft-evasion movement grew markedly as the war escalated. Methods of evasion became increasingly more sophisticated, while the evaders suffered no opprobrium from their classmates.

Some students elected to go abroad during the Vietnam years to study in foreign universities. Such study arrangements were completely legal.[134] Other students enrolled in officer-training programs on their home campuses. Such ROTC affiliations were considered to be a sensible alternative to serving on a Vietnam battlefield. Some students discovered that if they enrolled in the National Guard, they would also be protected from being sent to Vietnam. During the war years, most Guard units stayed at home, keeping an eye on possible violent dissent. At the same time, many students availed themselves of the services of the draft counselors who were springing up on every campus. There were religious counselors, left-wing counselors, guidance counselors, and many others. All of them helped potential draftees by pointing out the various legal expedients that could be employed to delay or prevent induction.[135]

A number of young men of college age during the Vietnam years found the idea of going abroad to study at a university, say, in England, France, or Switzerland, irresistible. Among them was a future President of the Unites States, William Jefferson Clinton. Other collegians, who opted for enrollment in their school's ROTC unit, would be exempt from the Vietnam draft during their years in college and this exemption would continue for two or three years afterwards if they became members of the reserves.[136] Art Harris, who later was a successful journalist, recalled: "I belonged to a 'subversive' outfit at Duke called ROTC. My dad told me he had spent too much money on me to have me become Vietnam cannon fodder."[137]

Since it was widely assumed that members of the National Guard would never be sent to Vietnam, service in the Guard became extremely popular with young men who were in college and many who were not. During 1968 the National Guard waiting list grew to one hundred thousand. Pentagon spokesmen reported in 1970 that 71 percent of all Reserve enrollees and 90 percent of all enlistments in the Guard came from people who admitted that they hoped to avoid the draft by signing up.

One million men became guardsmen and reservists during the Vietnam years. A future Vice President of the United States, Dan Quayle, was one of these.[138]

By and large, Pentagon officials were not overjoyed at the sudden vogue for National Guard service. One of them remarked acidly that many of the newly-hatched Guardsmen and reservists were "Sergeant Bilkos — trying to look brave while making sure someone else does the fighting." University men were often quite numerous in the reserve units. A woman from Massachusetts remembered that her husband's outfit was "a very academic unit. A lot from Harvard Law — bright, talented, and interesting." Her husband had a master's degree in business and journalism; on weekends he served as a clerk-typist in a reserve Civil Affairs unit. "He got into his uniform at 7 A.M. on Saturday," the woman recalled, "and got out of it as soon as he came home on Sunday. They had the short haircuts, the whole thing. .... It wasn't just Vietnam; it was the whole concept of the Army."[139]

Even college and university attendance itself, it developed, could be used by ingenious "students" as a means of delaying or evading the draft. Studies made during the mid-1960s revealed that a number of young men who might not otherwise have gone to college were now doing so in hopes that they would thereby get student deferments. College enrollments during the Vietnam years increased notably, especially in defense-related fields such as engineering and science. Enrollees were aware that their draft vulnerability would end at age twenty-six. As a result, graduate schools became extremely popular; a survey made by a graduate school dean found that 90 percent of the applicants to his institution admitted that anxiety about the draft was one of the main reasons for seeking admission. When graduate school deferments were ended in 1967, applications for graduate programs in such areas as liberal arts or business administration declined sharply. Deferments were still practically automatic in fields such as teaching, theology, engineering, and the sciences generally. Divinity schools now experienced a boom in student applications. A similar rush to teacher-training programs and graduate schools of engineering followed. It became difficult, in some cities, for recent teachers college graduates to find jobs in the school systems as the shifting draft regulations created an artificial glut. At the same time, it became increasingly difficult to get into medical schools and other advanced training programs in health services.[140]

Everything that could be used for legal draft exemption was employed. Family status was a means of escape for some students. A student who could demonstrate that he was the sole support of a widowed mother or dependent younger brothers or sisters could qualify for draft deferment. Originally, married men were automatically granted deferments, giving considerable encouragement to romance. When that exemption was revised so that it applied only to married men with children, a number of married students developed an interest in having a family.[141]

Such strategies, and many more, were the special province of the horde of draft counselors on the campuses. Counselors with a left-wing orientation worked hard to advise students how to escape the draft and worked also to gum up the conscription system. The "May 2nd Movement," for example, sent counselors to the College of the City of New York to inform students about techniques of legal draft evasion and to give encouragement to those "who object to fighting in an imperialist army."[142] The national leftist student organization, SDS, set up tables outside the centers where draftees took their physicals.[143] SDS representatives distributed a manual instructing students on ways to ensure rejection by army doctors. Innovative techniques in this undercover publication included the following: Make trouble at the induction center by wearing a protest sign and handing out anti-war leaflets; refuse to sign the prescribed loyalty oath; make it known that you are a homosexual; arrive drunk at the induction center; play "psycho" — tell them that "you're really a secret agent for the great God Johnson"; arrive at the center dirty and unkempt, or make sure that the examining doctors see obvious signs that you are a drug addict; inform the authorities that you are a bed-wetter.[144]

Some campus counselors advised their charges to emphasize physical ailments they thought they had or were able to fake on the chance that such conditions might get them rejected. Advisors at the University of Michigan boldly suggested: "Get a note from a cooperative doctor saying that you once attempted suicide." At Dartmouth, a new technique was proposed: "Get your face and hands all tattooed, preferably with obscene messages."[145] On some campuses, the religious chaplains did their best to help potential pacifist inductees build up a case for exemption as conscientious objectors.

One commentator sums up the medical rejection picture as follows:

> The white middle class knew how to face their medicals. A loophole in the law gave every registrant the right to choose the site of his pre-induction physical. Butte, Montana, was considered the spot for anyone with a doctor's letter; Little Rock, Arkansas, was for anyone with a note from a psychiatrist; Seattle, Washington, was for anyone carrying a medical message, "regardless of what the letter said."[146]

Whatever the circumstances, it is a fact that a number of young Americans were disqualified for the Vietnam draft because of medical disabilities. This group included the sons of some of the most prominent advocates of military intervention in Vietnam.[147]

A survey of the overall operation of the Vietnam draft compiled at Notre Dame University came up with interesting findings. Approximately fifteen million draft-age men in the United States were discovered to have avoided being conscripted for combat in Vietnam largely because they had taken action to prevent this from happening. The army that fought in Vietnam, stated Notre Dame investigators, was not composed primarily of college men; young college men somehow managed to avoid being drafted. As Bashkir and Straus put it, the draftees who fought and died in Vietnam were mostly "society's losers from the lower rungs of the class structure, high-school dropouts, members of minority groups."[148]

By 1969 the government was ready to take a new, long look at the draft and the war in Southeast Asia. The combined impact of campus and street demonstrations, spreading anti-war violence, all-out draft resistance by some and ingenious draft evasion by others, was undermining and, in some areas, practically paralyzing the Selective Service machinery. The induction center at Oakland, California, which administered the draft for the northern half of the state, reported in May 1969 that more than half of the men who had been ordered to show up for induction simply did not appear. Eleven percent of those who did report refused to enter the military. Other Selective Service centers were being raided by radical anti-war groups led by activists like Father Daniel Berrigan. Vitally important draft files were being destroyed.[149]

Conditions among American troops in Vietnam were not much better. In 1971 a Marine Corps Colonel stated in an article in the *Armed Forces Journal* that at least fourteen different groups critical of the war had been operating openly among American servicemen and that at least one hundred fourty-four "underground" newspapers and anti-war factsheets aimed at men in uniform were being published at or in the neighborhood of United States military bases. When massive anti-war demonstrations took place in the United States during October and November 1969, members of United States combat units in Vietnam wore black armbands to show their sympathy for the cause. The Colonel's article mentioned "booing and cursing of officers and even of hapless entertainers such as Bob Hope" and asserted that in the year 1970, two hundred nine United States officers who were killed at the front may have been the victims, not of the Vietcong, but of their own men. Desertion rates by that year were four times higher than they had been in 1966. Riots in army stockades were becoming much more frequent and difficult to control. Peace signs were being put up on the walls of mess halls and other buildings at military bases. "Pray-Ins" for peace were being conducted openly at military bases. The Colonel's study concluded: "By every conceivable indicator, our army that now remains in Vietnam is in a state approaching collapse."[150]

Lyndon Johnson, deciding not to seek reelection in 1968, was in effect driven out of office by the failure of his Vietnam policy. His successor, Richard Nixon, though proclaiming on every occasion that the United States would never be pushed out of Vietnam, in reality worked to speed up a policy of "Vietnamization" of the war. This approach, which in essence amounted to a gradual American withdrawal, was pictured by Nixon as a step intended to achieve "peace with honor."[151]

The real change in American policy by 1969 was revealed by the implementation of a new draft system. Since manpower stationed in Vietnam was gradually being reduced in size, it was possible for the Nixon Administration to cut down on draft calls at home. Late in 1969, the government announced a new Selective Service system, a draft "lottery." The new system was extremely important for American college and university students because it assured most of them that they would probably never be conscripted during their years of draft eligibility. Meanwhile, a special commission was set up to study the operation of Selective Service. The commission devoted a considerable amount of its time to studying the possibility of ending the draft altogether. In addition, it considered the measures that would be necessary to convert American military forces into an all-volunteer professional army made up of career specialists.[152]

From Peace Marching to Campus "Trashing"

During the years 1966 through 1970, campus protests against the continuing Vietnam conflict grew more numerous, more strident, and much more violent. Clearly there was more than just a coincidental connection between the many anti-war demonstrations during these five difficult years and the steady increase in the number of men taken in the draft.

By December 1967 the Johnson Administration had dispatched more than 475,000 servicemen to Vietnam. By this time, too, the anti-war movement had split openly into two factions: a peaceful protest wing and a violent, direct-action wing. The nonviolent activists staged massive peace parades during these years. On 15 April 1967 they mobilized hundreds of thousands of marchers, many of them college students, to demonstrate at United Nations Headquarters in New York. In mid-October of the same year, more than fifty thousand anti-Vietnam demonstrators, again predominantly college students, marched to the Pentagon in Washington, D.C., to proclaim their peace-now message.[153]

As Vietnam casualties mounted, the protests increased in size. On 26 April 1968, more than 200,000 students from high schools, colleges, and universities in the New York metropolitan area staged a day-long strike against the war. The strike was part of a worldwide "Day of Protest against the War," as crowds in Tokyo, Paris, Prague, and many other overseas cities joined in demonstrations against American intervention in Vietnam.[154]

All of this was just a prelude to "Vietnam Moratorium Day," 15 October 1969, when one of the biggest peace demonstrations of the period was held. On that day, two million Americans participated in anti-war rallies. Fifty members of the United States Congress joined in the protests.[155] A second "Moratorium Day" was scheduled for 15 November after President Nixon announced that he would not permit anti-war demonstrations to influence his policy. On that date, while the President professed to be preoccupied as he watched a Washington Redskins football game on television, between a quarter-and-a-half million peace demonstrators thronged the nation's capital. Commentators called the gathering the largest public protest demonstration ever held in Washington. Once again, large numbers of college and university students were on hand to swell the throng. At hundreds of campuses across the land, even at ultra-conservative schools like Vanderbilt, classes were suspended and anti-war rallies were held. In an eerie "March against Death," forty thousand of the marchers circled the White House again and again. On the college campuses, bells tolled solemnly and crosses were planted in memory of those Americans who had been slain in Vietnam.[156]

The peace marchers, however, did not go far enough to satisfy the radical wing of the anti-war movement. Campus extremists gained increasing prominence as the Administration refused to budge. Advocates of "direct-action" believed that Teach-Ins, peace marches, and sit-ins at draft boards were too ineffectual to force the authorities to end the war.[157]

Early examples of "direct-action" tactics came in 1966. In November of that year, a group of Brown University students were arrested for charging the stage in order to disrupt a speech being given at Pembroke College by General Earle Wheeler, chairman of the Joint Chiefs of Staff.[158] And at about the same time, a group of extremists at Harvard surrounded the automobile of Robert McNamara, Secretary of Defense in the Johnson Administration, refusing to let him leave the campus. McNamara had earlier tried to deliver a speech to the students but was shouted down by the angry crowd. The Secretary finally escaped his harassers via a series of steam tunnels.[159]

Students for a Democratic Society (SDS) took the lead in many of the violent campus actions. This New Left organization, which claimed by 1968 to have as many as seventy-five thousand members and hundreds of local chapters at the colleges, had Marxist antecedents. It was originally an offshoot of the Student League for Industrial Democracy, which, in turn, had evolved from the pre-World War I Intercollegiate Socialist League.[160] Mark Rudd was the youthful leader of an extremist (even for SDS) faction at Columbia University which called itself "the mother-fuckers." Rudd explained the "non-negotiable" demands of his group as follows:

> Liberal solutions ... partial understandings, compromises are not allowed anymore. The essence of the matter is that we are out for social and political revolution, nothing less. This, of course, puts the administration of Columbia University in somewhat of a bind ...[161]

Why did extremist elements in the anti-war movement, like Rudd's group at Columbia, turn on the universities instead of the government and target the former for "direct action"? Undoubtedly, the revelations in *Ramparts* and the *New York Times* about the secret links between the CIA and universities like Michigan State fueled the anger and resentment of campus radicals. The openly acknowledged research for the Pentagon that was going on at prestigious schools like Stanford and MIT greatly increased their ire. Radical activists considered such pursuits to be a horrendous distortion of the true purposes of higher learning.[162] Political groups found that they could attract substantial student support by openly attacking contract research for the military at the universities. Next to opposition to the draft this became their most popular issue. By contrast, the SDS attacks on war-related job recruiting and the campaign to abolish all military training at colleges and universities were much less popular.[163]

It should not be assumed, of course, that the crusade against classified research attracted universal student approbation. Some students at major universities, especially graduate students in science and engineering, had succeeded in obtaining fellowships and assistantships that involved work on military projects. Such appointments conferred on the researcher automatic draft exemption.[164]

Direct action against classified contract research, however, had distinct advantages over other possible objects for radical attack. It might be easier to pursue such a campaign to a successful conclusion. The Pentagon was far away and well-guarded; the university, on the contrary, was close at hand and relatively vulnerable.

The SDS anti-classified-research drive featured an all-out attack on the Institute of Defense Analysis (IDA), a consortium of twelve major universities that did much secret military research for the government. Technically, the Institute functioned as a separate entity from its university sponsors; in actuality, it was their creature. One of the first moves in the attack came at Princeton, where thirty-one students were arrested in October 1967 as they tried to block the entrance to a building where the

Institute had its headquarters.[165] At Columbia, the onslaught on the university's connection with IDA will be discussed later. At the University of Chicago, a student sponsored protest drove the IDA off the campus.[166] At the University of Pennsylvania, student and faculty pressures forced the school in September 1967 to end all classified military research on its campus. At Cornell, a similar campaign resulted in the termination of a contract to develop a counter-insurgency project for Thailand. At the University of Minnesota, it was announced that the institution would no longer sponsor a secret government project that involved studying the usefulness of drugs in the interrogation of war prisoners. New York University, for its part, decided not to renew a chemical warfare contract and announced that its restrictions on secret research projects would be considerably tightened.[167]

Perhaps the most dramatic move in the nationwide campaign against university-based military research came at Stanford in mid-April 1969. At that time, a band of anti-war students staged a nine-day occupation of the University's applied electronics laboratories, where secret research was being done for the government. The student occupiers announced that their primary objective was to end all military research at Stanford. The protesters eventually won a partial victory. A committee of the Stanford faculty adopted new guidelines that, in effect, banned all military research on the school's campuses. The secret contract research on chemical and biological warfare went on, however, at a facility in Menlo Park. This off-campus center, the Stanford Research Institute, was an affiliate of the University, though not an integral part of it.[168]

The most obstinate and unyielding opposition by any major university to the campaign against contract research occurred at the world-renowned Massachusetts Institute of Technology. In one year, 1969, MIT's so-called "T" Lab and its affiliate, the Lincoln Laboratory in nearby Lexington, Massachusetts, brought the school 110 million dollars in income. MIT's *entire* budget for that year was 218 million dollars. Some students at the Institute, not entirely as a joke, called their campus "The Second Pentagon."[169]

Three MIT graduate students proposed in 1969 a strike for a couple of days by personnel at all secret military research centers affiliated with universities. The purpose would be to dramatize the campaign against classified research. The plan was received enthusiastically by many institutions and a Science Action Coordination Committee was set up to implement it. Ultimately, on 4 March and 8 March 1969 faculty and students at thirty research-oriented universities joined in bringing all secret military projects to a halt.[170]

The faculty of MIT had formed its own Science Action Coordination Committee and this body issued the following statement:

Misuse of scientific and technical knowledge presents a major threat to the existence of mankind. Through its actions in Vietnam our government has shaken our confidence in its ability to make wise and humane decisions.[171]

A number of Harvard professors and students joined their MIT colleagues during the stoppage. George Wald, a professor of biology at Harvard and a recipient of the Nobel Prize, delivered an address in which he denounced what he viewed as a perversion of national values. The government, he contended, was mostly preoccupied with the business of killing instead of what should be its real purpose, namely, the safeguarding and fostering of life. No wonder, he said, college students were depressed and uneasy. "What we are up against is a generation that is by no means sure that it has a future."[172]

The nationwide strike by science researchers did not fully achieve its purpose. Universities such as Penn State that still insisted on performing secret work for the Pentagon refused to divest themselves of their contracts for such work.[173] In fact, certain schools, such as Southern Illinois University, introduced contract research where formerly there had been none. Southern Illinois announced in September 1969 that it had received a one million dollar government grant to set up a "Center for Vietnamese Studies." Demonstrations by students and faculty against the center broke out in February 1970 amid charges that the agency was not a scholarly subdivision but a government-subsidized project to perpetuate American influence in Vietnam. Scattered violence occurred during the demonstrating, and a number of students were arrested.[174]

At MIT, too, there was unyielding resistance to the campaign against classified research. In November 1969 hundreds of student demonstrators thronged the Institute's campus, demanding the immediate termination of all military-related research. President Howard W. Johnson flatly refused to negotiate with them and called for help from the police of Cambridge, Massachusetts. A melee followed, in which ten student protesters were injured. Incidentally, Johnson's actions flew in the face of recommendations sent to him by a special twenty-two-member student-faculty committee on research at MIT. The committee's report recommended that laboratories at MIT radically reduce work in weapons research and change their emphasis from military to civilian projects. The school's administration refused to go along with the recommendations of its own committee.[175]

SDS's campaign against on-campus job recruiting by representatives of the armed services and private corporations was only partially successful. To SDS, a military contractor such as the Dow Chemical Corporation, which supplied the army with napalm (a terror weapon and defoliant), was a symbol of all the horrors and injustices of the war. The student activists held that any hostile action was justifiable, including physical violence, to drive job recruiters for Dow and similar military contractors off the college campuses of America. SDS spokespersons said that universities, by allowing Dow, CIA, and Department of Defense recruiters on their campuses, were in effect collaborating with the war effort in Vietnam and signaling approval of it.[176]

The campus campaign against Dow drew much attention in the media. Dow Corporation management announced in February 1969 that there had been 203 campus demonstrations against its recruiters during the preceding three years, plus "several dozen more" off-campus protests at Dow offices, plants, and installations at home and overseas.[177] There were also angry campus attacks on job interviewers for Olin Mathieson, Litton Industries, and General Electric, as well as others representing the CIA, the Navy, and the Marines.[178]

Some of the anti-recruiter demonstrations turned ugly, with physical attacks on university property as well as against company and government representatives. At the University of Wisconsin, for example, the protest degenerated into a major riot in which sixty-five persons were injured, including three policemen.[179] At Harvard, two hundred student demonstrators imprisoned a Dow recruiter for nine hours; the University later put seventy-four of the protesters on probation for "forcible obstruction."[180] At San Jose State College in California, an anti-Dow demonstration became a full-fledged battle of students versus police. Tear gas was used, college windows were smashed, and a number of people were injured.[181] At the University of North Carolina, fifteen student demonstrators against Dow recruiters were arrested.[182] Dow refused to take its representatives off the campuses, but the CIA decided to follow a different tack. Officials of that top-secret agency grew tired of being a target for campus demonstrators. In December 1967 they directed that, wherever possible, CIA recruiting in the future be conducted at off-campus locations.[183]

Despite the vehemence of some of the anti-recruiter outbreaks, the SDS campaign was not wildly popular at many colleges. A number of students felt that they should be permitted to hear arguments from any source, and then make up their own minds. Eden Weinman, president of Columbia's sophomore class, declared in 1967: "Although many students feel that the war in Vietnam is wrong, people do not feel that suppression of certain types of speech is a suitable means of protest."[184]

There were also certain practical considerations involved in the situation. Many anti-Vietnam students did not feel that on-campus recruiting by Dow or the military affected their lives and career plans the way the draft did. For some, the issue was indeed a difficult one — moral responsibility versus expediency. Jobs with Dow or with the CIA would provide draft exemption. Students of "inconsistent conscience" (the words are Gabriel

Kolko's) who took such jobs would probably never be shipped to Vietnam.[185]

Whatever the reasons, students with strong anti-Vietnam War views expressed a measure of tolerance for job recruiters. A poll of Columbia College undergraduates in November 1967 disclosed that 67.3 percent, or two-thirds of the thirty-one hundred students voting, were in favor of open recruiting on their campus. A similar poll of campus opinion was conducted at CCNY in mid-February 1968. There, 11,900 CCNY students and 329 tenured faculty voted overwhelmingly in favor of permitting on-campus job recruiting.[186]

SDS also failed to achieve the total support it sought for its all-out campaign against ROTC. Anti-war partisans argued that ROTC was a local symbol of the war effort in Vietnam and, for that reason, must be terminated. A Harvard faculty member who sympathized with the SDS position charged that "a principal function of the American military establishment is to suppress and discourage popular revolution in the third world as well as to discourage dissent at home." For this reason, the professor concluded, "the training of junior officers at Harvard involves the University in complicity in the suppression of rights of popular revolution and self-determination."[187]

The radical opponents of ROTC could point to a well-established trend that seemed to favor their point of view. During the anti-war agitation of the 1920s and 1930s, activists at the colleges had launched numerous anti-ROTC campaigns. Indeed, as far back as the 1880s, student agitation against military training had erupted at a few state universities. So the current SDS-sponsored campaign was not really a new idea.

The drive against ROTC went the same way as the campaign against on-campus recruiters. There were dramatic demonstrations that drew public attention to the anti-Vietnam cause. There were violent clashes with university authorities and with the police. And there were occasional successes. All in all, though, effective student support for the effort did not manifest itself.

Anti-ROTC protests and "sit-ins" were staged at a number of campuses during 1968 and 1969. Occasionally, as at Miami University in Ohio, where violence erupted during the demonstrations against ROTC, state troopers were called in and tear gas was used. After a similar demonstration at Dartmouth, thirty-six student protesters were arrested.[188]

In many instances, as at Penn State, university faculties and administrations refused to abolish the Corps outright. They did, however, make a partial response to the protests by taking academic credit away from ROTC.[189] At the majority of campuses, ROTC had long since ceased to be required, but SDS denounced such concessions as only "half-a-loaf."[190]

The campaign's most dramatic success came at Harvard. There, after a long and bitter faculty debate, it was decided in 1969, that the University's ROTC program would be terminated by 30 June 1971, eliminating one of the oldest ROTC units at any American college.[191]

However, the SDS encountered rough going at conservative campuses. At the University of Oklahoma, for example, radical activists were unable to overcome strong student, alumni, and community support for on-campus officer-training. Some parents expressly sent their sons to the University so that these young men would have careers in the United States armed forces. Consequently, the general environment was hardly unfriendly to ROTC. By this time, Oklahoma's biggest income came from military bases.[192]

SDS's main problem, however, stemmed from the fact that many anti-war students did not necessarily favor abolition of the Corps. Such students were satisfied with discrediting ROTC, removing it from the regular academic curriculum and making it completely voluntary. There were practical considerations that operated here. After receiving officers' training at college, students who opted for ROTC could postpone active tours of duty for one, two, or even three years, while they went on to graduate and professional schools. By the time they finished such training, the Vietnam War might be over.[193]

A study of the ROTC contingent at Dartmouth in July 1968 illustrated why SDS was having such a difficult time implementing its uncompromising program. The survey revealed that the majority of Dartmouth Corpsmen were strongly opposed to the Vietnam War. After completing their officer training, most Dartmouth ROTC students hoped to attend a professional or graduate school and defer their active service. A number were planning to go to law school, while there was also much interest in journalism and city planning. Asked by the Army to indicate the branches of service they preferred, these collegians listed such services as the Finance Corps, the Adjutant General's Office (which handled legal affairs), the Medical Division, and the Transportation Corps. None listed the Infantry; only three listed the Artillery Corps. Dartmouth students were concerned about the way the general public might regard them, however. A number of them placed an advertisement in New Hampshire's most widely-circulated newspaper that declared:

DON'T CALL US DRAFT DODGERS.
... We believe in our country. We will all serve ... But we strongly oppose the war in Vietnam. We think it is tragic for Vietnam and for the United States. America has its own problems to solve.[194]

Students at other campuses, many of them similarly disapproving of the war, showed no overwhelming desire to abolish ROTC. At Brown, a poll of thirteen hundred students revealed that 68 percent believed ROTC should remain in some form. At Northeastern University in Boston, a similar poll found a large campus majority favoring continuance of ROTC. And at Tufts, a student poll showed majority sentiment for continuing ROTC, but only on a voluntary basis and with no academic credit.[195]

For a faction of radical extremists in SDS, the organization's various "direct-action" attacks on the war had not succeeded because its measures had not gone far enough in "radicalizing" students. These left-wing activists, like Mark Rudd at Columbia University, believed that the time had come to attack the universities directly. They advocated "trashing" the universities, occupying their buildings, and paralyzing their academic routines, thus destroying their potential to aid the military establishment.

Rudd's faction launched its attack on Columbia in April and May of 1968. His militants seized on two overriding issues as the basis for presenting a series of non-negotiable demands. These amounted to an ultimatum demanding that Columbia sever at once all remaining ties with the Institute for Defense Analysis. In addition, the University was told it must immediately cease construction of a new gymnasium on land that had been leased in Morningside Park. Afro-American militants wished the land in question to be devoted solely to the needs of the black community of Harlem. The Columbia administrators were given very little time to respond to the ultimatum. When they did not surrender immediately, student revolutionaries "occupied" four Columbia buildings; black activists took over a fifth.[196]

The Columbia faculty overwhelmingly condemned the occupation of university buildings but made attempts to mediate the conflict peacefully. All such efforts at compromise failed. Ultimately, on 30 April the Columbia authorities made the extremely difficult decision to summon police. In the subsequent "bust," nearly one thousand New York policemen removed students from the buildings, using very rough methods to carry out the mission. By the time order was restored to the Columbia campus, 148 persons had been injured and more than 700 arrested. The "bust," which was apparently more ruthless than the Columbia administration had anticipated, caused additional difficulties for the hapless University. The student body, enraged by what it saw as police brutality, developed sympathy for Rudd's followers.[197]

In the end, Columbia University suspended Mark Rudd and seventy-two of the most violent student "occupiers." A general sympathy strike, called by student leaders, brought all classes to a halt. Final examinations had to be called off and only two grades, "pass" or "fail," were given on the basis of previous course work. Mark Rudd was forced to leave the campus, but questions persisted about the management of the crisis. This led subsequently to the resignation of Columbia's president, Grayson

Kirk, and also his chief assistant, Vice-President David Truman. Obviously, there were few winners in this first dramatic example during the Vietnam War of a violent student attack on a major American university.[198]

Campus Violence Reaches Its Peak

The publicity generated by the Columbia takeover and "bust" gave rise to much apprehension that a nationwide student revolution was at hand. SDS extremists did little to quiet such fears, making highly emotional appeals for "two, three, many Columbias." Student unrest and violence reached greater heights than ever before. The Educational Testing Service released an estimate that over three thousand campus disturbances had broken out during the year 1968 alone. The majority of these incidents occurred in the months following the Columbia outbreak.[199]

During the succeeding academic year, 1969–70, there were many more violent campus incidents — 9,400 in all — of which at least 730 eventually led to forcible intervention of police and the arrest of student demonstrators. In this period, too, 410 of the disturbances led to some destruction of college property.[200]

A comprehensive study of the principal issues that set off the violent campus protests during 1968–70 found that the Vietnam War played a central role in most of them. While a great number of issues provoked campus outbreaks, the four leading causes were: United States military policy in Vietnam; Selective Service; ROTC on the campus; and secret military research at colleges and universities.[201]

Violence on the campus seemed to generate more militant attitudes among some faculty. Morton Fried, chairman of the Anthropology department at Columbia, told the *New York Times*: "The violence of the police raid was a watershed for many of us, certainly for me." One of the younger Columbia professors who refused to condemn the violent takeover of the university buildings, claimed that between two hundred and three hundred Columbia faculty members, mostly younger teachers like himself, identified themselves "with the politics of the New Left." Radical student protesters, marching on campuses throughout the nation, chanted: "Ho-Ho-Ho Chi Minh; The NLF is gonna win!"[202]

Columbia's violent scenario was now repeated in many places, including the hitherto sedate precincts of the Harvard Yard. By the spring of 1969, anti-Vietnam War sentiment had become so strong at that Ivy League school that the editors of the *Crimson* felt free to call on students to support the left-wing National Liberation Front in Vietnam. Nevertheless, the events that transpired on 9 April 1969 deeply shocked many members of the Harvard community. On that day, seventy extremist members of

SDS at Harvard, demanding the immediate abolition of ROTC, seized the principal administration building of the University. Staff personnel were expelled and negotiations with administration authorities were begun. These talks got nowhere, however, and at 4:45 A.M. the following morning, university officials called in the Cambridge police, plus six busloads of Massachusetts state troopers. These officers succeeded in evicting the student occupiers, but at a high cost. A total of 196 persons were arrested, and 48 individuals, 5 of them policemen, were sent to the hospital.[203]

As was the case at Columbia, the Harvard community reacted with indignation to the calling in of police. The student body went on strike for three days and the faculty condemned the president of the university and his assistants for bringing municipal police into Harvard Yard. In addition, the faculty recommended, 395 to 13, that all criminal charges against the student intruders be dropped. Later, some ten thousand persons gathered in Harvard's Soldier's Field to register a protest against the university administration. The faculty also took away all academic credit from ROTC.[204]

These actions did not quiet the rage of anti-war extremists, however. In late September of the same year, about twenty young people who, it was reported, "appeared to be of college age," invaded the Harvard Center for International Affairs. Identifying themselves as members of SDS, they terrorized the staff and evicted them from the building, stating that the Center was being attacked because of its close ties to the "war makers in Washington." Having "liberated" the building, the intruders disrupted a seminar, smashed windows, ransacked files, and painted anti-war slogans on the walls. An emergency call was put in to the campus police, but by the time they arrived, the demonstrators had fled. No staff member at the Center came forward to identify the intruders. One year later, in 1970, when a wave of terrorist bombings by anti-war extremists hit prominent universities, a bomb tore through the International Affairs Center, which was housed in Harvard's Semitic Museum, and blew a hole through its roof. Presidential advisor Henry Kissinger had an office in the center, but happened to be away when the explosion occurred. The Museum was not able to reopen until 1982.[205]

The swiftly spreading brushfire of campus rebellion soon reached Berkeley, California, the original center of student political protest. By the spring of 1969, mobs of anti-Vietnam War students were raging up and down the university campus. A struggle broke out over the control of a "People's Park" nearby. Ultimately, street-fighting flared up between student mobs and police wearing battlegear while helicopters sprayed tear gas on the area. Thousands of armed National Guardsmen were mobilized for patrol duty. These confrontations went on for four days, after which a "State of Civic Disaster" was proclaimed by the government.[206]

On Memorial Day of 1969, student radicals organized a protest march by thirty thousand people to demonstrate support for what they called "The Berkeley Liberation Program." This program called for all-out war against the University of California because it was allegedly "a major brain center for world domination." According to this plan, the South Campus area was to be converted into "a strategic free territory for revolution." W. J. Rorabaugh noted:

> By 1969 most members of the University community were angry and exhausted, almost shell-shocked . . . Prudent faculty members removed valuable possessions, including research notes, and took them home for safekeeping. It was difficult to work on campus, and the University's overall efficiency in its research and teaching dropped considerably.[207]

Conditions were not much better at another branch of the University of California located at Santa Barbara. There, in late February 1970, a thousand rioting students registered a violent protest against their country's current policies by seizing a three-block area in the business district near the University. They held out for six hours, in the meantime burning a branch of the Bank of America to the ground. Eventually the demonstrators were forcibly evicted by the police.[208] Major violence also flared up at Stanford, where extremists used arson as a means of anti-war protest and at Cornell, where heavily armed students threatened a shoot-out. The Cornell incident came to a head in December 1968, and involved a series of non-negotiable demands presented by militant Afro-American students. The protesters insisted on the immediate establishment of a Black Studies college. Without question, the majority of non-black students supported these demands. Even though at one point armed black militants threw the President of Cornell off a platform when he was trying to speak, opinion among the white students did not turn against the protesters, at least for the record. Lacking support from the university community, the president ultimately gave in to the the demands.[209]

At New York University, SDS demonstrators in December 1968 took control of the school's Loeb Center as part of an anti-war protest. Waving Vietcong flags and shouting obscenities, the demonstrators dismantled the loudspeaker system and made it impossible for the Ambassador of South Vietnam and James Reston, an editor from the *New York Times*, to deliver speeches they had prepared. The students draped a Nazi flag around the South Vietnamese envoy's neck and poured a pitcher of water on him. Employees of the Center finally succeeded in rescuing the ambassador and rushed him out of the hall.[210]

Much more was still to come. During the early morning hours of 24 August 1970, a powerful bomb exploded at the University of Wisconsin, killing a research worker, injuring four other persons, damaging Sterling Hall and a number of other campus buildings, and causing eight million dollars worth of damage. Sterling Hall, home of an Army-financed "Mathematics Research Center," had frequently been the target of anti-war demonstrations and protests. The person who was killed, thirty-three-year old Robert Fassnacht, was a post-doctoral research fellow in Physics. He had no connection with the Army Center and had been working late in a basement laboratory on a special project of his own. There had been many violent incidents in the campus anti-war campaign, but the Wisconsin bombing shocked the nation more than any of the others.[211]

At this point, the war still showed no signs of ending. And as it ground on, the tragic chain of violent outbreaks on American college campuses headed towards a terrible denouement. President Nixon continued to be committed to helping his nation's South Vietnamese ally even as he moved gradually to reduce America's direct military involvement in Southeast Asia. The American people were almost completely taken by surprise, however, when Nixon announced on 30 April 1970 that he was sending United States troops into hitherto neutral Cambodia. The reason for this action, the President explained, was that the North Vietnamese army and the Vietcong were using Cambodian territory as "a privileged sanctuary" from which they could launch attacks on the United States forces still remaining in Vietnam.

Nixon's action, which was seen by many as widening the Indochina conflict rather than shutting it down, burst with the force of a bombshell onto the college and university campuses. Almost immediately, student anti-war leaders called for a nationwide strike to protest what they declared was a disastrous and unconscionable move. In this instance, they received approval and cooperation from a number of college faculties and administrators. Thus, Nixon's "get tough" decision had the unanticipated effect of triggering something unique in the history of American education, a nationwide shutdown of the country's colleges and universities.[212]

More than 130 institutions quickly cancelled all classes for the remainder of the spring semester. Final examinations were either called off or made optional. Students left for home and campuses were deserted. What had happened was essentially a general strike by academe that paralyzed American higher education. The Urban Research Corporation's study of the shutdown reported that at least 760 campuses played a significant role in the national protest. Sixty percent of the college enrollment in 1970, which totaled seven and one-half million, went out on strike. This amounted to more than four million participants. Perhaps with some degree of exaggeration, Fred Halstead called it "the biggest student strike in world history."[213]

Angered by the campus reaction to his Cambodia decision, Nixon at a Pentagon appearance referred to his student critics as "bums." His uncompromising attitude did not especially reassure the presidents of America's leading colleges and universities. Alarmed by the dangerous potentialities of the situation, thirty-seven of them sent the President an urgent letter on 4 May urging that he demonstrate "unequivocally your determination" to put an end to the United States military involvement in Indochina. They told him that the American invasion of Cambodia and the continued United States bombing of North Vietnam was generating "severe and widespread apprehensions on our campuses." They implored Nixon "to consider the incalculable dangers of an unprecedented alienation of America's youth."[214]

The Cambodian invasion had thus set off angry protests at hundreds of colleges. But these embittered outbursts were mild compared to the wild rage that engulfed academe as a result of another dramatic and unhappy event. Campus demonstrations had led in some places to scattered violence necessitating the calling in of police. At Kent State University in Northern Ohio, rampaging bands of students got out of control as they protested Nixon's Cambodian move. On the night of 2 May, the protesters burned the school's ROTC building to the ground. The Kent State administration thereupon appealed for help to Governor Rhodes. Rhodes responded by dispatching units of the Ohio National Guard to the Kent State campus "to restore law and order." As the Guardsmen arrived, a curfew was imposed on the entire town of Kent. The angry students ignored this and continued to riot. For the third night in a row they rampaged through the town, smashing windows and setting fires. On campus, they repeatedly attacked university property. On Monday, 4 May, hundreds converged on the University Commons to attend a protest rally. The National Guardsmen drove them back with tear gas and the demonstrators responded by hurling rocks, chunks of pavement, and smoking canisters at the Guardsmen. One platoon of soldiers seemed at this point to be moving away, but suddenly turned, aimed its rifles at the demonstrators, and fired. When the smoke cleared away, it became apparent that the Guardsmen had killed outright four students and wounded eight others.[215]

An Ohio state official quickly issued a statement asserting that the troops had opened fire only because they were being shot at by a sniper. "They were under standing orders to take cover," said the spokesman, "and return any fire." This explanation did not stand up, however. Within days, officials of the Ohio National Guard admitted that they had been unable to find any evidence of sniper fire at the troops on 4 May.[216]

News of the Kent State tragedy, spreading across the country, greatly intensified the student strike that was in progress. From coast to coast "there was an immediate outburst of protests with an emotional intensity bordering on hysteria."[217] In California, the disturbances became so threatening that the Governor ordered all universities in the state to be closed.[218] Later President Nixon acknowledged that the days following the Kent State killings were "among the darkest" his Administration ever had to face.[219]

Unhappily, there seemed to be no end to the campus violence. At Jackson State College in Mississippi, black students about this time were rioting as they protested a number of things, including the Vietnam War and the drafting of college students. On 14 May a squad of white city policemen and state highway patrolmen opened fire on them. Two of the students were killed and fourteen others were wounded.[220]

President Nixon decided to appoint a special commission to investigate the nature and causes of the widespread campus unrest. This body published a report in October 1970 that summarized the results of a detailed investigation of the Kent State and Jackson State tragedies. The Commission severely criticized the Ohio National Guard for issuing loaded weapons to the personnel it had dispatched to control disorderly crowds. This policy, it stated, was in direct violation of Department of the Army guidelines. Such actions must never occur again, the Commission declared. The findings on Jackson State were similarly negative. The Commission found that "unreasonable, unjustified overreaction" on the part of the Mississippi police and state troopers had led them to fire "indiscriminately into a crowd of students."[221]

Did the nationwide campus strike of May 1970 have an impact on national policy? There is considerable evidence that it did. Nixon and his Administration seemed to moderate their policies on Southeast Asia as the college and university shutdown developed. The President told an anxious group of visiting university presidents at this time that he and Vice President Agnew would henceforth desist from referring to student demonstrators in harsh and inflammatory terms. More important, on 8 May, the President announced at a press conference that he would withdraw all United States troops from Cambodia by the end of June.[222]

The Decline of "The Movement": Causes and Consequences

After Cambodia, after Kent State and Jackson State, campus protest reached an all-time peak; it seemed inevitable that "The Movement" would explode into open rebellion. Surprisingly, the precise opposite happened. "There is no doubt," a contemporary observed, "that both activism and radical sentiments declined considerably during the 1970–1971 academic year."[223]

When undergraduates returned to their campuses in the fall of 1970, they found that "an era had ended ... Protest stopped."[224] The number and size of anti-war marches and demonstrations reported in the mass media declined noticeably.[225] Traditionally conservative campuses, such as that at Vanderbilt, returned to their usual conservatism.[226] Schools like Stanford, which had been radical and activist, became relatively quiet.[227] A number of the extremist leaders had dropped out of school. Professors noted with surprise that their students were now putting more emphasis on getting high grades than on attending protest demonstrations.[228] "Classes are well attended," reported *Time Magazine*. "Library lights burn into the night."[229] Once again, students seemed to be interested in "getting into graduate school and striving for good jobs in the establishment."[230] And this trend seemed to be worldwide. Gianni Statera, researching student activism in Europe during these years, found that protest movements in the universities of such countries as France, West Germany, and Italy had "begun a stage of decline" in 1969.[231]

Why was this happening? One important cause may have been the cyclical factor. Some historians, such as Arthur Levine, believe that "societies are like people. They go through periods of wakeful, strenuous, and even frenetic activity, and then must rest ... and the cycle goes on and on."[232] Ladd and Everett made an effort to apply Levine's approach to the history of American higher education. They theorized that colleges went through periods of active on-campus protest. The Vietnam anti-war movement, they wrote, was only the latest example of such a development. But that most recent wave, they predicted, "would also ebb."[233] David Riesman was another scholar who took the cyclical interpretation seriously. He saw the slowing down of campus anti-Vietnam War agitation as possibly constituting a new phase in "the recurrent cycles of activism and withdrawal" that had characterized the behavior of American college students in past eras."[234] In this connection, Seymour Lipset suggested a pattern that might characterize such recurrent ideological swings. He noted that the college population "turns over almost completely within half a decade." Thus, one college class will be entering school just as their predecessors, whose militancy might have been shaped by earlier events, are leaving. For the new arrivals, the developments that had played such a vital part in the lives of the graduates were nothing more than history.[235]

One of the most influential cycles shaping campus viewpoints may well have been the business cycle. A period of economic decline had begun in 1970, depressing the labor market for college graduates. This downturn was especially difficult for graduate students; the graduate schools had become glutted and good jobs were hard to get. The situation became particularly grim for newly graduated Ph.D.'s in the humanities, an area that had produced many of the anti-war protesters.[236] At big state universities, the changing economic conditions were especially hard to take.

The result was that students on all levels had "to study hard and compete strenuously with each other for the good grades which will determine their personal economic futures."[237] As for political protest, many students began to view such activism as potentially hazardous. "In a buyer's market, few are willing to jeopardize a job or program in defense of principle." They tended to be "less willing to make waves."[238] Professors, too, became less adventurous and independent-minded. Increases in the cost of living began to outpace pay raises for faculty members. Many universities were faced with a decline in federal grants and state appropriations. Tighter controls accordingly were imposed on allocations of funds to faculty. All of this may have had a sobering effect on the outlook of potentially activist but vulnerable professors.[239]

The overall situation was hardly improved by the internal dissension and factionalism that tore apart the anti-war movement. Originally a broad and pluralistic phenomenon, the campus anti-war crusade, in the words of David Caute, "yielded at last to the fanatical violence of small, embittered factions."[240] This bitter infighting alienated many moderate students who had opposed the Vietnam war and the draft but were not ready to follow the lead of violent extremists. The annual meeting of SDS in June 1969 illustrated dramatically the fragmentation of "The Movement." At that gathering, several extremist factions — the "Weathermen," the "Crazies," and the "Motherfuckers" — split off from the central core. SDS now ceased to exist as a coherent national group on American campuses. The successor factions sought total revolution through violent "direct action" against "the pig power structure." The concluding sentence of Mark Rudd's open letter to President Grayson Kirk of Columbia suggested their intellectual level: "Up against the wall, mother-fucker!"[241]

We may gain additional clues to the sophistication of these extremists from a speech delivered by a "Mother-fucker" to the SDS national council:

> What I'm saying is, it's bullshit, dig it, bullshit to support repression anywhere. Dig. Look at Cuba, China. The German SDS had its conference in Yugoslavia — that's freedom? That's bullshit, man:
> You're all fucked up if you can support that in the cause of internationalism. That's bullshit.[242]

"New Left" campus extremists were no longer primarily concerned with ending the Vietnam War. America was ugly and evil to them. Third-world revolutionaries such as Che Guevara, the Vietnamese NLF, and the Palestinian terrorists were their heroes and models for action. This was the mood when the NYU Washington Square student council, in November 1968, declared its solidarity with the National Liberation Front of South Vietnam and called for "a popular socialist revolution."[243]

Fragmentation of the broad anti-war movement was also hastened by the splitting off from the old coalition of diverse special-interest groups. The activists who were now withdrawing in considerable numbers were not preoccupied with the end of the war, but with "Gay Liberation"; or with the welfare of Chicanos, Native-Americans, and Asian-Americans; or with environmentalism, "Women's Liberation," and "Black Power."

Radical feminists insisted, on campus and off, that the gender issue was preeminent. They denounced the anti-war leadership as all-male and not sufficiently interested in giving women an equal role in "The Movement." Women must follow their own separate path to fulfill their goals, said the feminists. Years later, a feminist at Barnard College, studying the sixties, expressed a similar point of view. Most of the leaders of the anti-war movement had been men, she complained. "I've been finding out about the SDS. They were really sexist."[244]

Extreme advocates of "Black Power," as represented most dramatically by Huey Newton's Black Panthers, rejected the student anti-war leadership as much too moderate, too white, and excessively tainted by racism. Nothing less than an armed attack on the entire white structure would satisfy the Panthers.[245] More moderate black campus leaders did not go that far, but they were much less concerned with the Vietnam War than with what they perceived to be their own issues. These included the establishment of Black Studies departments, appointment of more black faculty, liberalization of admissions policies for black students, plus better campus housing, guidance, job counseling, and social facilities for black students. One study of campus protest during 1969–70 found that nearly half of the incidents involved "Black Power" demands; only 22 percent were directly related to Vietnam issues.[246]

A conference of black leaders in Washington in June, 1972, issued a statement denouncing the anti-war movement as "racist." They complained that the anti-war campaign did not emphasize sufficiently the "racist" character of the conflict in Southeast Asia and that the anti-war leaders did not offer sufficient backing to black candidates for political office.[247]

Increasingly, extremists and special-interest activists began to disrupt meetings of the student anti-war coalition. When the Student Mobilization Committee (Student Mobe) met in mid-February 1970 to draw up plans for massive anti-war demonstrations, extremists did their best to upset the proceedings. Spokesmen for the "Independent Radical Caucus," brushing aside anti-war themes, demanded active support for Black Panthers, Gay rights, and Women's Lib. They called for support for Ahmed Evans, a black nationalist sentenced to death for his role in a shoot-out with police. They insisted on civil disobedience and street violence rather than peace marches and campus demonstrations. When outvoted, they chanted "barnyard epithets" and sailed paper airplanes, made from folded position papers, around the hall.[248]

When Student Mobe finally held anti-war rallies in mid-April 1970, the extremists sought to turn them into violent clashes with the police. At an anti-war rally at Columbia University, radicals disrupted the proceedings by smashing windows and hurling paint. They brushed aside the anti-war message of the participants and demanded all-out support for the Black Panthers. More than two hundred policemen were summoned to Morningside Heights to restore order.[249]

In Boston, where a hundred thousand peace demonstrators gathered that spring on the Common, radical groups split off from the main rally. The extremists marched across a Charles River bridge to Cambridge and rampaged through Harvard Square, where they set fires and smashed shop windows. The Massachusetts National Guard had to be mobilized to aid Cambridge police in controlling the violence. More than two hundred persons were injured and $100,000 worth of property was damaged or destroyed. At the anti-war rallies the mainline demonstrators had been chanting "Peace Now"; the radicals, with clenched fists, responded, "Revolution Now!"[250]

A particularly disturbing aspect of the April 1970 Cambridge riot was that many of the so-called "student" radicals were apparently not college students at all. It later became clear that most of the Cambridge rioters who were protesting the trial of Bobby Seale, national chairman of the Black Panther party, had never attended either Harvard or MIT. Besides terrorizing Harvard Square and destroying property, the rioters gathered outside the gates to Harvard Yard, gates that had been hurriedly shut against them. There they taunted the students who were watching from the university residence hall windows, with such jeers as: "How are the nation's elite doing tonight?" At Berkeley, security officials reported much the same phenomenon. Rioters who had poured onto the University of California's campus came from local schools but were definitely not college students. Again the main emphasis seemed to be on freeing Black Panther leaders rather than ending the war in Vietnam.[251]

The President's Commission on Campus Unrest noted in its report that there had been numerous bomb threats to American colleges and universities during the period from 1 January 1969 to 15 April 1970.[252] In only one case, however, did terroristic actions actually cause a loss of life. That happened, as we have noted, at the University of Wisconsin. It is ironic, in this connection, that the Madison bombers missed their main objective. Intending to blow up the Army Mathematics Research Center, they demolished the Department of Physics instead.[253]

The actions of the terrorists and extremists predictably created a conservative backlash against all campus anti-war activists. Todd Gitlin, himself an anti-war organizer, took note of this phenomenon when he remarked: "Public opinion did turn steadily against the war, but, if anything, as the war became steadily less popular, so did the movement against it, maybe even faster."[254]

Campus attitudes reflected this change in perceptions. Professors who had earlier sponsored "Teach-Ins" against the war were now increasingly repelled by the actions of the minority of student extremists. They found it impossible to accept "buildings occupied and polluted ... library files overturned and damaged ... offices ransacked ... fellow teachers humiliated in the classroom and in public."[255] Many students who had marched and demonstrated against the war were not prepared to condone the latest forms of extremist violence. Those young people lived in "genuine fear" of what some crazy bomb-thrower might do to their school.[256]

Sensationalist television coverage gave the general public the impression that the extremists and terrorists represented all campus anti-war activists. Many voters, shocked by such lurid images, turned increasingly to right-wing politicians like Governor Wallace of Alabama and Governor Reagan of California. The nation's Vice-President, Spiro Agnew, courted instant popularity by launching vitriolic attacks on all liberals, whether on or off the campuses. President Hayakawa of San Francisco State became one of the most popular college presidents in the land because he was perceived as having taken a tough stand against campus rioters.[257]

It was paradoxical that just as the anti-war movement in academe was foundering in bitter factionalism and losing much of its luster with the general public, the cause for which it had fought so long was coming closer and closer to success. All through 1971 and 1972, the American war effort in Vietnam was steadily winding down. The watchword of the Nixon Administration had become "Vietnamization" of the Southeast Asia conflict. Monthly draft calls were becoming smaller and smaller. General Lewis B. Hershey, arguably one of the most unpopular government officials as viewed by college students, was removed from his position as Director of Selective Service. The draft itself had now been placed on a lottery basis. The new system reassured students in older age categories and those who had drawn higher numbers (such as 200 through 400) that it was extremely unlikely that they would ever be drafted. They could now plan their education and prepare for business and professional careers without fear of disruption due to the war.[258]

Many college presidents felt that the changes in the draft would inevitably take the "steam out of the student movement against the Vietnam War."[259] At the same time, a government commission was hard at work studying the possibility of terminating Selective Service altogether and replacing it with an all-volunteer professional army.

As American forces hastened their withdrawal from Southeast Asia, Washington's allies in South Vietnam found themselves increasingly powerless to resist strong attacks launched by the North Vietnamese army and the Vietcong. Their perilous situation had the effect of reviving peace negotiations, which had been under way in Paris for some time. On 27 January 1973 the United States (representing South Vietnam) finally signed an ambiguous cease-fire agreement with the North Vietnamese and the Vietcong. For Americans, this meant the war was over. The longest military conflict in American history and one of the least popular ones had been terminated at last. Of all of America's wars, the Vietnam conflict had proved to be the fourth most costly in terms of human casualties.[260]

One hundred thousand demonstrators showed up in Washington on 20 January 1973, inauguration day, for what was indisputably "the last peace march." It was obvious by that time that peace in Vietnam was finally at hand. Many of the marchers were still outraged, however, by the Christmas bombing of Hanoi, which Nixon had ordered to put pressure on the peace negotiations. For many of the marchers, though, there was also a sense of sadness and nostalgia. This was very likely their last peace demonstration. "These marches . . . had been among the great experiences of their lives. This communion . . . this coming together in a common cause, might never happen again."[261]

Did the colleges play a significant part in generating effective opposition to America's intervention in the Vietnam War? The evidence seems rather conclusive that they did so. The campus anti-war movement of the 1960s was a remarkable phenomenon by any standard of evaluation. Such deep-seated opposition at the nation's colleges to the policies of the nation's government is really without precedent in American history.[262] One observer remarked that, except for Russia in 1905 and 1917, the American academics and students who opposed government policy constituted "the most effective anti-war movement within any big power while the shooting was going on."[263] John K. Galbraith added the observation that "not since 1848 has there been anything so universal."[264] Sympathy with the American campus rebels ignited student revolutions in France, Britain, Poland, Czechoslovakia, Italy, Latin America, and East Asia.[265]

The widespread politicalization of American colleges during the Vietnam War was perhaps matched in United States history only by the campus activism that flared up two centuries earlier during the American Revolution. The general strike on most campuses in 1970 against the Cambodian incursion was also essentially without precedent. And faculty political activism reached new peaks, most notably in the case of the Harvard professorial delegation that went to Washington in 1970 specifically to tell

Henry Kissinger, a former colleague, that he must work to end the war quickly.[266]

Contemporary observers felt that the principal factor unleashing student unrest during the '60s and early '70s was the Vietnam War. Thus, the Cox Commission, appointed in 1968 to investigate the disturbances at Columbia, very quickly came to the conclusion that Vietnam was the main culprit. As Dean David B. Truman put it:

> The Vietnam war is the overriding concern of nearly all students. For them it is a matter of life or death — to kill or be killed. For many, it is an immoral war and all who support it are immoral; it should be stopped at once ...[267]

When the President's Commission on Campus Unrest held its hearings, very similar views were expressed. United States Senators, prominent educational leaders, a number of student spokesmen, and many other witnesses were unanimous in telling the Commission that there would be no peace on the campuses until there was peace in Vietnam.[268]

The college anti-war movement had to accomplish what it could in spite of a number of serious limitations that inhibited its effectiveness. Anti-war academics never were able to establish a permanent national lobbying group or a grassroots political organization to advance their views. They had no important newspapers, magazines, or radio stations under their control. Their outreach to other influential segments in society, namely organized labor or the farmers, was not very successful. And college students, the main base for campus protests, were "an unreliable constituency for an opposition movement" because they were mostly transients and their anti-war efforts would necessarily tend to be seasonal and sporadic.[269]

Despite such difficulties, the college anti-war movement eventually came to exercise a rather remarkable veto power over the actions of American presidents. This veto power was most evident when government authorities contemplated major escalations of the Vietnam conflict. Late in 1966, for example, Pentagon officials urged President Johnson to bomb Hanoi and destroy North Vietnam's industrial capacity. David Halberstam reports what Johnson told the generals on that occasion: "I have one more problem for your computer — will you feed into it how long it will take five hundred thousand angry Americans to climb that White House wall out there and lynch their President if he does something like that?"[270]

One of the most important and influential campaigns against the war that originated on the college campuses was the nationwide drive against secret, classified, war-related research at the major universities.[271] Another significant movement that involved collegians was the so-called "Children's Crusade" in New Hampshire. In February of 1968 Senator Eugene

McCarthy, a strong opponent of the war, ran in the New Hampshire presidential primary against his party's White House incumbent, Lyndon Johnson. College student volunteers from all over the country poured into the state to work for McCarthy's campaign. Thanks to their enthusiastic help, the Senator did unexpectedly well in the primary. President Johnson clearly viewed the New Hampshire result as a kind of referendum on his Vietnam policies. In March 1968 he startled the country by taking himself out of the presidential campaign.[272]

In 1971 Kenneth Galbraith summed up the contributions that he felt had been made by colleges and universities to help bring the Vietnam War to a close:

> It was the universities — not the trade unions, nor the free-lance intellectuals, nor the press, nor the businessmen . . . which led the opposition to the Vietnam war, which forced the retirement of President Johnson, which are forcing the pace of our present withdrawal from Vietnam . . .[273]

6

Comparisons and Conclusions

THE principal theme of this book, that colleges and universities have played a vital role during times of great crisis in American history, was recognized and elucidated as early as 1782. In that year, a committee of the Pennsylvania Assembly declared in a report to the public: "Colleges have a powerful Influence on the Interest and Government of Every State."[1] Very true indeed. The historical record shows that the colleges and universities of America have responded actively and helpfully in all the major crises confronting their country.

Institutions of higher education experienced waves of student and faculty activism. During periods of decisive change, campus communities actively met the challenges of their time.[2] Repeatedly, colleges became "politicized" by such momentous developments as the American Revolution, the War Between the States, the global conflicts of the twentieth century, and the nation's controversial involvement in Southeast Asia.

In reviewing patterns of collegiate activism during five of the most significant crises in American history, certain similar reactions may be discerned, while at the same time points of essential difference become obvious. One important element of continuity is the intense politicalization of college life that occurs during difficult times. Student leaders organize demonstrations; activist professors and college presidents stir their students to action; excitement and enthusiasm become the prevailing campus mood.

There are other continuities as well. One of them, it must be stated, is the violence that often accompanied campus activism. This, a frequent feature of Vietnam-era demonstrations, appeared somewhat more sporadically in earlier times. It should be remembered, however, that early episodes of campus violence focused mainly on dissatisfaction with disciplinary regulations or the quality of food in college dining halls, rather than questions of political principle or fundamental ideology.

A somewhat less portentous similarity between eighteenth-century and twentieth-century campus activism was the expression of protest through modes of attire. In the Revolutionary era, this involved wearing conspicuously simple, domestically-produced broadcloth to support the Patriot cause. During the Vietnam years the "new campus look" was achieved by wearing dirty T-shirts and crumpled jeans to demonstrate disapproval of conservatively-attired government officials.

Another recurring pattern was rather widespread campus opposition to military training and the draft. As early as the 1880s, opposition to on-campus officer training made an appearance. Attacks on ROTC began in 1916 and 1917, became a nationwide phenomenon during the 1930s, and flared up violently as a means of protest against the Vietnam War. As for the draft, there was opposition to conscription during the Civil War on campuses in both the North and the South. Ingenious methods were devised to evade it and full advantage was taken of all available legal exemptions. During the Vietnam conflict, the aversion to the draft was, if anything, much greater, and the methods that were devised to defy or evade it became much more complex.

Notable differences in the reaction of college communities to challenges confronting the country appeared almost as frequently as similarities. One obvious contrast appears in the role played by the world of academe in two periods of supreme crisis, the Revolution and Vietnam. In the first instance, the college campuses helped initiate colonial resistance, supported the Revolutionary war for independence, and played an important part in prosecuting it to a successful conclusion. In the Vietnam period, many members of campus communities were opposed from the beginning to the current American policy, which involved armed intervention in Southeast Asia. They protested bitterly against their government's actions and worked assiduously to build a public sentiment that would demand an end to American involvement.

Another salient difference between earlier and later collegiate responses to national crises pertained to the nature of the campus constituency that was involved. In the eighteenth and nineteenth centuries, the members of academe constituted what might be called an elite class in American society. As such, their views carried considerable weight. In the twentieth century, with the rise of mass higher education, this may not have been true to the same extent, even though the leaders of the most prestigious universities were still listened to very carefully by political leaders and the general public. Even more important, perhaps, was the gradual breakdown of the unity of campus communities. In earlier times, colleges were relatively homogeneous in the sense that they were largely liberal-arts oriented. By the twentieth century, the "multi-versity" had become so complex and diverse that it was no longer easy to mobilize a unified, all-embracing response to critical events. Concerns that were all-important to students of the humanities and the theoretical sciences did not necessarily stir to action those who were majoring in business, engineering, education, or agriculture.

Differences between campus reactions in the eighteenth and mid-nineteenth centuries and those in the twentieth century derived also from the contrasting views young people had of their relationship to families, older contemporaries, and their own colleges and universities. The earlier student activists had not generally responded to crisis situations by conflicting with their parents, their colleges, and the older citizens in their community. Instead, they worked in harmony with these contemporaries, on campus and off, to attain the goals they sought. By the Vietnam period, however, many campus activists professed to be alienated from all older individuals. Their response to a crisis was to battle the establishment both on their own campus and in the society outside. A "generation gap" existed that had not been a significant factor in earlier student movements.

Such differences did not, however, alter the basic role of American colleges and universities in times of trial. There was a fundamental continuum here from the Revolution to Vietnam. Members of academic communities sought time after time during these two centuries, to help resolve the nation's major crises constructively. Students and professors rallied to the cause of colonial rights and subsequently to that of independence. They supported the aims of their embattled sections, North and South, during the Civil War. They responded to the global crises of the twentieth century by providing alternate scenarios about the wisest course their nation should follow and by influencing the actions that their government ultimately pursued. In all five of the crucial periods that helped shape the development of the American nation, colleges and universities, while not the ultimate decision makers, played an important part in determining what those decisions would be.

Notes

Chapter 1. The American Revolution

1. John F. Roche, *The Colonial Colleges in the War for American Independence* (New York: Associated Faculty Press, Inc., 1986), 57.

2. Thomas J. Wertenbaker, *Princeton, 1746–1896* (Princeton: Princeton University Press, 1946), 56; Larry R. Gerlach, *Prologue to Independence* (New Brunswick, NJ: Rutgers University Press, 1976), 117–18; Sheldon S. Cohen and Larry R. Gerlach, "Princeton in the Coming of the American Revolution," *New Jersey History* 92 (Summer 1974): 73–74.

3. Howard H. Peckham, "*Collegia ante-bellum*," *Pennsylvania Magazine of History and Biography* 95 (January 1971): 57.

4. Louis L. Tucker, *Puritan Protagonist* (Chapel Hill, NC: University of North Carolina Press, 1962), 253–61.

5. Roche, *The Colonial Colleges in the War for American Independence*, 48

6. Gerlach, *Prelude to Independence*, 117.

7. Brooks M. Kelley, *Yale: A History* (New Haven: Yale University Press, 1974), 83.

8. Roche, *The Colonial Colleges in the War for American Independence*, 21.

9. As quoted in Robson, *Educating Republicans: The College in the American Revolution* (Westport, CT: Greenwood Press, 1985), 67–68.

10. Cohen and Gerlach, "Princeton in the Coming of the American Revolution": 75–76.

11. Philip Freneau, "A Poem on the Rising Glory of America," in Harry H. Clark, ed., *Poems of Freneau* (New York: Hefner Publishing Co., 1929), 3–17.

12. Walter C. Bronson, *History of Brown University* (Providence, RI: Brown University, 1914), 41–43; 63–65.

13. Wilkes was a bitter critic of George III and had been expelled from the British Parliament because of his extreme views. He was finally put in prison for libels against the King that had been published in the forty-fifth issue of a periodical that Wilkes sponsored.

The quotation may be found in Steven J. Novak, *The Rights of Youth* (Cambridge, MA: Harvard University Press, 1977), 5.

14. The Townshend Acts had placed duties on all imports of paper into the colonies.

For the campus boycotts, see William C. Lane, "The Printer of the Harvard Theses of 1771," vol. 26, *Colonial Society of Massachusetts Publications* (Boston: C.S.M., 1924–26), 1–15.

15. Peckham, "*Collegia ante-bellum*," 60. Peckham quotes these lines from a poetic dialogue that was presented by candidates for the Master's Degree at the 1770 commencement. They were indeed published in the *Pennsylvania Gazette* for 14 June 1770, but the name of the author of this rhapsodic invocation unfortunately was not given.

16. Cohen and Gerlach, "Princeton in the Coming of the American Revolution": 78–80.

17. James Madison to James Madison, Sr., 23 July 1770.

The letter may be found in William T. Hutchinson and William M. S. Rachal, eds., *The Papers of James Madison* (Chicago: University of Chicago Press, 1962), 1:49−50.

18. The quotation from *The Pennsylvania Gazette* for 18 October 1770 may be found in Wertenbaker, *Princeton, 1746−1896*, 57; on this incident, see also Cohen and Gerlach, "Princeton in the Coming of the American Revolution": 76.

19. Wertenbaker, *Princeton, 1746−1896*, 57−58.

20. Charles C. Beatty to Rev. Enoch Beatty, 31 January 1774, as quoted in Robson, *Educating Republicans*, 69.

21. Gerlach, *Prologue to Independence* 197−98.

22. Roche, *The Colonial Colleges in the War for American Independence*, 54.

23. Gerlach, *Prologue to Independence*, 198; Cohen and Gerlach, "Princeton in the Coming of the American Revolution": 80−81.

24. Wertenbaker, *Princeton, 1746−1896*, 57.

25. This statement was printed in the *Newport Mercury* for 12 September 1774, and is quoted in Peckham, "'Collegia ante-bellum'": 52; On the 1774 commencement, see also Bronson, *History of Brown University*, 65.

26. This quotation may be found in Samuel Eliot Morison, *Three Centuries of Harvard* (Cambridge, MA: Harvard University Press, 1936), 145−46.

27. The quotation and other foregoing material comes from Kelly, *Yale: A History*, 89−90.

28. Alexander Cowie, *John Trumbull, Connecticut Wit* (Westport, CT: Greenwood Press, 1972), 57−60; 133−138; Victor E. Gimmestad, *John Trumbull* (New York: Twayne Publishers, 1974).

29. A large number of the Princeton graduates from these years later held office in the new American Revolutionary governments. See Robson, *Educating Republicans*, 70.

30. Morison, *Three Centuries of Harvard*, 147.

31. David F. Hawke, *Benjamin Rush: Revolutionary Gadfly* (Indianapolis, IN: Bobbs-Merrill, 1971), 54−59.

32. David C. Humphrey, *From King's College to Columbia, 1746−1800* (New York: Columbia University Press, 1976), 140−41; 151−153; also see William H. W. Sabine, ed., *Historical Memoirs of William Smith, 1778−1783* (New York: Arno Press, Inc., 1971), 57−58.

33. Peckham, "'Collegia ante-bellum'": 63.

34. Humphrey, *From King's College to Columbia*, 152.

35. Robert P. Thomson, "The Reform of the College of William and Mary," *Proceedings of the American Philosophical Society* 115 (1971): 200−203.

36. The quotation from James Madison, *An Oration in Commemoration of the Founders of William and Mary College* is included in Roche, *Colonial Colleges in the War for American Independence*, 41; also see Peckham, "'Collegia ante-bellum'": 68−69.

37. For sketches of politically active faculty during these years, see "Naphtali Dagget," s.v., *Dictionary of American Biography; The John Bogart Letters* (New Brunswick, NJ: Rutgers College, 1914), 6−26; "John Winthrop," s.v., *Dictionary of American Biography*; "John Warren," s.v., *Dictionary of American Biography*: "Joseph Willard," s.v. *Dictionary of American Biography*; "Samuel Langdon," s.v., *Dictionary of American Biography*.

38. Cohen and Gerlach, "Princeton in the Coming of the American Revolution": 85.

39. Cohen and Gerlach, "Princeton in the Coming of the American Revolution": 88−89.

40. This quotation comes from Morison, *Three Centuries of Harvard*, 136.

41. Robson, *Educating Republicans*, 70–86.

42. Both the Harvard College Library Charging List for 1773 through 1776 and Benjamin Wadsworth's Notebook for the years 1766 and 1767 (Harvard College Archive) are cited by Robson, *Educating Republicans*, 88–89.

43. Morison, *Three Centuries of Harvard*, 141–42.

44. Peckham, "Collegia ante-bellum": 52–61.

45. Cohen and Gerlach, "Princeton in the Coming of the American Revolution": 81.

46. Charles Beatty to Betsy Beatty, 28 May 1775, as quoted in Robson, *Educating Republicans*, 70.

47. Robson, *Educating Republicans*, 62.

48. This quotation, from a letter Robert Sill sent to Nathan Hale, may be found in Kelley, *Yale*, 84.

49. Roche, *Colonial Colleges in the War for American Independence*, 77.

50. Chew's address was published in the *Pennsylvania Gazette* for 31 May 1775, and is quoted in Robson, *Educating Republicans*, 91.

51. Lyon G. Tyler, *Williamsburg, The Old Colonial Capital* (Richmond, VA: Whittet & Shepperson, 1907).

52. John Witherspoon, "Thoughts on American Liberty," *The Works of John Witherspoon* (Philadelphia: Woodward, 1800).

53. Reuben A. Guild, *History of Brown University* (Providence, RI: Providence Press Company, 1867), 285–87.

54. George P. Schmidt, *Princeton and Rutgers: The Two Colonial Colleges of New Jersey* (Princeton: Van Nostrand, 1964), 12–14.

55. The quotation is from Joseph Willard, *The Duty of the Good and Faithful Soldier*, Mendam, Massachusetts, 25 March 1781 (Boston: Printed by T. and J. Fleet, 1781). Also see Morison, *Three Centuries of Harvard* 135–37; Peckham, "Collegia ante-bellum": 54; *Dictionary of American Biography*, s.v., "Joseph Willard."

56. Franklin B. Dexter, ed., *The Literary Diary of Ezra Stiles* (New York: Charles Scribners' Sons, 1901), 1:136–37; 382–85; 427; 521; 584. 2:21–26.

57. Albert F. Gegenheimer, *William Smith, Educator and Churchman* (Philadelphia: University of Pennsylvania Press, 1943), 143–65; Charles J. Stillé, *A Memoir of the Rev. William Smith, DD* (Philadelphia: Moore & Sons, 1869), 42–45.

58. *Dictionary of American Biography*, s.v., "William Smith."

59. Edward P. Cheyney, *History of the University of Pennsylvania* (Philadelphia: University of Pennsylvania Press, 1940), 104–12.

60. *Dictionary of American Biography*, s.v., "Myles Cooper."

61. Humphrey, *From King's College to Columbia*, 127–29; 151–54.

62. William Smith, *Historical Memoirs of William Smith*, 1:222–25; Clarence H. Vance, "Myles Cooper," *Columbia University Quarterly* (fall 1930); 22:262–64; 271–78.

63. Thomson, "The Reform of the College of William and Mary" 200–205.

64. Cohen and Gerlach, "Princeton in the Coming of the American Revolution": 200–205.

65. Russell F. Weigley, ed., *Philadelphia, A Three-Hundred Year History* (New York: W. W. Norton & Co., 1982), 145–48.

66. The material from the records of the Harvard College Overseers, vol. 3, is cited by Roche, *Colonial Colleges in the War for American Independence*, 89–90.

67. *Dictionary of American Biography*, s.v., "William Samuel Johnson"; Humphrey, *From King's College to Columbia*, 268−84.

68. Weigley, ed., *Philadelphia*, 145−46.

69. Gegenheimer, *William Smith* 180−83.

70. Cheyney, *History of the University of Pennsylvania* 120−25; Robert L. Brunhouse, *The Counter-Revolution in Pennsylvania, 1776−1790* (New York: Octagon Books, 1971), 72−79.

71. Cheyney, *History of the University of Pennsylvania*, 125−28.

72. The quotations may be found in Howard Miller, *The Revolutionary College* (New York: New York University Press, 1976), 133−38.

73. An account of this commencement was published in *The Pennsylvania Journal*, 12 July 1780, and is quoted in Roche, *The Colonial Colleges in the War for American Independence*, 151.

74. Brunhouse, *The Counter-Revolution in Pennsylvania*, 152−54; Miller, *The Revolutionary College*, 132−34.

75. Cheyney, *History of the University of Pennsylvania* 148−49; Horace Wemyes Smith, *Life and Correspondence of the Rev. William Smith, D.D.* (Philadelphia: Ferguson Bros & Co., 1880) 2:21−33.

76. Smith, *Life and Correspondence of The Rev. William Smith*, 2:28−33; Gegenheimer, *William Smith*, 80−87.

77. Cheyney, *History of the University of Pennsylvania*, 149−52.

78. Weigley, *Philadelphia* 161; also see Gegenheimer, *William Smith*, 87−89.

79. Cheyney, *History of the University of Pennsylvania*, 154−58.

80. Gegenheimer, *William Smith*, 89−92.

81. The quotation is from Weigley, ed., *Philadelphia*, 167; also see the evaluation in Cheyney, *History of the University of Pennsylvania*, 149.

82. Thomson, "Reform of the College of William and Mary": 201−4.

83. Thomson, "Reform of the College of William and Mary": 205−6.

84. Peckham, "*Collegia Ante-Bellum*": 68−69.

85. Julian P. Boyd, ed., *The Papers of Thomas Jefferson* (Princeton: Princeton University Press, 1950), 2:305−39; 526−45.

86. Thomson, "Reform of William and Mary": 206−10.

87. Paul L. Ford, ed., *The Works of Thomas Jefferson* (New York: G.P. Putnam Publishers, 1904), 3:250−59.

88. Thomson, "Reform of William and Mary": 209−12.

89. Thomson, "Reform of William and Mary": 208−14.

90. Peckham, "*Collegia ante-bellum*": 69−71.

91. John S. Brubacher and Willis Rudy, *Higher Education in Transition* (New York: Harper & Bros., 1958), 19−20.

92. Robson, *Educating Republicans*, 110−14.

93. President James Manning of the College of Rhode Island to a friend in England, 13 November 1776. The quotation is from Bronson, *History of Brown University*, 66; also see *Dictionary of American Biography* s.v., "James Manning."

94. Robson, *Educating Republicans*, 97.

95. This quotation comes from Kelley, *Yale, A History*, 84.

96. Kelley, *Yale, A History*, 84−85.

97. Morison, *Three Centuries of Harvard*, 146−49.

98. Morison, *Three Centuries of Harvard*, 149.

99. Peckham, "*Collegia ante-bellum*", 57.

100. Cheyney, *History of the University of Pennsylvania*, 115−17.

101. This quotation may be found in Smith, *Life and Correspondence of Rev.*

William Smith, 1:570−71.

102. Wertenbaker, *Princeton, 1746−1896*, 61−62.

103. Roche, *The Colonial Colleges in the War for American Independence*, 155−57.

104. Bogart, *Letters With Notes*, 14.

105. See Bronson, *History of Brown University*, 67−75; Morison, *Three Centuries of Harvard*, 151−53. For additional descriptions of disruptions of colleges caused by the war, see James Madison to Ezra Stiles, 19 June 1782 in Isabel M. Calder, ed., *Letters and Papers of Ezra Stiles* (New Haven: Yale University Library, 1933).

106. Reuben A. Guild, *Life, Times, and Correspondence of James Manning* (Boston: Gould and Lincoln, 1864), 336−40. James Manning's report is dated 17 June 1782, and is quoted in Bronson, *History of Brown University*, 71−72.

107. Kelley, *Yale: A History*, 86−87.

108. Kelley, *Yale: A History*, 95−96.

109. Edmund Morgan, *The Gentle Puritan: Ezra Stiles* (New Haven: Yale University Press, 1962), 334−38.

110. Humphrey, *From King's College to Columbia*, 153−56.

111. Thomas Jones reported the looting in his *History of New York during the Revolutionary War*, vol. 1, and is quoted in Roche, *The Colonial Colleges in the War for American Independence*, 85.

112. The quotation is cited in Richard P. McCormick, *Rutgers: A Bicentennial* (New Brunswick, NJ: Rutgers University Press, 1966), 16; Also see William H. S. Demarest, *A History of Rutgers College, 1766−1924* (New Brunswick, NJ: Rutgers University Press, 1924), 116−17; 133−35.

113. Wertenbaker, *Princeton, 1746−1896*, 58−60.

114. Roche, *The Colonial Colleges in the War for American Independence*, 105−7.

115. Rush is quoted in Wertenbaker, *Princeton, 1746−1896*, 61.

116. Wertenbaker, *Princeton, 1746−1896*, 61−62.

117. Wertenbaker, *Princeton, 1746−1896*, 62.

118. Roche, *The Colonial Colleges in the War for American Independence*, 107−9.

119. Cheyney, *History of the University of Pennsylvania*, 116−17.

120. Miller, *The Revolutionary College*, 133−35.

121. Tyler, *Williamsburg, the Old Colonial Capital*, 165−71.

122. Lyon G. Tyler, *The College of William and Mary in Virginia, 1693−1907* (Richmond, VA: Whittet & Shepperson, 1907), 58−59.

123. Tyler, *Williamsburg, the Old Colonial Capital*, 166−69; Tyler, *The College of William and Mary in Virginia*, 54−58.

124. The quotation was taken from *The Pennsylvania Packet* for 15 July 1776. It is cited in Cohen and Gerlach, "Princeton in the Coming of the American Revolution": 83.

125. Wertenbaker, *Princeton, 1746−1896*, 58−62; Gerlach, *Prelude to Independence*, 274−75; 322−24.

126. The quotation comes from a sermon delivered by Dr. John Witherspoon on 17 May 1776. The title of the sermon was "The Dominion of Providence over the Passions of Men." It may be found in Roche, *The Colonial Colleges in the War for American Independence*, 92.

127. The dominant college ideology during the Revolution is summed up quite succinctly in Robson, *Educating Republicans*, 71−75.

128. See Novak, *The Rights of Youth*, 2–6.

129. Andrew Eliot's statement is quoted by Morison in *Three Centuries of Harvard*, 138.

130. Ezra Stiles's address, "The United States Elevated to Glory and Honor," is cited by Robson, *Educating Republicans*, 116.

Chapter 2. The Civil War

1. Seymour M. Lipset and Gerald Schaflander, *Passion and Politics* (Boston: Little Brown & Co., 1972), 128–30; George P. Fisher, *Life of Benjamin Silliman* (New York: Scribner's, 1866), 2:336–37.

2. Andrew Dickson White, *Autibiography* (London: Macmillan, 1905), 1:348–49; Lipset and Schaflander, *Passion and Prejudice*, 130.

3. Brubacher and Rudy, *Higher Education in Transition*, 53.

4. Robert S. Fletcher, *History of Oberlin College* (New York: Arno Press, 1971), 1:184–86.

5. Brubacher and Rudy, *Higher Education in Transition*, 66; Arthur C. Cole, *The Irrepressible Conflict, 1850–1865* (New York: Macmillan, 1934), 213–14; For the interrelations between the home mission movement as it involved the colleges and the anti-slavery crusade, see Dwight L. Dumond, *Anti-Slavery Origins of the Civil War* (Ann Arbor, MI: University of Michigan Press, 1939), 28–77, and Gilbert H. Barnes, *The Anti-Slavery Impulse, 1830–1844* (Gloucester, MA: Peter Smith, 1957), 34–70.

6. Fletcher, *History of Oberlin College*, 1:181–84; 186–92; 2:771–74; Cole, *The Irrepressible Conflict*, 214.

7. Charles H. Rammelkamp, *Illinois College, A Centennial History* (New Haven, CT: Yale University Press, 1928), 101–2; Charles E. Frank, *Pioneer's Progress: Illinois College, 1829–1979* (Carbondale, IL: Southern Illinois University Press, 1979), 39–45; Merton L. Dillon, *Elijah P. Lovejoy, Abolitionist Editor* (Urbana, IL: University of Illinois Press, 1961), 61–62; 140; Ernest E. Calkins, *They Broke the Prairie* (New York: Charles Scribner's Sons, 1937), 82–83; 226–27; *Dictionary of American Biography*, s.v., "Jonathan Blanchard"; "Edward Beecher"; Julian M. Sturtevant."

8. Arthur G. Beach, *A Pioneer College: The Story of Marietta* (Marietta, OH: Privately printed, 1935), 133–35.

9. James O. Oliphant, *The Rise of Bucknell University* (New York: Appleton-Century Crofts, 1965), 90–92.

10. Thomas N. Hoover, *The History of Ohio University* (Athens, OH: Ohio University Press, 1954), 117–18.

11. Claude M. Fuess, *Amherst, The Story of a New England College* (Boston: Little, Brown, & Co., 1935), 186.

12. Oliphant, *Rise of Bucknell University*, 20.

13. Rammelkamp, *Illinois College*, 202–3.

14. James I. Osborne and Theodore G. Gronert, *Wabash College: The First Hundred Years* (Crawfordsville, IN: R.E. Banta, 1932) 119–20.

15. Rammelkamp, *Illinois College*, 198–201.

16. Louis C. Hatch, *The History of Bowdoin College* (Portland, ME: Loring, Short, and Harmon, 1927), 116–17.

17. Osborne and Gronert, *Wabash College*, 119–21.

18. Osborne and Gronert, *Wabash College*, 119–21.

19. Arthur J. Hope, *Notre Dame—One Hundred Years* (South Bend, IN: Icarus Press, Inc., 1978), 116–17.

20. Wertenbaker, *Princeton, 1746–1896*, 265–66.

21. The Princeton incident was reported in the *American and Commercial Advertiser* of Baltimore, 5 December 1859. For this account, see *The Princeton Alumni Weekly* 7 April 1909, 9:406–7.

22. Hatch, *History of Bowdoin*, 116.

23. Samuel E. Morison, *Three Centuries of Harvard* (Cambridge, MA: Harvard University Press, 1936), 302.

24. Arthur C. Cole, *A Hundred Years of Mount Holyoke College* (New Haven, CT: Yale University Press, 1946), 176.

25. Oliphant, *Rise of Bucknell University*, 90.

26. Hoover, *History of Ohio University*, 118.

27. Fletcher, *History of Oberlin College*, 1:843.

28. Virginius Dabney, *Mr. Jefferson's University: A History* (Charlottesville, VA: University of Virginia, 1981), 25–26.

29. Walter L. Fleming, *Louisiana State University, 1860–1896* (Baton Rouge, LA: Louisiana State University Press, 1936), 94–97.

30. Ellsworth Eliot, Jr., *Yale in the Civil War* (New Haven, CT: Yale University Press, 1932), 17–18; 23–24.

31. Fletcher, *History of Oberlin College*, 1:844–45.

32. Beach, *A Pioneer College: Marietta*, 134.

33. Thomas D. Clark, *Indiana University: Volume 1, The Early Years* (Bloomington, IN: Indiana University Press, 1970), 104–6.

34. Kent Sagendorph, *Michigan: The Story of the University* (New York: E.P. Dutton & Co., Inc., 1948), 103–7. On the Ann Arbor situation, see also Howard H. Peckham, *The Making of the University of Michigan, 1877–1967* (Ann Arbor, MI: University of Michigan Press, 1967), 46–48.

35. Morison, *Three Centuries of Harvard*, 302–3.

36. Glenn Weaver, *The History of Trinity College* (Hartford, CT: Trinity College Press, 1967), 1:130–31.

37. David Heim, *A Student's View of the College of St. James* (Lewiston, NY: Edwin Mellon Press, 1968), 114–15.

38. George H. Callcott, *A History of the University of Maryland* (Baltimore: Maryland Historical Society, 1966), 157–58.

39. Allen Cabaniss, *The University of Mississippi: The First Hundred Years* (Hattiesburg, MS: University and College Press of Mississippi, 1971), 50–51.

40. William Couper, *One Hundred Years at V.M.I.*, (Richmond, VA: Garrett and Massie, Inc., 1939), 2:22–25.

41. E. Merton Coulter, *College Life in the Old South* (Athens, GA: University of Georgia Press, 1951), 236–37 (reprint of 1928 edition).

42. Dabney, *Mr. Jefferson's University*, 25.

43. James Sellers, *History of the University of Alabama* (University, AL: University of Alabama Press, 1953), 260–67.

44. Cabaniss, *The University of Mississippi: The First Hundred Years* 50–51; Daniel W. Hollins, *The University of South Carolina* (Columbia, SC: University of South Carolina Press, 1951), 1:212–15.

45. Coulter, *College Life ini the Old South*, 237.

46. Rachel B. Stillman, *Education in the Confederate States of America, 1861–1865* (Ph.D. Dissertation, The University of Illinois, 1972), 74–79.

47. Morison, *Three Centuries of Harvard*, 302−3; Kelley, *Yale: A History*, 196−97; Rammelkamp, *Illinois College*, 196; B. Wallace Chessman, *Ohio Colleges and the Civil War* (Columbus, OH: Ohio State University Press, 1963), 4−7.

48. This quotation is from J. M. Ludlow's manuscript "Reminiscences of Princeton" and may be found in Wertenbaker, *Princeton, 1746−1896*, 266.

49. Chessman, *Ohio Colleges and the Civil War*, 6.

50. Cheyney, *History of the University of Pennsylvania*, 250.

51. These and other quotations from Francis Sellers' scrapbook may be found in James H. Morgan, *Dickinson College: The History of One Hundred Fifty Years, 1783−1933* (Carlisle, PA: Dickinson College, 1933), 311−12.

52. Fletcher, *History of Oberlin College*, 1:845.

53. *The Princetonian*, 1 March 1941, 1−2.

54. Ernest C. Marriner, *The History of Colby College* (Waterville, MD: Colby College Press, 1963), 153−54.

55. Walter Havighurst, *The Miami Years, 1809−1959* (New York: G.P. Putnam's Sons, 1958), 114−15.

56. Beach, *A Pioneer College: Marietta*, 135.

57. Fletcher, *History of Oberlin College*, 1:845.

58. The quotations are from Nora C. Chaffin, *Trinity College, 1839−1892* (Durham, NC: Duke University Press, 1950), 220−22.

59. Dabney, *Mr. Jefferson's University*, 27.

60. Hollis, *The University of South Carolina*, 1:214−15.

61. Thomas G. Dyer, *The University of Georgia: A Bicentennial History* (Athens, GA: University of Georgia Press, 1985), 103−4.

62. Wayland F. Dunaway, *History of the Pennsylvania State College* (Lancaster, PA: Pennsylvania State College, 1946), 39−40.

63. Fletcher, *History of Oberlin College*, 1:846.

64. Jesse L. Rosenberger, *Rochester: The Making of a University* (Rochester, NY: The University of Rochester, 1927), 150−51.

65. James F. A. Pyre, *Wisconsin* (New York: Oxford University Press, 1920), 147.

66. Chaffin, *Trinity College, 1839−1892*, 22; Cabaniss, *The University of Mississippi: The First Hundred Years*, 51.

67. McCormick, *Rutgers*, 78; David B. Skillman, *The Biography of a College, Lafayette* (Eastern, PA: Lafayette College, 1932), 1:245.

68. Fuess, *Amherst*, 187.

69. *New York Times*, 9 August 1865, 5.

70. Eliot, *Yale in the Civil War*, 11; Rosenberger, *Rochester: The Making of a University*, 153−54; Wertenbaker, *Princeton, 1746−1896*, 270−71; Marriner, *The History of Colby College*, 154; McCormick, *Rutgers*, 77−78; Weaver, *The History of Trinity College*, 1:250−51; Skillman, *Biography of a College*, 248.

71. *New York Times*, 25 July 1865, 1.

72. Morison, *Three Centuries of Harvard*, 303.

73. Chessman, *Ohio Colleges and the Civil War*, 5.

74. Beach, *A Pioneer College: Marietta*, 134−36.

75. Clark, *Indiana University: Volume 1, The Early Years*, 10.

76. James A. Woodburn, *History of Indiana University* (Bloomington, IN: Indiana University, 1940), 162−63.

77. Pyre, *Wisconsin*, 146−47.

78. Chessman, *Ohio Colleges and the Civil War*, 23−24.

79. Osborne and Gronert, *Wabash College*, 121−24.

80. Rammelkamp, *Illinois College*, 204–5.
81. William L. Fisk, *A History of Muskingum College* (New Concord, OH: Muskingum College, 1972), 73.
82. The reminiscence may be found in John S. Nollen, *Grinnell College* (Iowa City, IA: State Historical Society, 1953), 61.
83. Eliot, *Yale in the Civil War*, 15–16; 20.
84. Kelley, *Yale: A History*, 197–98.
85. Weaver, *The History of Trinity College*, 1:130–31.
86. The quotation about "the laboring classes" appeared in the *Yale Literary Magazine* in July 1863. See Eliot, *Yale in the Civil War*, 6–7; 14.
87. Eliot, *Yale in the Civil War*, 16.
88. *New York Times*, 29 July 1864, 4.
89. Chessman, *Ohio Colleges and the Civil War*, 13; Hoover, *History of Ohio University*, 118–19.
90. Fisk, *A History of Muskingum College*, 73.
91. Chessman, *Ohio Colleges and the Civil War*, 19–20.
92. John Strietelmeier, *Valparaiso University's First Century* (Valparaiso, IN: Valparaiso University, 1959), 8–9.
93. Oliphant, *Rise of Bucknell University*, 103–4.
94. Chessman, *Ohio Colleges and the Civil War*, 12.
95. Newell Y. Osborne, *A Select School* (Alliance, OH: Mount Union College, 1967), 508.
96. Nollen, *Grinnell College*, 62.
97. Strietelmeier, *Valparaiso University's First Century*, 9–10.
98. Pyre, *Wisconsin*, 150–52.
99. William W. Sweet, *Indiana Asbury-DePauw University, 1837–1937* (Cincinnati, OH: The Abingdon Press, 1937), 108–9.
100. Strietelmeier, *Valparaiso University's First Century*, 8.
101. Chessman, *Ohio Colleges and the Civil War*, 26; Osborne and Gronert, *Wabash College*, 127.
102. Hoover, *History of Ohio University*, 125–26; Chessman, *Ohio Colleges and the Civil War*, 27.
103. Sweet, *Indiana Asbury-DePauw University, 1837–1937*, 107.
104. Rammelkamp, *Illinois College*, 210–11.
105. Chessman, *Ohio Colleges and the Civil War*, 23–24.
106. Oliphant, *Rise of Bucknell University*, 106.
107. Pyre, *Wisconsin*, 156.
108. Leon B. Richardson, *History of Dartmouth College* (Hanover, NH: Dartmouth College Publications, 1932), 2:517–18.
109. Chessman, *Ohio Colleges and the Civil War*, 26.
110. Oliphant, *Rise of Bucknell University*, 107.
111. Sweet, *Indiana Asbury-DePauw University, 1837–1937*, 111–12.
112. Chessman, *Ohio Colleges and the Civil War*, 26–27.
113. Hoover, *History of Ohio University*, 123.
114. Chessman, *Ohio Colleges and the Civil War*, 23.
115. Skillman, *Biography of a College*, 249–50.
116. Chessman, *Ohio Colleges and the Civil War*, 11–12; 24; 26.
117. Pyre, *Wisconsin*, 156.
118. Wertenbaker, *Princeton, 1746–1896*, 275–76.
119. Oliphant, *Rise of Bucknell University*, 107–8; Chessman, *Ohio Colleges and the Civil War*, 25–26.

120. Morgan, *Dickinson College: The History of One Hundred Fifty Years, 1783–1933*, 314; Skillman, *Biography of a College*, 246.

121. See "A Letter from Sixty-Three, Nassau Hall," *Newark Daily Advertiser*, 13 September 1862. This may be found in the Princeton University Archives, Princeton, NJ.

122. Chessman, *Ohio Colleges and the Civil War*, 16–17.

123. Chessman, *Ohio Colleges and the Civil War*, 17–18.

124. Hoover, *History of Ohio University*, 122–24.

125. Skillman, *Biography of a College* 246–47; Morgan, *Dickinson College: The History of One Hundred Fifty Years, 1783–1933*, 314–15; Charles H. Glatfelter, *A Salutary Influence: Gettysburg College, 1832–1985* (Gettysburg, PA: Gettysburg College, 1987), 1:183.

126. Morgan, *Dickinson College: The History of One Hundred Fifty Years, 1783–1933*, 314–17.

127. Glatfelter, *A Salutary Influence*, 1:185.

128. Glatfelter, *A Salutary Influence*, 1:185.

129. This recollection may be found in Glatfelter, *A Salutary Influence*, 1:185–86.

130. Glatfelter, *A Salutary Influence*, 1:186–87.

131. Joseph H. Dubbs, *History of Franklin and Marshall College* (Lancaster, PA: Franklin and Marshall College Alumni Association, 1903), 304–6; Oliphant, *Rise of Bucknell University* 104–5; Glatfelter, *A Salutary Influence*, 1:189.

132. Agnes L. Starrett, *Through One Hundred and Fifty Years: The University of Pittsburgh* (Pittsburgh, PA: University of Pittsburgh Press, 1937), 148–49.

133. Fisk, *A History of Muskingum College*, 71–72; Havighurst, *The Miami Years*, 120–22.

134. *New York Times*, 13 July 1862, 1.

135. *New York Times*, 25 June 1862, 5.

136. *New York Times*, 8 August 1862, 8; 11 August 1862, 2.

137. Fuess, *Amherst*, 87.

138. Theiss, *Centennial History of Bucknell University* (Williamsport, PA: Bucknell University, 1946), 446–47.

139. This quotation may be found in "Recollections of Professor T. W. Hunt, Princeton, Class of 1865," *New York Sun*, 14 May 1911, 5.

140. Clay McCauley, "The College during the Civil War," Part I, *Princeton Alumni Weekly*, 17, 25 October 1916, 87.

141. Osborne and Gronert, *Wabash College*, 124–25.

142. Fisk, *A History of Muskingum College*, 72–73.

143. Fisk, *A History of Muskingum College*, 73.

144. Osborne and Gronert, *Wabash College*, 124–25.

145. Rammelkamp, *Illinois College*, 205–6.

146. Francis Wayland, *No Failure for the North* (New York: Loyal Publication Society, 1864), 5–6.

147. Weaver, *The History of Trinity College*, 132–34.

148. Wertenbaker, *Princeton, 1746–1896*, 267–69.

149. Theodore W. Hunt, "College and Civil War Reminiscences," *Princeton Alumni Weekly* 17, 23 May 1917, 760–61.

150. Hatch, *History of Bowdoin College*, 121.

151. Peckham, *The Making of the University of Michigan*, 47–55.

152. Chessman, *Ohio Colleges and the Civil War*, 18–23.

153. Richardson, *History of Dartmouth College*, 474–75; also see Richard

Hofstadter and Wilson Smith, ed., *American Higher Education: A Documentary History* (Chicago: University of Chicago Press, 1961), 1:472–73.

154. Morison, *Three Centuries of Harvard*, 303–4.

155. Eliot, *Yale in the Civil War*, 8–9; 14–20.

156. Marriner, *The History of Colby College*, 152–53.

157. Julian I. Lindsay, *Tradition Looks Forward: The University of Vermont, 1791–1954* (Burlington, VT: University of Vermont, 1954), 221–22.

158. Robert I. Gannon, *Up to the Present: The Story of Fordham* (Garden City, NY: Doubleday & Co., 1967), 59–60.

159. David R. Dunigan, *A History of Boston College* (Milwaukee, WI: Bruce Publishing Co., 1947), 51–52.

160. Skillman, *Biography of a College*, 240–44.

161. Clark, *Indiana University: Volume 1, The Early Years*, 105.

162. Richard R. Duncan, "The Impact of the Civil War on Education in Maryland," *Maryland Historical Magazine*, 61 (March 1966): 40–42.

163. Heim, *A Student's View of the College of St. James* 17–18; 126–28; Duncan, "The Impact of the Civil War on Education in Maryland," 38–42.

164. Callcott, *A History of the University of Maryland*, 155–63.

165. Duncan, "The Impact of the Civil War on Education in Maryland," 37–43; Callcott, *A History of the University of Maryland*, 163–65.

166. Daniel E. Huger Smith, *A Charlestonian's Recollections, 1846–1913* (Charleston, SC: Carolina Art Association, 1960), 62–63; Dabney, *Mr. Jefferson's University*, 24–31.

167. James E. Scanlon, *Randolph-Macon College* (Charlottesville, VA: University Press of Virginia, 1983), 59–60.

168. William Colper, *One Hundred Years at V.M.I.* (Richmond, VA; Garrett and Massie, Inc., 1939), 70–72.

169. Chaffin, *Trinity College*, 233.

170. Allen E. Ragen, *History of Tusculum College, 1794–1944* (Bristol, TN: Tusculum Sesquicentennial Committee, 1945), 56–59.

171. Winsted P. Bone, *A History of Cumberland University* (Lebanon, TN: Published by the author, 1935), 82–86.

172. Chaffin, *Trinity College*, 225–228.

173. Chaffin, *Trinity College*, 226.

174. Chaffin, *Trinity College*, 223–25.

175. Letter from Fletcher B. Watson to "Pa," 7 May 1861, as quoted in Chaffin, *Trinity College*, 222.

176. Coulter, *College Life in the Old South*, 240; Dyer, *The University of Georgia*, 105–6.

177. Hollis, *The University of South Carolina*, 1:220–21.

178. The quotation from Longstreet may be found in Edwin L. Green, *a History of the University of South Carolina* (Columbia, SC: The State Company, 1916), 73–74.

179. Sellers, *History of the University of Alabama*, 270–75.

180. Sellers, *History of the University of Alabama*, 275–76.

181. Sellers, *History of the University of Alabama*, 276–77.

182. Dyer, *The University of Georgia*, 107–9.

183. Cabaniss, *The University of Mississippi*, 56–57.

184. Hollis, *The University of South Carolina*, 1:203–4; Green, *a History of the University of South Carolina*, 74–77.

185. Chaffin, *Trinity College*, 232–33; 246–47.

186. Bone, *A History of Cumberland University*, 82–83.

187. Dyer, *The University of Georgia*, 104–5.

188. Stillman, *Education in the Confederate States of America*, 85–86; 338–40; 418–22.

189. Dyer, *The University of Georgia*, 105–6.

190. Stillman, *Education in the Confederate States of America*, 179–81.

191. Stillman, *Education in the Confederate States of America*, 417–19.

192. Dyer, *The University of Georgia*, 105–6.

193. Stillman, *Education in the Confederate States of America*, 179–80.

194. Sellers, *History of the University of Alabama*, 264.

195. Dyer, *The University of Georgia*, 104–6.

196. Hollis, *The University of South Carolina*, 1:219–20.

197. Stillman, *Education in the Confederate States of America*, 284–86.

198. Stillman, *Education in the Confederate States of America*, 285.

199. Derrell Roberts, "The University of Georgia and Georgia's Civil War G.I. Bill," *Georgia Historical Quarterly* 49, December 1965, 417–22.

200. Sellers, *History of the University of Alabama*, 275–87.

201. Lyon G. Tyler, *The College of William and Mary in Virginia* (Richmond, VA: Whittet & Shepperson, 1907), 82–84; Fleming, *Louisiana State University*, 106–17.

202. Cabaniss, *The University of Mississippi*, 57–58.

203. James H. Easterby, *History of the College of Charleston* (Charleston, SC: The College of Charleston, 1935), 149–51.

204. Green, *a History of the University of South Carolina* 77–78; Hollis, *The University of South Carolina*, 1: 226–27.

205. The quotation, from Professor Ellis's address, "Oberlin and the American Conflict," is taken from Fletcher, *History of Oberlin College* 1:885.

206. Bronson, *History of Brown University*, 355.

207. This account was published in *The Princeton Standard*, 7 April 1865. It is cited in Wertenbaker, *Princeton University, 1746–1896*, 269–70.

208. Eliot, *Yale in the Civil War*, 17.

209. Bronson, *History of Brown University*, 355–57.

210. Havighurst, *The Miami Years*, 123–24.

211. Chessman, *Ohio Colleges and the Civil War*, 26–27.

212. Gannaway's memoir, "Trinity College in War Times," is quoted extensively in Chaffin, *Trinity College*, 247–49.

213. This observation comes from Chessman, *Ohio Colleges and the Civil War*, 27.

214. Hunt, "College and Civil War Reminiscences," 760.

215. McCormick, *Rutgers, A Bicentennial History*, 78; McCormick, "Rutgers and the Civil War," 60.

216. Chessman, *Ohio Colleges and the Civil War*, 27.

217. Cheyney, *History of the University of Pennsylvania*, 253.

218. Fleming, *Louisiana State University*, 98–112; Cabaniss, *The University of Mississippi: The First Hundred Years*, 52–54.

219. Parker's views are summarized in Lorraine A. Williams, *The Civil War and Intellectuals of the North* (Washington, DC: Ph.D. Dissertation, American University, 1955), 137–38; 173–74; 230–33; see also *Dictionary of American Biography*, s.v. "Joel Parker."

220. Merle Curti, *Growth of American Thought* (New York: Harper and Bros., 1943), 462–66; *Dictionary of American Biography*, s.v. "Oliver Wolcott Gibbs"; "Joseph Leidy."

221. *Dictionary of American Biography*, s.v., "Theophilus Parsons"; also see the biographical sketch of another pro-Union professor at Harvard Law School, *Dictionary of American Biography*, s.v., "Emory Washburn."

222. Frank Freidel, *Francis Lieber: Nineteenth Century Liberal* (Baton Rouge, LA: Louisiana State University Press, 1947), 318–23.

223. Curti, *Growth of American Thought*, 474; Freidel, *Francis Lieber*, 312–37.

224. Freidel, *Francis Lieber*, 329–30.

225. Green, *a History of the University of South Carolina*, 75–77; *Dictionary of American Biography*, s.v., "John LeConte"; "Joseph LeConte."

226. Hollis, *The University of South Carolina*, 1:219–20; 227–28; *Dictionary of American Biography*, s.v., "Maximilian La Borde."

227. Dabney, *Mr. Jefferson's University*, 26–27.

228. Hoover, *History of Ohio University*, 124–25.

229. Curti, *Growth of American Thought*, 467–69.

230. Brubacher and Rudy, *Higher Education in Transition*, 65–67.

231. Curti, *Growth of American Thought*, 468–70.

232. Brubacher and Rudy, *Higher Education in Transition*, 65–68.

233. Chaffin, *Trinity College*, 251–52.

234. Easterby, *History of the College of Charleston*, 153.

235. Brooks, *The University of Georgia*, 47–48; Dyer, *The University of Georgia*, 108–9.

236. Cabaniss, *The University of Mississippi*, 60–62.

237. *New York Times*, 16 July 1865, 2; 31 July 1865, 8; 9 August 1865, 5; *Princetonion* 17 May 1931, 1.

238. Wertenbaker, *Princeton, 1746–1896*, 270; Morison, *Three Centuries of Harvard*, 303.

239. Pyre, *Wisconsin*, 149.

Chapter 3. The American Campus and the Great War in Europe, 1914–1917

1. William W. Sweet, *Indiana Asbury-DePauw University, 1837–1937* (Cincinnati, OH: Abingdon Press, 1937), 214.

2. These quotations may be found in Page Smith, *America Enters the World* (New York: McGraw-Hill Book Co., 1985), 436.

3. The atmosphere of the American campus on the eve of World War I is well described in a number of works. See Edward A. Birge, "A Change of Educational Emphasis," *Atlantic Monthly* 103, February 1909, 190–93; Burgess Johnson, "Campus Against Classroom," *Harper's Magazine* 167, July 1933, 218–19; Henry S. Canby, *Alma Mater: The Gothic Age of the American College* (New York: Farrar, Straus & Giroux, 1936), 121–36; Wilbur C. Abbott, "The Guild of Students," *Atlantic Monthly* 128, November 1921, 623–24; Stephen Vincent Benet, *The Beginning of Wisdom* (New York: Holt, Rinehart & Winston, 1921), especially 125–29; Laurence R. Veysey, *The Emergence of the American University* (Chicago: University of Chicago Press, 1965), 272–79.

4. Morris Bishop, *A History of Cornell* (Ithaca, NY: Cornell University Press, 1962), 425.

5. William Summerscales, *Affirmation and Dissent* (New York: Teachers College, Columbia, 1970), 45–46.

6. Claude Fuess, *Amherst, the Story of a New England College* (Boston: Little, Brown & Co., 1935), 314.

7. George W. Pierson, *Yale College* (New Haven, CT: Yale University Press, 1952), 448.

8. Louis R. Wilson, *The University of North Carolina* (Chapel Hill, NC: University of North Carolina Press, 1957), 261–62.

9. Lucy L. Notestein, *Wooster of the Middle West*, (Wooster, OH: The College of Wooster, 1971), 2:168–69.

10. Paul M. Brechtel, *Wheaton College: A Heritage Remembered* (Wheaton, IL: Harold Shaw Publishers, 1984), 80.

11. Cedric Cummins, *The University of Dakota, 1862–1966* (Vermilion, SD: Dakota Press, 1975), 129–30.

12. Pierson, *Yale College*, 447.

13. Samuel E. Morison, *Three Centuries of Harvard* (Cambridge, MA: Harvard University Press, 1935), 450–51.

14. Howard H. Peckham, *The Making of the University of Michigan* (Ann Arbor, MI: University of Michigan Press, 1967), 127.

15. Fuess, *Amherst*, 315.

16. Julius T. Willard, *History of the Kansas State College* (Manhattan, KS: Kansas State College Press, 1940), 303–4.

17. Mark Sullivan, *Our Times: Over Here, 1914–1918* (New York: Charles Scribner's Sons, 1933), 5:134–35.

18. Albion W. Small, "Germany and American Opinion," *Sociological Review* 8, April 1915, as cited in Carol S. Gruber, *Mars and Minerva* (Baton Rouge, LA: Louisiana State University Press, 1975), 55.

19. Gruber, *Mars and Minerva*, 52.

20. Reginald McGrane, *The University of Cincinnati* (New York: Harper & Row, 1963), 232–36.

21. Herman F. Eschenbacher, *The University of Rhode Island* (New York: Appleton-Century-Crofts, 1967), 185–86.

22. James Osborne and Theodore Gronert, *Wabash College* (Crawfordsville, IN: R.E. Banta, 1932), 317.

23. Charles W. Eliot, "The No-Faith Doctrine of Germany," *New York Times*, 15 May 1915, 12.

24. Gruber, *Mars and Minerva*, 80.

25. Pierson, *Yale College*, 449–50.

26. *New York Times*, 13 January 1915, 11.

27. John P. Finnegan, *Against the Specter of a Dragon* (Westport, CT: Greenwood Press, 1974), 27–30; 60–64.

28. *New York Times*, 31 January 1915, 4; 12 March 1915, 7; 30 November 1915, 3.

29. See General Wood's speech at Princeton, 15 April 1915, as reported in the *New York Times*, 16 April 1915, 14.

30. George P. Schmidt, *The Liberal Arts College* (New Brunswick, NJ: Rutgers University Press, 1957), 288–90.

31. Brubacher and Rudy, *Higher Education in Transition*, 225–28.

32. Earl D. Ross, *A History of the Iowa State College* (Ames, IA: The Iowa State College Press, 1942), 302–3; John Milton Cooper, Jr., *The Vanity of Power* (Ph.D. Dissertation, Columbia University, 1968), 67–69.

33. Finnegan, *Against the Specter of a Dragon*, 58–62.

34. *New York Times*, 5 January 1915, 3.

35. *New York Times*, 24 January 1915, 5; "Training soldiers at college," *Literary Digest* 50 (6 February 1915): 242.

36. *New York Times*, 14 May 1915, 5.

37. Finnegan, *Against the Specter of a Dragon*, 62–66.

38. "Students in Military Training Camps," *School and Society* 4 (2 September 1916): 366.

39. "Students in Military Training Camps," 336.

40. Paul K. Conkin, *Gone with the Ivy* (Knoxville, TN: University of Tennessee Press, 1985), 232; Charles W. Eliot, "A New Kind of Army Needed," *New York Times Magazine*, Section 7, 11 March 1917, 1–3.

41. Doris G. Rodin, *The Opposition to the Establishment of Military Training in the United States* (Master of Arts Thesis, American University, 1949), 26–28; 41–42.

42. *New York Times*, 18 October 1916, 3.

43. *New York Times*, 28 September 1916, 7.

44. Kelley, *Yale: A History*, 349–51; Pierson, *Yale College*, 463.

45. Gruber, *Mars and Minerva*, 49–51; 69–70; 80–81.

46. Albert Bushnell Hart, *The War In Europe: Its Causes and Results* (New York, D. Appleton & Co., 1914).

47. *New York Times*, 10 January 1915, 9.

48. *New York Times*, 22 March 1915, 6.

49. Verne A. Stadtman, *The University of California, 1868–1968* (New York: McGraw-Hill, 1970), 193–95.

50. John W. Burgess, *The European War of 1914* (Chicago: A.C McClure & Co., 1915).

51. Gruber, *Mars and Minerva*, 47–51.

52. Lillian Wald summed up many of these arguments in an address delivered in April 1916. See *New York Times*, 7 April 1916, 3; A similar line of reasoning may be found in a pamphlet, *A Letter from the Collegiate Anti-Militarism League, and a Reply* (San Francisco: Blair-Murdock Co., Printers, 1915).

53. "Training Soldiers at College," *Literary Digest*, 6 February 1915, 50: 243.

54. Summerscales, *Affirmation and Dissent*, 47.

55. Summerscales, *Affirmation and Dissent*, 46–49.

56. *New York Times*, 7 March 1915, Section III, 2.

57. Henry D. Sheldon, *History of the University of Oregon* (Portland, OR: Binfords & Mort, 1940), 191–92.

58. *New York Times*, 16 January 1915, 8.

59. Summerscales, *Affirmation and Dissent*, 46–48.

60. *New York Times*, 16 February 1915, 5; 12 March 1915, 7; 29 March 1915, 7.

61. *New York Times*, 14 April 1915, 9; 12 May 1915, 4; 4 July 1915, Section II, 10; 19 September 1915, Section II, 5; Seymour M. Lipset, *Passion and Politics* (Boston: Little, Brown and Co., 1972), 150–51.

62. *New York Times*, 12 May 1915, 4; Peckham, *The Making of the University of Michigan*, 128; Carl F. Price, *Wesleyan's First Century* (Middletown, CT: Wesleyan University, 1932), 191–92.

63. As quoted in J. Donald Adams, *Copey of Harvard* (Boston: Houghton, Mifflin Co., 1960), 207–8.

64. "Princeton Students Opposed to Military Training," *Advocate of Peace* April 1916, 78: 112–13, as cited in Rodin, *Opposition to the Establishment of Military Training*, 72.

65. Norman Thomas, "A Defense of Dissenters," *Princeton Alumni Weekly*, 15

March 1916, 16: 526–27, as quoted in Bernard K, Johnboll, ed., *Norman Thomas on War* (New York: Garland Publishing, 1974), 27–28.

66. *New York Times*, 15 May 1916, 12; 31 May 1915, 6; 1 June 1915, 14.

67. *New York Times*, 14 April 1915, 9.

68. *New York Times*, 25 July 1915, Section II, 11.

69. Peckham, *The Making of the University of Michigan*, 127–128; Fuess, *Amherst*, 316.

70. *New York Times*, 15 November 1915, 4.

71. W. Freeman Galpin, *Syracuse University* (Syracuse, NY: Syracuse University Press, 1960), 2: 375–76.

72. *New York Times*, 19 February 1916, 18; 22 February 1916 7; 23 February 1916, 22.

73. *New York Times*, 31 March 1916, 5.

74. *New York Times*, 7 April 1916, 3.

75. S. Willis Rudy, *The College of the City of New York, A History* (New York: City College Press, 1949), 347; *New York Times*, 31 March 1916, 5.

76. Finnegan, *Against the Specter of a Dragon*, 135.

77. *New York Times*, 28 April 1916, 10; 4 May 1916, 10.

78. Clark, *Indiana University*, 2:176.

79. *New York Times*, 20 April 1916, 6.

80. "Even if no good is done to the two Belgians, such an impressive showing of our sympathy and our unanimity will do us some good." Letter from 93 American professors to the U.S. Secretary of State, 7 June 1916. This quotation may be found in Gruber, *Mars and Minerva*, 68.

81. Adams, *Copey of Harvard*, 200–212.

82. Arthur A. Ekirch, Jr., *The Colleges and the Military* (Colorado Springs, CO: Ralph Myles, Publisher, 1972), 182–84.

83. Professor Hayes's statement was published in the *Columbia Spectator* for 16 January 1917, and is quoted, together with the *Spectator*'s account of the Earl Hall meeting in Summerscales, *Affirmation and Dissent*, 49–50.

84. Summerscales, *Affirmation and Dissent*, 50.

85. Summerscales, *Affirmation and Dissent*, 48–52.

86. *New York Times*, 5 February 1917, 11.

87. *New York Times*, 6 February 1917, 6.

88. *New York Times*, 7 February 1917, 6.

89. *New York Times*, 14 February 1917, 5.

90. *New York Times*, 21 February 1917, 12.

91. *School and Society* 10 March 1917, 5:284.

92. *New York Times*, 7 February 1917, 6.

93. *New York Times*, 8 February 1917, 22.

94. John Barnard, *From Evangelicalism to Progressivism at Oberlin College* (Columbus, OH: Ohio State University Press, 1969), 125–26.

95. Kent Sagendorph, *Michigan: The Story of the University* (New York: E.P. Dutton & Co., 1948) 258–260.

96. Samuel Servin and Iris Wilson, *Southern California and its University* (Los Angeles, CA: The Ward Ritchie Press, 1964), 251; 259–62.

97. "Freedom of Speech at Harvard University," *School and Society* 1 (8 May 1915): 668; *New York Times*, 13 March 1915, 4; Morison, *Three Centuries of Harvard*, 453–56.

98. *New York Times*, 9 February 1917, 4.

99. *New York Times*, 30 March 1917, 4.

100. *New York Times*, 16 February 1917, 3.

101. *New York Times*, 30 March 1917, 11.

102. Rudy, *The College of the City of New York: A History*, 348−49; *New York Times*, 30 March 1917, 4.

103. "Silentia Vobiscum," an editorial in the *Harvard Crimson*, 4 April 1917, as quoted in *Harvard Magazine* 96 Number 2 (November−December, 1993): 56.

104. Phelps's statement is quoted in Kelley, *Yale: A History*, 349; See also Pierson, *Yale College*, 450, and *New York Times*, 7 April 1916, 3.

105. *New York Times*, 28 February 1917, 13.

106. Summerscales, *Affirmation and Dissent*, 52−54.

107. *New York Times*, 27 March 1917, 11.

108. *New York Times*, 30 March 1917, 11; Pierson, *Yale College*, 465−66; Kelley, *Yale: A History*, 350.

109. Charles Chatfield, *For Peace and Justice* (Boston: Beacon Press, 1973), 26−27.

110. *New York Times*, 23 March 1917, 1.

111. Russell E. Miller, *Light on the Hill* (Boston: Beacon Press, 1966), 480; McCormick, *Rutgers: A Bicentennial History*, 164−65; James H. Easterly, *History of the College of Charleston* (Charleston, SC: College of Charleston, 1935), 187−88; Sagendorph, *Michigan: The Story of the University*, 235−38; Servin and Wilson, *Southern California and its University*, 65−66; Cedric Cummins, *The University of South Dakota, 1862−1966*, 131−33; Arthur J. May, *History of the University of Rochester* (Rochester, NY: University of Rochester, 1977), 164; Harold W. Cary, *The University of Massachusetts: A History of One Hundred Years* (Amherst, MA: University of Massachusetts, 1962), 131−32; Arthur J. Hope, *Notre Dame: One Hundred Years* (South Bend, IN: Icarus Press, Inc., 1978), 318; *School and Society* 5 (26 May 1917): 614−15; "College Mobilization," *Literary Digest* 54 (7 April 1917): 984.

112. Morison, *Three Centuries of Harvard*, 458.

113. Sweet, *Indiana Asbury-DePauw University*, 215.

114. Conkin, *Gone with the Ivy*, 233.

115. Galpin, *Syracuse University*, 2:379.

116. Bishop, *A History of Cornell*, 428−29.

117. George W. Knepper, *New Lamps for Old* (Akron, OH: University of Akron, 1970), 128−29.

118. "Who Willed American Participation?", *New Republic* 10 (14 April 1917): 308, as quoted in Gruber, *Mars and Minerva*, 82.

119. Pierson, *Yale College*, 446.

120. Ross, *A History of the Iowa State College*, 315−16.

121. Summerscales, *Affirmation and Dissent*, 68.

Chapter 4. The Second World War: From Peace Strikes to Pearl Harbor

1. *New York Times*, 29 November 1925, 4; 1 December 1925, 21; 17 January 1926, 1.

2. Rudy, *The College of the City of New York, A History*, 406−7.

3. *New York Times*, 7 May 1927, 4; 26 October 1928, 25; *The Campus* (CCNY), 18 November 1927, 2.

4. Calvin B. T. Lee, *The Campus Scene, 1900−1970* (New York: David McKay Company, 1970), 40−44; Lipset, *Passion and Politics*, 160−74; Philip G. Altbach

and Robert Laufer, eds., *The New Pilgrims* (New York: David McKay Co., Inc., 1972), 16–29.

5. Stadtman, *The University of California*, 301–2.

6. Harold Seidman, "The Colleges Renounce War," *Nation* 136 (17 May 1933): 554–55.

7. Rudy, *The College of the City of New York, A History*, 417–20.

8. Eileen M. Eagan, *The Student Peace Movement in the United States* (Ph.D. Dissertation, Temple University, 1979), 147–49.

9. James C. Carey, *Kansas State University: The Quest for Identity* (Lawrence, KS: Regents Press of Kansas, 1977), 157–59.

10. Stadtman, *The University of California* 303; Eagan, *The Student Peace Movement in the United States*, 1–3; 152–73.

11. Clifford Griffin, *The University of Kansas, A History* (Lawrence, KS: University Press of Kansas, 1974), 485–88; Conkin, *Gone with the Ivy*, 415–16; Stadtman, *The University of California*, 302–4.

12. Eagan, *The Student Peace Movement in the United States*, 1–2; Arthur J. May, *History of the University of Rochester* (Rochester, NY: University of Rochester, 1977), 267–68; John M. Cooper, *The Vanity of Power* (Ph.D. Dissertation, Columbia University, 1968), 337–38; Stadtman, *The University of California*, 303–4; Lipset, *Passion and Politics*, 179–89.

13. Eagan, *The Student Peace Movement in the United States*, 229–30.

14. John T. Cunningham, *University in the Forest* (Florham Park, NJ: Afton Publishing Co., 1972), 215–16.

15. Frederick Meiners, *A History of Rice University* (Houston, TX: Rice University Studies, 1982), 132–33.

16. Eagan, *The Student Peace Movement in the United States*, 230.

17. Eagan, *The Student Peace Movement in the United States*, 229.

18. Notestein, *Wooster of the Middle West*, 2:253–54.

19. Leslie Hanawalt, *The History of Wayne State University* (Detroit, MI: Wayne State University Press, 1968), 249–51.

20. W. Freeman Galpin and Oscar T. Barck, Syracuse University (Syracuse, NY: Syracuse University Press, 1984), 3:326–27.

21. Eagan, *The Student Peace Movement in the United States*, 225–42.

22. Chatfield, *For Peace and Justice*, 295–97; Galpin and Barck, *Syracuse University* 3:327–28; Eagan, *The Student Peace Movement in the United States*, 230–48.

23. Hanawalt, *The History of Wayne State University*, 249–50.

24. Raphael Hamilton, *The Story of Marquette University* (Milwaukee, WI: Marquette University Press, 1953), 338.

25. Peckham, *The Making of the University of Michigan*, 194–95.

26. Robert K. Root, *The Princeton Campus in World War II* (Princeton, NJ: Ms, Princeton University Archives, 1950), 1–2.

27. May, *History of the University of Rochester*, 267–68.

28. Eagan, *The Student Peace Movement in the United States*, 244–45.

29. Irwin Ross, "The Student Union and the Future," *New Republic* 102 (8 January 1940): 48–50.

30. *New York Times*, 13 February 1940, 1–2; 10–11; Irwin Ross, Youth Goes to Washington," *New Republic* 102 (26 February 1940): 275–76.

31. James Wechsler, "Politics on the Campus," *Nation* 149 (30 December 1939): 732–33; Hamilton, *The story of Marquette University*, 342–43.

32. Griffin, *The University of Kansas, A History*, 486.

33. McCormick, *Rutgers: A Bicentennial History*, 254.

34. Cunningham, *University in the Forest*, 216−17.

35. Root, *The Princeton Campus in World War II*, 3.

36. *New York Times*, 23 April 1940, 9.

37. Calcott, *History of the University of Maryland*, 335.

38. Victor Hicken, *The Purple and the Gold* (Macomb, IL: Western Illinois University Foundation, 1970), 95−96.

39. Peckham, *The Making of the University of Michigan*, 196−98.

40. Gerald McDevitt, *The University of Santa Clara* (Stanford, CA: Stanford University Press, 1979), 258−59.

41. Stadtman, *The University of California*, 302−5.

42. *New York Times*, 5 November 1939, Section 2, 6.

43. *New York Times*, 11 November 1939, 5.

44. Stadtman, *The University of California*, 305.

45. Peckham, *The Making of the University of Michigan*, 196.

46. Galpin and Barck, *Syracuse University*, 3: 329−30.

47. *New York Times*, 22 September 1939, 21.

48. Galpin and Barck, *Syracuse University*, 3: 329−31.

49. Peckham, *The Making of the University of Michigan*, 196.

50. Ernest H. Wilkins, "The College Faces War and Peace," *School and Society* 51 (6 January 1940): 1−7.

51. *New York Times*, 1 June 1940, 7.

52. *New York Times* 26 May 1940, 2.

53. *New York Times*, 1 June 1940, 8.

54. *New York Times*, 1 June 1940, 8.

55. *New York Times*, 21 May 1940, 12.

56. J. Juan Reid, *Colorado College* (Colorado Springs, CO: The Colorado College, 1979), 151.

57. Hamilton, *The Story of Marquette University*, 343−44.

58. Galpin and Barck, *Syracuse University*, 3: 328.

59. *New York Times*, 2 June 1940, 20−21.

60. *New York Times*, 18 June 1940, 11.

61. Eagan, *The Student Peace Movement in the United States*, 272−73.

62. Mark L. Chadwin, *The Hawks of World War II* (Chapel Hill, NC: University of North Carolina, 1968), 122−23; Walter Johnson, *The Battle Against Isolation* (Chicago: University of Chicago Press, 1944), 71−75; 108−10.

63. Michelle Ely Stenehjem, *An American First* (New Rochelle, NY: Arlington House Publishers, 1976), 15−27.

64. Kelley, *Yale: A History*, 395−98.

65. *New York Times*, 9 September 1940, 7; 31 October 1940, 3.

66. Morris B. Stanley, *The America First Committee* (Master of Arts Thesis, Emory University, 1942), 57−59.

67. Charles Seymour, "War's Impact on the Campus," *New York Times Magazine* (29 September 1940): 15−16.

68. Chadwin, *The Hawks of World War II*, 8−9.

69. Irwin Ross, "College Students and the War," *New Republic* 103 (15 July 1940): 80−81.

70. Reid, *Colorado College*, 150−51.

71. *New York Times*, 1 June 1940, 8.

72. *New York Times*, 25 May 1940, 6.

73. Geoffrey Perett, *Days of Sadness, Years of Triumph* (New York: Coward,

McCann & Geoghegan, 1979), 111–12.

74 Paul P. Cram, "Undergraduates and the War," *Atlantic Monthly* 166 (October 1940): 410–16.

75. Ross, "College Students and the War," 80.

76. Seymour, "War's Impact on the Campus," 15; note a similar analysis by Professor J. H. Newlon, Teachers College, Columbia, in the *New York Times*, 11 July 1940, 21.

77. William H. Attwood, "Facing the Future," *NEA Service* (June 1941). Princeton University Archives, Princeton, NJ.

78. *New York Times*, 6 August 1940, 1.

79. George Knepper, *One Hundred Years of Urban Higher Education* (Akron, OH: The University of Ohio, 1970), 251.

80. Hamilton, *The Story of Marquette University*, 343.

81. Leal A. Headley and Merrill E. Jarchow, *Carleton: The First Century* (Northfield, MN: Carleton College, 1966), 348.

82. *New York Times*, 1 August 1940, 14.

83. Root, *The Princeton Campus in World War II*, 4.

84. Knepper, *One Hundred Years of Urban Higher Education*, 251.

85. Hamilton, *The Story of Marquette University*, 344–45.

86. Clark, *Indiana University*, 3:119.

87. *New York Times*, 29 July 1940, 6.

88. *New York Times*, 6 August 1940, 3.

89. "The Pasadena Meeting of the Association of American Colleges," *School and Society* 53 (25 January 1941): 124–25.

90. Galpin and Barck, *Syracuse University*, 3:328.

91. *New York Times*, 13 September 1940, 9.

92. *New York Times*, 4 July 1940, 8; *School and Society*, 6 July 1940, 52:4–5; 17 August 1940, 102; 30 November 1940, 548–49.

93. *New York Times*, 8 July 1940, 2; 29 September 1940, sec. 2, 6.

94. *New York Times*, 29 September 1940, sec. 2, 6.

95. Dabney, *Mr. Jefferson's University*, 328; Calcott, *History of the University of Maryland*, 335; Hanawalt, *The History of Wayne State University*, 252; *School and Society*, 7 September 1940, 52:158–59; 26 October 1940, 388–89.

96. *New York Times*, 27 October 1940, sec. 2, 6; 24 November 1940, 4; Reginald C. McGrane, *The University of Cincinnati* (New York: Harper & Row, 1962), 299–300.

97. *New York Times*, 7 December 1940, 11; 23 December 1940, 8; 29 February 1941, sec. 2, 6; "ROTC Courses in the Colleges and Universities," *School and Society*, 8 March 1941, 53:306–7. See also the issue of 22 March 1941, 365.

98. *New York Times*, 11 December 1940, 9; 17 December 1940, 20; 10 June 1941, 31.

99. *New York Times*, 23 February 1941, sec. 2, 6.

100. *New York Times*, 26 February 1941, 11.

101. *New York Times*, 14 May 1941, 13.

102. *New York Times*, 8 December 1940, 64.

103. *New York Times*, 30 January 1941, 4.

104. *New York Times*, 22 December 1940, 24.

105. *School and Society*, 4 January 1941, 53:14.

106. Archibald Macleish, "To the Class of 41," *Nation* 152 (21 June 1941): 717–18.

107. *New York Times*, 23 April 1941, 23.

108. "Have the young gone sour?" *New Republic* 104 (13 January 1941): 39–40.

109. Chadwin, *The Hawks of World Ward II*, 188.

110. Stadtman, *The University of California*, 306.

111. *School and Society*, 10 May 1941, 53:594.

112. Chadwin, *The Hawks of World War II*, 168.

113. Stenehjem, *An American First*, 78–79; 102–16.

114. *New York Times*, 23 April 1941, 23; Joseph L. Jaffe, Jr., *Isolationism and Neutrality in Academe* (Ph.D. Dissertation, Case Western Reserve University, 1979), 318–29.

115. "Keep out of War," *Newsweek* 16 (30 December 1940): 9.

116. *School and Society*, 4 January 1941, 53:14; *New York Times*, 24 January 1941, 5; Jaffe, *Isolationism and Neutrality in Academe*, 21–59; 82–117.

117. Stenehjem, *An American First*, 79–80.

118. *New York Times*, 22 December 1940, 24.

119. *New York Times*, 24 April 1941, 6; 25 April 1941, 12; James E. Pollard, *History of the Ohio State University* (Columbus, OH: Ohio State University Press, 1952), 352–54.

120. Peckham, *The Making of the University of Michigan*, 202; *New York Times*, 25 February 1941, 11.

121. *New York Times*, 7 February 1941, 8.

122. *New York Times*, 4 February 1941, 8.

123. Jaffe, *Isolationism and Neutrality in Academe*, 318–22.

124. Jaffe, *Isolationism and Neutrality in Academe*, 125–28; 324–330.

125. *New York Times*, 4 March 1941, 1–9.

126. *New York Times*, 5 March 1941, 9.

127. "Policy Pro and Con," *Newsweek* 17 (4 April 1941): 17–19; "Present State and Trends of Public Opinion, *New York Times*, 11 May 1941, sec. 4, 3.

128. *New York Times*, 23 March 1941, sec. 7, 4.

129. *New York Times*, 20 April 1941, 18.

130. *New York Times*, 24 April 1941, 6.

131. *New York Times*, 10 May 1941, 3.

132. *New York Times*, 9 May 1941, 9.

133. Peckham, *The Making of the University of Michigan*, 203–4.

134. *New York Times*, 6 May 1941, 4.

135. *New York Times*, 10 May 1941, 3.

136. Root, *The Princeton Campus in World War II*, 5.

137. Eagan, *The Student Peace Movement in the United States*, 292–95.

138. Root, *The Princeton Campus in World War II*, 9–10.

139. Peckham, *The Making of the University of Michigan*, 203.

140. *New York Times*, 23 October 1941, 3.

141. *New York Times*, 4 November 1941, 4.

142. *New York Times*, 27 November 1941, 26.

143. *New York Times*, 17 August 1941, 27.

144. Root, *The Princeton Campus in World War II*, 8.

145. Hanawalt, *The History of Wayne State University*, 251–52.

146. *New York Times*, 24 October 1941, 6.

147. Galpin and Barck, *Syracuse University*, 3:332; *New York Times*, 30 November 1941, 11.

148. *New York Times*, 6 December 1941, 6.

149. Griffin, *The University of Kansas, A History*, 487.

150. *New York Times*, 9 December 1941, 64.
151. McCormick, *Rutgers University*, 255.
152. Knepper, *One Hundred Years of Urban Higher Education*, 253.
153. Galpin and Barck, *Syracuse University*, 3:304.
154. McGrane, *The University of Cincinnati*, 301–2.
155. *New York Times*, 29 December 1941, 29.

Chapter 5. The Vietnam Era

1. Gail Kennedy, ed., *Education at Amherst* (New York: Harper & Row, 1955), 290–92.
2. Philip G. Altbach and Patti M. Peterson, "Before Berkeley," in Philip G. Altbach and Patti M. Peterson, eds., *The New Pilgrims* (New York: David McKay, 1972), 25.
3. Ellen W. Schrecker, *No Ivory Tower: McCarthyism and the Universities* (New York: Oxford University Press, 1986), 8–11; 338–41.
4. Brubacher and Rudy, *Higher Education in Transition*, 349.
5. Frederick W. Obear, "Student Activism in the Sixties," in Julian Foster and Durward Long, eds., *Protest! Student Activism in America* (NY: W. Morrow & Co., 1970), 14.
6. Obear, "Student Activism in the Sixties," 15.
7. James P. O'Brien, "The Development of the New Left," *Annals of the American Academy of Political and Social Science* 395 (May 1971): 15–25.
8. Edward Bloomburg, *Student Violence* (Washington, DC: Public Affairs Press, 1970), 36–42; John R. Silber, "Respect for the Law on the Campus," *Educational Record*, 51 (Spring 1970): 130–33.
9. Lee, *The Campus Scene, 1900–1970*, 119.
10. William O'Neill, *Coming Apart* (Chicago: Quadrangle Books, 1974), 149–55.
11. Edward J. Bacciocco, *The New Left in America* (Stanford, CA: Hoover Institution Press, 1974), 149–55.
12. Anthony Esler, *Bombs, Beards, and Barricades* (New York: Stein and Day, 1972), 268–69.
13. Bacciocco, *The New Left in America*, 153–54; see also Lee, *The Campus Scene*, 120–21.
14. William J. McGill, *The Year of the Monkey* (New York: McGraw-Hill, 1982), 202–4; Robert Nisbet, *The Degradation of the Academic Dogma* (New York: Basic Books, 1970), 72–74.
15. Lee, *The Campus Scene*, 119–120; Frederick S. Allen, *The University of Colorado* (New York: Harcourt Brace Jovanovich, 1976), 226–28.
16. The quotation by Professor William Petersen of the University of California at Berkeley may be found in Bacciocco, *The New Left in America*, 155.
17. Thomas Powers, *The War at Home* (New York: Grossman Publishers, 1973), 33–35; Sam Angeloff, "Go to V.D.C. House," *Life*, 59 (10 December 1964): 114–15.
18. Bacciocco, *The New Left in America*, 154–55; Powers, *The War at Home*, 34.
19. Obear, "Student Activism in the Sixties," 18; Lee, *The Campus Scene*, 120.
20. Bacciocco, *The New Left in America*, 157.

21. Powers, *The War at Home*, 36–37.

22. Sandy Vogelgesang, *The Long Dark Night of the Soul* (New York: Harper & Row, 1974), 69–75.

23. Helen L. Horowitz, *Campus Life* (New York: Alfred A. Knopf, 1987), 232.

24. Fred Halstead, *Out Now!* (New York: Monad Press, 1978), 21–22; Powers, *The War at Home*, 35; Obear, "Student Activism in the Sixties," 18–19.

25. Halstead, *Out Now!*, 31–32; Powers, *The War at Home*, 53–54.

26. Quotation is from Halstead, *Out Now!*, 33.

27. Louis Menashe and Ronald Radosh, eds., *Teach-Ins, U.S.A.* (New York: Frederick A. Praeger, 1967), 3–4.

28. *New York Times*, 1 March 1965, 17.

29. *New York Times*, 20 February 1965, 2; 2 March 1965, 22.

30. *New York Times*, 3 March 1965, 13.

31. *New York Times*, 3 April 1965, 3.

32. Menashe and Radosh, eds., *Teach-Ins, U.S.A.*, 5–8.

33. *New York Times*, 25 March 1965, 9; 27 March 1965, 47; 9 April 1965, 65; 24 April 1965, 1; Erwin Knoll, "Revolt of the Professors," *Saturday Review* 48 (19 June 1965): 65–66.

34. "Teach-Ins," *New Republic*, 152 (17 April 1965): 9; O'Nell, *Coming Apart*, 142; W. J. Rorabaugh, *Berkeley at War* (New York: Oxford University Press, 1989), 92–94; Menashe and Radosh, eds., *Teach-Ins, U.S.A.*, 11; James Reston, "Washington: The Decline of Serious Debates," in *New York Times*, 21 April 1965, 44.

35. Lee, *The Campus Scene*, 124.

36. See the discussion of "Vietnam Day" in Berkeley in Rorabaugh, *Berkeley at War*, 91–92; also see the letter of Professor Marvin Harris to the Editor of the *New York Times*, 28 April 1965, 44; Menashe and Radosh, eds., *Teach-Ins, U.S.A.*, 96.

37. Menashe and Radosh, eds., *Teach-Ins, U.S.A.*, 11.

38. Mitchel Levitas, "Vietnam Comes to Oregon U," *New York Times Magazine* (9 May 1965): 25–26; 89–92; "Up All Night," *Nation* 200 (31 May 1965): 574.

39. *New York Times*, 15 May 1965, 63; 16 May 1965, 1; "Highbrow to Highbrow," *Newsweek* (65 Nov 24 May 1965): 28; "Keep it Rolling," *Nation* 200 (31 May 1965): 575.

40. *New York Times*, 14 May 1965, 16; 16 May 1965, 62; Elinor Langer, "National Teach-In," *Science* 148 (21 May 1965): 1075–76.

41. Webster Schott, "The Teach-In: New Forum for Reason," *Nation* 200 (31 May 1965): 575–76; Langer, "National Teach-In," 1076.

42. *New York Times*, 24 April 1965, 1; Melvin Small, *Johnson, Nixon, and the Doves* (New Brunswick, NJ: Rutgers University Press, 1988), 36–42; Charles De Benedetti and Charles Chatfield, *An American Ordeal* (Syracuse, NY: Syracuse University Press, 1990), 115–16; 124–26.

43. O'Neill, *Coming Apart*, 143–45.

44. Christopher Lasch, "New Curriculum for the Teach-Ins," *Nation* 201 (18 October 1965): 239–40; Thomas R. Brooks, "Voice of the New Campus 'Underclass,'" *New York Times Magazine* (7 November 1965): 138–39.

45. Powers, *The War at Home*, 72.

46. Powers, *The War at Home*, 72.

47. *New York Times*, 18 April 1965, 1–3; 23 October 1965, 1; 17 November 1965, 1; 43–44; 28 November 1965, 1; Obear, "Student Activism in the Sixties," 18–19.

48. O'Neill, *Coming Apart*, 145; De Benedetti and Chatfield, *An American Ordeal*, 117–20.

49. The quotation is from "They Marched, Doubting They Will Overcome," *New Republic* 152 (30 October 1965): 9; also see Rorabaugh, *Berkeley at War*, 93–95; O'Neill, *Coming Apart*, 144; "The Demonstrators, Why?" *Newsweek* 66 (1 November 1965): 25.

50. *New York Times*, 16 October 1965, 1–2; 17 October 1965, 43; 20 November 1965, 6; Rorabaugh, *Berkeley at War*, 95–98; "The Battle of Vietnam Day," *Newsweek* 66 (25 October 1965): 98.

51. Powers, *The War at Home*, 85; Brooks, "Voice of the New Campus 'Underclass'," 138; "The Demonstrators, Why?" 32; "Storm at Home," *Senior Scholastic* 87 (4 November 1965): 18.

52. Small, *Johnson, Nixon, and the Doves*, 44–46.

53. *New York Times*, 5 May 1965, 16.

54. *New York Times*, 7 May 1965, 2.

55. Allen, *The University of Colorado*, 228–29; Menashe and Radosh, eds., *Teach-Ins, U.S.A.*, 273–78.

56. *New York Times*, 14 November 1966, 41; 13 December 1966, 20; 3 June 1969; 33; "HUAC Eyes the Campus," *Nation* 203 (12 December 1966): 628.

57. *New York Times*, 13 December 1966, 20.

58. *New York Times*, 14 November 1966, 41; Small, *Johnson, Nixon, and the Doves*, 46.

59. "Vietnam: Growing War and Campus Protests Threaten Student Deferments," *Science* 150 (17 December 1965): 1567–68.

60. *New York Times*, 12 January 1966, 8; 30 November 1967, 17; David Caute, *The Year of the Barricades* (New York: Harper & Row, 1988), 129–30; "The Draft in the Ivory Tower," *The Saturday Review* 51 (20 January 1965): 61–62; E. M. Schreiber, "Opposition to the Vietnam War among American Students and Faculty," 293–95.

61. Small, *Johnson, Nixon, and the Doves*, 46–47.

62. *New York Times*, 16 February 1967, 26; Small, *Johnson, Nixon, and the Doves*, 41.

63. Small, *Johnson, Nixon, and the Doves*, 45–46.

64. *New York Times*, 10 December 1965, 1; 16.

65. Small, *Johnson, Nixon, and the Doves*, 45–48.

66. *New York Times*, 16 February 1967, 26; 16 May 1967, 34; Powers, *The War at Home*, 180–82; Small, *Johnson, Nixon, and the Doves*, 47–48.

67. "The Demonstrators, Why?," 25.

68. McGill, *The Year of the Monkey*, 45.

69. See the Associated Press survey published in the *New York Times* for 29 October 1965, 4.

70. Everett Ladd and Seymour Lipset, *The Divided Academy* (New York: McGraw-Hill, 1975), 32.

71. Horowitz, *Campus Life*, 241.

72. Horowitz, *Campus Life*, 241–42.

73. Lee, *The Campus Scene*, 127; 142.

74. "Now a Backlash to Anti-Vietnamese Protests," *U.S. News and World Report* 59 (8 November 1965): 11; *New York Times*, 19 April 1965; 6; 29 April 1965, 22; 18 October 1965, 22; 21 October 1965, 1; 28 October 1965, 1; 14 November 1965, 9; 25 November 1965, 10.

75. Horowitz, *Campus Life*, 238–39.

76. Ladd and Lipset, *The Divided Academy*, 32—33.

77. *New York Times*, 28 April 1968, 73.

78. Horowitz, *Campus Life*, 238; Caute, *The Year of the Barricades*, 375—76.

79. Obear, "Student Activism in the Sixties," 19—20; Brooks, "Voice of the New Campus 'Underclass'," 138; Horowitz, *Campus Life*, 234—36.

80. "The Demonstrators, Why?," 31—32; McGill, *The Year of the Monkey*, 53—55.

81. Alexander Kendrick, *The Wound Within* (Boston: Little, Brown & Co., 1974), 265—69; Esler, *Bombs, Beards, and Barricades* 279—81.

82. These remarks may be found in Bacciocco, *The New Left in America*, 157.

83. Everett C. Ladd, Jr., "Professors and Political Petitions," *Science* 163 (28 March 1969): 1425—27.

84. Ladd, "Professors and Political Petitions," 1426; 1430.

85. Irving Kristal, "Teaching In, Speaking Out: The Controversy Over Vietnam," *Encounter*, 25 (August 1965): 65—70.

86. Ladd, "Professors and Political Petitions" 1426; William F. Buckley, Jr., "Hope in Academe," *Washington Star Syndicate* (1 September 1966).

87. Ladd, "Professors and Political Petitions," 1428.

88. Seymour M. Lipset, "Introduction," in Seymour M. Lipset and Philip G. Altbach, eds., *Students in Revolt* (Boston: Houghton, Mifflin, 1969), xxxii.

89. Robert A. McCaughey, "Opposition to the Vietnam War: A Reconsideration," *Minerva* 14 (August 1976): 320—21.

90. McCaughey, "Opposition to the Vietnam War," 321.

91. "They Said It," *The Saturday Review* 51 (20 January 1968): 61.

92. "They Said It," 61—62.

93. Nisbet, *The Degradation of the Academic Dogma*, 72—74.

94. McCaughey, "Opposition to the Vietnam War," 325—27.

95. Lipset, "Introduction," xxxii.

96. McCaughey, "Opposition to the Vietnam War," 307.

97. *New York Times*, 16 January 1967, 8; 22 January 1967, 9; 3 March 1967, 5; 26 March 1967, Section 4, 7; 28 September 1967, 7; 9 October 1967, 38; 23 January 1969, 15; "A Letter to the President from 462 Yale Faculty Members," *New York Times*, 29 January 1967, Section 4, 5; "To Neutralize South Vietnam — A Proposal," *Princeton Alumni Weekly* 69 (29 October 1968): 9; 15.

98. *New York Times*, 12 October 1969, 1.

99. *New York Times*, 27 September 1969, 1.

100. *New York Times*, 8 October 1969, 1; "Opposition to the War Put on Record," *Science* 166 (17 October 1969): 352.

101. *New York Times*, 30 December 1966, 5; 15; 17 January 1968, 6.

102. Caute, *The Year of the Barricades*, 378—79.

103. *New York Times*, 23 September 1969, 7.

104. Caute, *The Year of the Barricades*, 380—86: Vogelgesang, *The Long Dark Night of the Soul* 70—72.

105. Kerr's statement is quotd in Ladd and Lipset, *The Divided Academy*, 33.

106. Lee, *The Campus Scene*, 127: Horowitz, *Campus Life*, 235—37.

107. Lawrence M. Bashkir and William Straus, *Chance and Circumstance* (New York: Alfred A.. Knopf, 1971), 6: See also Michael Levitas, "2-S — Too Smart to Fight?" *New York Times Magazine*, 24 April 1966, 27, 125—132.

108. *New York Times*, 25 March 1966, 1.

109. "The Draft in the Ivory Tower," 61.

110. Levitas, "2-S — Too Smart to Fight?" 127—32.

111. *New York Times*, 18 May 1966, 11.

112. Jerry L. Avorn, ed., *Up Against the Ivy Wall* (New York: Atheneum Press, 1969), 10–11.

113. *U.S. News and World Report* 59 (8 November 1966): 11; "The Draft in the Ivory Tower," 61.

114. Caute, *The Year of the Barricades*, 128.

115. Richard L. Howell, *Harvard University and the Indo–China War* (Ph.D. Dissertation, Michigan State University, 1988), 22–23.

116. Caute, *The Year of the Barricades*, 128–29.

117. Gene Graham, "Turmoil in the Graduate Schools," *New York Times Magazine* (7 April 1968): 59.

118. "The Draft in the Ivory Tower," 61.

119. Caute, *The Year of the Barricades*, 128–30; 134–36.

120. Lee, *The Campus Scene*, 128–30; Bashkir and Straus, *Chance and Circumstance* 203–5.

121. Myra MacPherson, *Long Time Passing* (Garden City, NY: Doubleday & Co., 1984), 380–83; Bashkir and Straus, *Chance and Circumstance*, 63–66.

122. *New York Times*, 25 March 1966, 3; Lee, *The Campus Scene*, 133–34; Caute, *The Year of the Barricades*, 125–28.

123. Caute, *The Year of the Barricades*, 128–29.

124. Caute, *The Year of the Barricades*, 129–30; 135–36.

125. Bashkir and Straus, *Chance and Circumstance*, 68–75; MacPherson, *Long Time Passing*, 380–82.

126. *New York Times*, 26 March 1966, 2.

127. *New York Times*, 15 April 1967, 17.

128. Rorabaugh, *Berkeley at War*, 120–21.

129. *New York Times*, 11 June 1968, 43.

130. *New York Times*, 13 June 1968, 14.

131. Noel Perrin, "College Seniors and the War," *New Yorker* 44 (20 July 1968): 57–58.

132. *New York Times*, 10 June 1969, 49.

133. *New York Times*, 3 June 1969, 15.

134. Caute, *The Year of the Barricades*, 129–30.

135. Brooks, "Voice of the New Campus 'Underclass'," 138–39.

136. Caute, *The Year of the Barricades*, 128.

137. MacPherson, *Long Time Passing*, 144.

138. Caute, *The Year of the Barricades*, 128–29.

139. MacPherson, *Long Time Passing*, 144–45.

140. Perrin, "College Seniors and the War," 7–8; 29–33.

141. Bashkir and Straus, *Change and Circumstance*, 7–8.

142. *New York Times*, 29 October 1965, 3.

143. Brooks, "Voice of the New Campus 'Underclass'," 137–39.

144. "The ABC's of 'Draft Dodging,'" *Newsweek* 66 (1 November 1965): 32; Levitas, "2-S – Too Smart to Fight?" 129.

145. Lee, *The Campus Scene*, 129–30; Perrin, "College Seniors and the War," 59.

146. Caute, *The Year of the Barricades*, 127–28.

147. Bashkir and Straus, *Chance and Circumstance*, 29–30.

148. Bashkir and Straus, *Chance and Circumstance*, 31–33.

149. Lawrence S. Wittner, *Cold War America* (New York: Holt, Rinehart & Winston, 1978), 351–54.

150. De Benedetti and Chatfield, *An American Ordeal*, 230–33; Wittner, *Cold War America*, 352–56.

151. Wittner, *Cold War America*, 350–53.

152. Bashkir and Straus, *Chance and Circumstance*, 27–29.

153. *New York Times*, 7 August 1966, 3; 28 February 1967, 18; 11 May 1967, 9; 10 October 1967, 2; 22 October 1967, 58.

154. *New York Times*, 27 May 1968, 1–2; 20.

155. *New York Times*, 16 October 1969, 14–15; 19.

156. *New York Times*, 16 November 1969, 1; 21; Wittner, *Cold War America*, 352; Thomas M. Gannon, "A Report on the Vietnam Moratorium," *America* 121 (1 November 1969): 380–82.

157. Donald T. Williams, "The Awesome Effectiveness of Confrontation," *Educational Record* 51 (Spring 1970): 130–33; Kendrick, *The Wound Within*, 265–66.

158. *New York Times*, 16 November 1966, 5.

159. *New York Times*, 8 November 1966, 1; 20.

160. Philip C. Altbach and Patti Peterson, "Before Berkeley: Historical Perspectives on Student Activism," *Annals of the American Academy of Political and Social Science* 395 (May 1971): 1–14; Lee, *The Campus Scene*, 135.

161. Mark Rudd, "Symbols of the Revolution," in Avorn, ed., *Up Against the Ivy Wall*, 291.

162. Powers, *The War at Home*, 181–82.

163. Herbert A. Deane, "Reflections on Student Radicalism," in Avorn, ed., *Up Against the Ivy Wall*, 286–87; Lee, *The Campus Scene* 136–37; Carnegie Commission on Higher Education, *Dissent and Disruption* (New York: McGraw-Hill, 1971), 78–79.

164. Gabriel Kolko, "Untangling the Alliances," *Nation*, No. 205 (18 December 1967): 645–46.

165. *New York Times*, 24 October 1967, 1.

166. Julian Foster and Durward Long, eds., *Protest!* (New York: William Morrow & Co., 1970), 20–22.

167. Kolko, "Untangling the Alliances," 646–48.

168. John Walsh, "Confrontation at Stanford: Exit Classified Research," *Science* 164 (2 May 1969): 534–36; Lee, *The Campus Scene*, 134.

169. "Go Back! Go Back!" *Newsweek* 174 (17 November 1969): 79–80.

170. Lee, *The Campus Scene*, 134.

171. Howell, *Harvard University and the Indo-China War*, 46.

172. Howell, *Harvard University and the Indo-China War*, 48–49.

173. Michael Bezilla, *Penn State, An Informal History* (University Park, PA: Pennsylvania State University Press, 1985), 296–97; 350–51.

174. *New York Times*, 23 February 1970, 24.

175. "Go Back! Go Back!," 79–80.

176. Foster and Long, eds., *Protest!*, 20; John L. Shover, "Preparation for Dow Day," *Nation* 205 (18 December 1967): 648–49.

177. *New York Times*, 2 February 1969, 53.

178. *New York Times*, 12 March 1969, 30; 1 April 1969, 38; 3 April 1969, 39; 5 April 1969, 1.

179. *New York Times*, 19 October 1967, 18.

180. Robert J. Samuelson, "War on Campus: What Happened when Dow Recruited at Harvard," *Science* 158 (8 December 1967): 1289–93.

181. *New York Times*, 21 November 1967, 8.

182. *New York Times*, 19 March 1968, 27.

183. *New York Times*, 15 November 1967, 10.

184. *New York Times*, 2 November 1967, 95; Conrad Hilberry, "Civil Disobedience at Oberlin," *Educational Record* 49 (Spring 1968): 132−37.

185. Kolko, "Untangling the Alliances," 647.

186. Avorn, ed., *Up Against the Ivy Wall*, 11; *New York Times*, 2 November 1967, 95; 15 February 1968, 30.

187. Howell, *Harvard University and the Indo-China War*, 39.

188. Lee, *The Campus Scene*, 134−35; *New York Times*, 16 April 1969, 53; 28 April 1969, 29.

189. Bezilla, *Penn State*, 297−98.

190. *New York Times*, 16 April 1969, 53.

191. Howell, *Harvard University and the Indo-China War*, 79−80.

192. *New York Times*, 25 April 1969, 29.

193. Halstead, *Out Now!*, 526−33; Lee, *The Campus Scene*, 135.

194. Perrin, "College Seniors and the War," 58−59.

195. Lee, *The Campus Scene*, 135−36.

196. *New York Times*, 14 March 1968, 45; 28 April 1968, 1; 12 May, 1968, 1; 69; Bacciocco, *The New Left in America*, 202−06; Caute, *The Year of the Barricades*, 165−72.

197. *New York Times*, 22 May 1968, 32; Caute, *The Year of the Barricades*, 173−80.

198. Kendrick, *The Wound Within*, 265−66; 290−92; *New York Times*, 5 June 1967, 24; 22 May 1968, 32.

199. Irwin Unger, *The Movement: A History of the American New Left* (New York: Dodd, Mead and Co., 1975), 114−15.

200. Horowitz, *Campus Life*, 294−95.

201. Alan E. Bayer and Alexander W. Astin, "Violence and Disruption on the U.S. Campus, 1968−1969," *Educational Record* 50 (Fall 1969): 344−45.

202. *New York Times*, 12 May 1968, 1−2; 69.

203. *New York Times*, 13 April 1969, 62; Lee, *The Campus Scene*, 140; "Harvard and Beyond: The University under Siege," *Time* 94 (18 April 1969): 47−48.

204. *New York Times*, 19 September 1969, 28; Seymour Lipset and David Riesman, *Education and Politics at Harvard* (New York: McGraw-Hill Book Co., 1975), 212−29.

205. *New York Times*, 26 September 1969, 95; Howell, *Harvard University and the Indo-China War*, 53−94; 156−57; "Turmoil at the Harvard Semitic Museum," *Biblical Archeology Review* 20 (March-April 1994): 64−65.

206. Wittner, *Cold War America*, 352−54.

207. Rorabaugh, *Berkeley at War*, 160−62.

208. Wittner, *Cold War America*, 354−55.

209. Caute, *The Year of the Barricades*, 425; 427; *New York Times*, 8 October 1992, Section B, 29.

210. *New York Times*, 5 December 1968, 2.

211. *New York Times*, 25 August 1970, 1.

212. *New York Times*, 2 May 1970, 1; 3 May 1970, 5; 5 May 1970, 18.

213. *New York Times*, 24 June 1970, 29; "The Events of May," *Princeton Alumni Weekly* 70 (19 May 1970): 8−13; Halstead, *Out Now!*, 561.

214. *New York Times*, 2 May 1970, 1; 5 May 1970, 1.

215. *New York Times*, 3 May 1970, 5; 4 May 1970, 11; 5 May 1970, 1; 17.

216. *New York Times*, 6 May 1970, 1.

217. McGill, *The Year of the Monkey*, 202; *New York Times*, 9 May 1970, 10.
218. Rorabaugh, *Berkeley at War*, 169.
219. Small, *Johnson, Nixon, and the Doves*, 201–3.
220. *New York Times*, 16 May 1970, 1; 5.
221. *New York Times*, 2 October 1970, 1; 5 October 1970, 1; 38.
222. Halstead, *Out Now!*, 556–58.
223. Lipset, *Passion and Politics*, 195.
224. Horowitz, *Campus Life*, 19.
225. Small, *Johnson, Nixon, and the Doves*, 211.
226. Paul K. Conkin, *Gone with the Ivy* (Knoxville, TN: University of Tennessee Press, 1985), 630.
227. Stephen R. Weissman, "No Retreat from Commitment," *Nation* 216 (18 June 1973): 781–82.
228. Seymour M. Lipset, "The American University, 1964–1974," in Paul Seabury, ed., *Universities in the Western World* (New York: Free Press, 1975), 143–44.
229. "From Rags to Reform," *Time* 96 (30 November 1970): 38.
230. Brubacher and Rudy, *Higher Education in Transition*, 353.
231. Gianni Statera, *Death of a Utopia* (New York: Oxford University Press, 1975), 219–20.
232. Arthur Levine, *When Dreams and Heroes Died* (San Francisco: Jossey-Bass Publishers, 1980), 118.
233. Ladd and Lipset, *The Divided Academy*, 300.
234. Riesman's evaluation is quoted in Lipset, *Passion and Politics*, 195.
235. Lipset, "The American University, 1964–1974," 146.
236. Weissman, "No Retreat from Commitment," 783.
237. Lipset, "The American University, 1964–1974," 146–47.
238. "From Rags to Reform," 38.
239. Lipset, "The American University, 1964–1974," 146.
240. Caute, *The Year of the Barricades*, 310–11.
241. Wittner, *Cold War America*, 354–355.
242. Quotation may be found in O'Neill, *Coming Apart*, 292. O'Neill explains that the New Left extremists had developed an argot, "borrowed largely from the Ghetto."
243. Bacciocco, *The New Left in America*, 215; O'Neill, *Coming Apart*, 294; *New York Times*, 26 November 1968, 10.
244. Caute, *The Year of the Barricades*, xiii; "Columbia Alumni Quietly Recall '68 Protest": *New York Times*, 25 April 1988, 32.
245. Bacciocco, *The New Left in America*, 221.
246. *New York Times*, 15 November 1968; 29; 25 April 1969, 29; 30 April 1969, 29–30; 14 January 1970, 13.
247. Halstead, *Out Now!* 681–82.
248. *New York Times*, 6 February 1970, 7.
249. *New York Times*, 16 April 1970, 1; 44.
250. *New York Times*, 17 April 1970, 42.
251. *New York Times*, 17 April 1970, 42; Howell, *Harvard University and the Indo-China War*, 144–46.
252. Small, *Johnson, Nixon, and the Doves*, 174.
253. See Tom Bates, *RADS: The 1970 Bombing of the Army Math Research Center at the University of Wisconsin* (New York: Harper Collins, 1992), 185–210.
254. Todd Gitlin, "Home Front Resistance to the Vietnam War," in Harrison

E. Salisbury, ed., *Vietnam Reconsidered: Lessons from a War* (New York: Harper & Row, 1984), 73.

255. Robert A. Nisbet, "Who Killed the Student Revolution?" *Encounter* 34 (February 1970): 17.

256. Lee, *The Campus Scene*, 140–142; O'Neill, *Coming Apart*, 303–4.

257. Nisbet, "Who Killed the Student Revolution?" 18; Avorn, ed., *Up Against the Ivy Wall*, 289–290; Small, *Johnson, Nixon, and the Doves*, 174–75; *New York Times*, 28 September 1967, 20.

258. *New York Times*, 18 September 1969, 12; Samuel Lubell, "That Generation Gap," in Daniel Bell and Irving Kristol, eds., *Confrontation: The Student Rebellion and the Universities* (New York: Basic Books, 1969), 66–68;

259. C. Vann Woodward, "What Became of the 1960s?" *New Republic* 171 (9 November 1974): 18–21; Lubell, "That Generation Gap," 67.

260. *New York Times*, 24 January 1973, 1; 28 January 1973, 1.

261. Richard J. Walton, "The Last March," *Nation* 216 (5 February 1973): 164.

262. Ladd, "Professors and Political Petitions," 1425.

263. Halstead, *Out Now!*, 709; see also Powers, *The War at Home*, 180–81.

264. Quotation may be found in De Benedetti and Chatfield, *An American Ordeal*, 217.

265. Foster and Long, eds., *Protest!*, 22–23.

266. Howell, *Harvard University and the Indo-China War*, 220–21.

267. *Crisis at Columbia: Report of the Fact-Finding Commission* (New York: Vintage Books, 1968), 10.

268. *New York Times*, 16 July 1970, 1.

269. Foster and Long, eds., *Protest!*, 9–10; O'Neill, *Coming Apart*, 244–45; 303–4; Ladd and Lipset, *The Divided Academy*, 25–26.

270. This quotation is from Gitlin, "Home Front Resistance to the Vietnam War," 73.

271. McGill, *The Year of the Monkey*, 202–3; Kolko, "Untangling the Alliances," 648–49.

272. Lee, *The Campus Scene*, 129–31.

273. This quotation may be found in Lipset, *Rebellion in the Universities*, 14.

Chapter 6. Comparisons and Conclusions

1. This quotation from *The Journal of the Pennsylvania House of Representatives*, 1782, may be found in Roche, *The Colonial Colleges in the War for American Independence*, 148.

2. Ladd and Lipset, *The Divided Academy*, 303.

Bibliography

Primary Sources

"Affairs at Princeton College," and "The Charge on Nassau Hall," *Newark Daily Advertiser*, 11 September 1863, Princeton: Princeton University Archives, Clippings Collection.

Attwood, William H. "Gypped Out of Future," *NEA Service*. Princeton: Princeton University Archives, World War II Collection, 1941.

Bogart, John. *Letters, 1776–1782, With Notes*. New Brunswick, NJ: Rutgers College, 1914.

Boyd, Julian P., ed. *The Papers of Thomas Jefferson*, Vol. 2. Princeton: Princeton University Press, 1950.

Calder, Isabel, M., ed. *Letters and Papers of Ezra Stiles*. New Haven: Yale University Library, 1933.

"Civil War Times at College," *New York Sun*, 14 May 1911. Princeton: Princeton University Archives, Civil War Collection.

Collegiate Anti-Militarism League, *A Letter, And a Reply*. San Francisco: The Blair and Murdock Printers, 1915.

Cox Commission. *Crisis at Columbia: Report of the Fact–Finding Commission*. New York: Vintage Books, 1968.

Digest of Reports of the Carnegie Commission on Higher Education. New York: McGraw-Hill Book Co., 1974.

Guild, Reuben A. *Life, Times, and Correspondence of James Manning*. Boston: Gould and Lincoln, 1864.

Hutchinson, William T., and William M. S. Rachal, eds., *Papers of James Madison*, Vol. 1. Chicago: University of Chicago Press, 1962.

Hein. David, ed. *The Letters of W. Wilkins Davis, 1842–1866: A Student's View of the College of St. James on the eve of the Civil War*. Lewiston, NY: Edwin Mellen Press, 1988.

Mathis, Ray, ed. *Uncle Tom Reed's Memoir of the University of Georgia*. Athens: University of Georgia Libraries, 1974.

Morse, Richard M. "Letter to his Parents," 26 February 1944 (Ms). Princeton: Princeton University Archives, World War II Collection.

Root, Robert K. *The Princeton Campus in World War II* (Ms). Princeton: Princeton University Archives, 1950.

Sabine, William H. W., ed. *Historical Memoirs of William Smith, 1778–1783*. New York: Arno Press, 1971.

Smith, Daniel E. H. *A Charlestonian's Recollections, 1846–1913*. Charleston, SC: Carolina Art Association, 1950.

Smith, Horace Wemyss. *Life and Correspondence of the Rev. William Smith, D. D.*, Vol. 2. Philadelphia: Ferguson Bros. & Co., 1880.

Stillé, Charles J. *A Memoir of the Rev. William Smith*. Philadelphia: Moore & Sons, 1869.

Willard, Joseph. "The Duty of the Good and Faithful Soldier," A Sermon preached at Mendon, 25 March 1781. Boston: T&J Fleet, 1781.

Biographical Dictionaries and Collections

Dictionary of American Biography

Shipton, Clifford K., ed., *New England Life in the 18th Century: Lives of Harvard College Graduates*. Cambridge, MA: Belknap Press of Harvard University Press, 1963.

Newspapers

New York Times
   1860–1865
   1914–1917
   1932–1941
   1963–1973

Dissertations and Theses

Cooper, John M., Jr. "The Vanity of Power: 1914–1917.: Dissertation. Columbia University, 1968.

Eagan, Eileen M. "The Student Peace Movement in the United States: 1930–1941." Dissertation. Temple University, 1979.

Howell, Richard L. "Harvard University and the Indochina War." Dissertation. Michigan State University, 1988.

Jaffe, Joseph L., Jr. "Isolation and Neutrality in *Academe*: 1938–1941." Dissertation. Case Western Reserve University, 1979.

Rodin, Doris G. "Opposition to Military Training in Schools and Colleges in the United States: 1914–1940." Master's Thesis. American University, 1949.

Stillman, Rachel B. "Education in the Confederate States of America: 1861–1865." Dissertation. Illinois University, 1972.

Williams, Lorraine A. "The Civil War and Intellectuals of the North." Dissertation. American University, 1955.

Books

Adams, J. Donald. *Copey of Harvard: A Biography of Charles Townsend Copeland*. Boston: Houghton, Mifflin Co., 1960.

Alberts, Robert C. *Pitt: The Story of the University of Pittsburgh, 1787–1987*. Pittsburgh: University of Pittsburgh Press, 1986.

Allen, Frederick I., et al. *The University of Colorado, 1876–1976*. New York: Harcourt Brace Jovanovich, 1976.

Altbach, Philip G., and Robert S. Laufer. *The New Pilgrims: Youth Protest in Transition*. New York: David McKay, 1972.

Altbach, Philip G., ed. *University Reform*. Cambridge, MA: Schenkman Publishing Co., 1974.

Austin, Mary S. *Philip Freneau: The Poet of the Revolution*. Detroit: Gale Research Co., 1968.

Avorn, Jerry L. *Up Against the Ivy Wall: A History of the Columbia Crisis*. New York: Atheneum Press, 1969.

Bacciocco, Edward J., Jr. *The New Left in America: Reform to Revolution, 1956 to 1970*. Stanford, CA: Hoover Institution Press, 1974.

Bander, Edward J., ed. *Turmoil on the Campus*. New York: H. W. Wilson Co., 1970.

Baritz, Loren. *Backfire*. New York: William Morrow, 1985.

Barnard, John. *From Evangelicalism to Progressivism at Oberlin College: 1866–1917*. Columbus: Ohio State University, 1969.

Barnes, Gilbert H. *The Anti-Slavery Impulse: 1830–1844* (1938). Gloucester, MA: Peter Smith, 1957.

Bashkir, Lawrence M., and William A. Straus, *Chance and Circumstance: The Draft, The War, and The Vietnam Generation*. New York: Alfred A. Knopf, 1978.

Beach, Arthur G. *A Pioneer College: The Story of Marietta*. N.P.: Privately printed, 1935.

Bechtel, Paul M. *Wheaton College: A Heritage Remembered*. Wheaton, IL: Harold Shaw Publishers, 1984.

Bell, Daniel, and Irving Kristol, eds. *Confrontation: The Student Rebellion and the Universities*. New York: Basic Books, 1969.

Benet, Stephen Vincent. *The Beginning of Wisdom*. New York: Holt, Rinehart & Winston, 1921.

Bezilla, Michael. *Penn State: An Illustrated History*. University Park: Pennsylvania State University Press, 1985.

Bishop, Morris. *A History of Cornell*. Ithaca, NY: Cornell University Press, 1962.

Bloomberg, Edward. *Student Violence*. Washington, DC: Public Affairs Press, 1970.

Bohi, Mary. *History of Wisconsin State University, Whitewater*. Whitewater: Whitewater State University Foundation, 1967.

Bone, Winsted, P. *A History of Cumberland University*. Lebanon, TN: Published by the author, 1935.

Bowden, Mary W. *Philip Freneau*. Boston: Twayne Publishers, 1976.

Bradshaw, Herbert C. *History of Hampden-Sidney College*, Vol. 1. Durham, NC: Seeman Printery, 1976.

Bronson, Walter C. *History of Brown University: 1764–1914*. Providence: Brown University, 1914.

Brooks, Robert P. *The University of Georgia*. Athens: University of Georgia Press, 1956.

Brubacher, John S., and Willis Rudy. *Higher Education in Transition*. New York: Harper & Row, 1976.

Bruce, Philip A. *History of the University of Virginia*, Vols. 3 and 5. New York: Macmillan, 1921 and 1922.

Brunhouse, Robert L. *The Counter-Revolution in Pennsylvania: 1776–1790*. New York: Octagon Books, 1971.

Cabaniss, Allen. *The University of Mississippi: Its First Hundred Years*. Hattiesburg: University and College Press of Mississippi, 1971.

Calkins, Ernest E. *They Broke the Prairie*. New York: Scribner's, 1937.

Callcott, George H. *A History of the University of Maryland*. Baltimore, Maryland Historical Society, 1966.

Canby, Henry S. *Alma Mater: The Gothic Age of the American College*. New York: Farrar, Straus & Giroux, 1936.

Carey, James C. *Kansas State University: The Quest for Identity*. Lawrence: The Regents Press of Kansas, 1977.

Cary, Harold W. *The University of Massachusetts: A History of One Hundred Years*. Amherst: University of Massachusetts, 1962.

Caute, David. *The Year of the Barricades*. New York: Harper & Row, 1988.

Chadwin, Mark L. *The Hawks of World War II*. Chapel Hill: University of North Carolina Press, 1968.

Chaffin, Nora C. *Trinity College: 1839–1892*. Durham, NC: Duke University Press, 1950.

Chamberlin, Ralph V. *The University of Utah: 1850–1950*. Salt Lake City: University of Utah Press, 1960.

Chatfield, Charles. *For Peace and Justice, 1914–1941*. Boston: Beacon Press, 1973.

Chessman, G. Wallace. *Ohio Colleges and the Civil War*. Columbus: Ohio State University Press, 1963.

Cheyney, Edward P. *History of the University of Pennsylvania: 1740–1940*. Philadelphia: University of Pennsylvania Press, 1940.

Clark, Harry H. *The Poems of Philip Freneau*. New York: Hafner Publishing Co., 1929.

Clark, Thomas D. *Indiana University: Midwestern Pioneer*, Vols. 1, 2, and 3. Bloomington: Indiana University Press, 1970, 1973, 1977.

Clough, Wilson O. *History of the University of Wyoming: 1887–1937*. Laramie: University of Wyoming, 1937.

Cole, Arthur C. *A Hundred Years of Mount Holyoke College*. New Haven: Yale University Press, 1940.

Cole, Arthur C. *The Irrepressible Conflict: 1850–1865*. New York: Macmillan, 1934.

Cole, Wayne S. *America First: The Battle Against Intervention*. Madison: University of Wisconsin Press, 1953.

Conant, James B. *My Several Lives*. New York: Harper & Row, 1970.

Conkin, Paul K. *Gone with the Ivy: A Biography of Vanderbilt University*. Knoxville: University of Tennessee Press, 1985.

Coon, Horace. *Columbia: Colossus on the Hudson*. New York: E.P. Dutton, 1947.

Coulter, E. Merton. *College Life in the Old South*. Athens: University of Georgia Press, 1951.

Coulton, Thomas E. *A City College in Action*. New York: Harper & Bros., 1955.

Couper, William. *One Hundred Years at V.M.I.*, Vol. 2. Richmond, VA: Garrett and Massie, 1939.

Cowie, Alexander. *John Trumbull: Connecticut Wit*. Westport, CT: Greenwood Press, 1972.

Cremin, Lawrence A. *American Education: The Colonial Experience*. New York: Harper & Row, 1970.

Cummins, Cedric. *The University of South Dakota: 1862–1966*. Vermillion, SD: Dakota Press, 1975.

Cunningham, John T. *University in the Forest: The Story of Drew University*. Florham Park, NJ: Afton Publishing Co., 1972.

Curti, Merle E. *Peace or War: The American Struggle*. New York: Garland Publishing, Inc., 1972.

Curti, Merle E., and Vernon Carstensen, *The University of Wisconsin: A History*, Vols. 1 and 2. Madison: University of Wisconsin Press, 1949.

Dabney, Virginius. *Mr. Jefferson's University: A History*. Charlottesville: University Press of Virginia, 1981.

De Benedetti, Charles with Charles Chatfield, *An American Ordeal*. Syracuse: Syracuse University Press, 1990.

De Benedetti, Charles. *The Peace Reform in American History*. Bloomington: Indiana University Press, 1980.

Demarest, William H. S. *A History of Rutgers College: 1766–1924*. New Brunswick, NJ: Rutgers College, 1924.

Dillon, Merton L. *Elijah P. Lovejoy: Abolitionist Editor*. Urbana: University of Illinois Press, 1961.

Dubbs, Joseph H. *History of Franklin and Marshall College*. Lancaster, PA: Franklin and Marshall College Alumni Association, 1903.

Dumond, Dwight L. *Anti-Slavery Origins of the Civil War*. Ann Arbor: University of Michigan Press, 1939.

Dunaway, Wayland F. *History of the Pennsylvania State College*. Lancaster: Pennsylvania State College, 1946.

Dunigan, David R. *A History of Boston College*. Milwaukee, WI: Bruce Publishing Co., 1947.

Durkin, Joseph T. *Georgetown University*. Garden City, NY: Doubleday, 1964.

Dyer, Thomas G. *The University of Georgia: A Bicentennial History*. Athens: University of Georgia Press, 1985.

Dyson, Walter. *Howard University: The Capstone of Negro Education*. Washington, DC: The Graduate School of Howard University, 1941.

Earnest, Ernest. *Academic Procession*. Indianapolis, IN: Bobbs-Merrill, 1953.

Easterby, James H. *History of the College of Charleston*. Charleston, SC: The College of Charleston, 1935.

Eaton, Edward D. *Historical Sketches of Beloit College*. New York: A. S. Barnes, 1935.

Ekirch, Arthur A., Jr. *The Civilian and the Military: A History of the American Antimilitarist Tradition*. Colorado Springs: Ralph Myles, Publisher, 1972.

Eliot, Ellsworth, Jr. *Yale in the Civil War*. New Haven, CT: Yale University Press, 1932.

Eschenbacher, Herman F. *The University of Rhode Island*. New York: Appleton-Century-Crofts, 1967.

Esler, Anthony. *Bombs, Beards, and Barricades*. New York: Stein and Day, 1972.

Fashing, Joseph J., and Steven E. Deutsch. *Academics in Retreat*. Albuquerque: University of New Mexico Press, 1971.

Finnegan, John P. *Against the Specter of a Dragon: The Campaign for American Military Preparedness*. Westport, CT: Greenwood Press, 1974.

Fisher, George P. *Life of Benjamin Silliman*, Vol. 2. New York: Scribner's, 1866.

Fisk, William L. *A History of Muskingum College*. New Concord, OH: Muskingum College, 1978.

Fleming, Walter L. *Louisiana State University: 1860–1896*. Baton Rouge: Louisiana State University Press, 1936.

Fletcher, Robert S. *History of Oberlin College*, Vols. 1 and 2 (1943). New York: Arno Press, 1971.

Foster, Julian, and Durward Long eds. *Protest! Student Activism in America*. New York: William Morrow & Co., 1970.

Frank, Charles E. *Pioneer's Progress: Illinois College, 1859–1979*. Carbondale: Southern Illinois University Press, 1979.

Freidel, Frank. *Francis Lieber: Nineteenth-Century Liberal*. Baton Rouge: Louisiana State University Press, 1947.

Fuess, Claude M. *Amherst: The Story of a New England College*. Boston: Little, Brown and Co., 1935.

Galpin, W. Freeman and Oscar T. Barck, Jr. *Syracuse University*, Vols. 2 and 3. Syracuse: Syracuse University Press, 1960, 1984.

Gannon, Robert I. *Up to the Present: The Story of Fordham*. Garden City, NY: Doubleday, 1967.

Gates, Charles M. *The First Century of the University of Washington*. Seattle: University of Washington Press, 1961.

Gegenheimer, Albert F. *William Smith: Educator and Churchman*. Philadelphia: University of Pennsylvania Press, 1943.

Geiger, Louis G. *University of the Northern Plains: A History of the University of North Dakota*. Grand Forks: University of North Dakota Press, 1958.

Gerlach, Larry R. *Prologue to Independence*. New Brunswick, NJ: Rutgers University Press, 1976.

Giffin, Frederick C. *Six Who Protested: Radical Opposition to the First World War*. Port Washington, NY: Kennikat Press, 1977.

Glatfelter, Charles H. *A Salutary Influence: Gettysburg College, 1832–1985*, Vols. 1 and 2. Gettysburg, PA: Gettysburg College, 1987.

Gray, James. *The University of Minnesota: 1851–1951*. Minneapolis: University of Minnesota Press, 1951.

Green, Edwin L. *A History of the University of South Carolina*. Columbia: The State Company, 1916.

Griffin, Clifford S. *The University of Kansas: A History*. Lawrence: University Press of Kansas, 1974.

Gruber, Carol S. *Mars and Minerva*. Baton Rouge: Louisiana State University Press, 1975.

Guild, Reuben A. *History of Brown University*. Providence, RI: Providence Press Company, 1867.

Hackett, Alice P. *Wellesley: Part of the American Story*. New York: E.P. Dutton, 1949.

Halstead, Fred. *Out Now! A Participant's Account*. New York: Monad Press, 1978.

Hamilton, Raphael N. *The Story of Marquette University*. Milwaukee: The Marquette University Press, 1953.

Hanawalt, Leslie L. *A Place of Light: The History of Wayne State University*. Detroit: Wayne State University Press, 1968.

Harrison, Lowell H. *Western Kentucky University*. Lexington: The University Press of Kentucky, 1967.

Hatch, Louis C. *The History of Bowdoin College*. Portland, ME: Loring, Short, & Harmon, 1927.

Havighurst, Walter. *The Miami Years, 1809–1959*. New York: G.P. Putnam's, 1958.

Hawke, David F. *Benjamin Rush: Revolutionary Gadfly*. Indianapolis: Bobbs-Merrill, 1971.

Headley, Leal, and Merrill E. Jarchow, *Carleton: The First Century*. Northfield, MN: Carleton College, 1966.

Hicken, Victor. *The Purple and the Gold: The Story of Western Illinois University*. Macomb: Western Illinois University Foundation, 1970.

Hofstadter, Rochard, and Wilson Smith, eds. *American Higher Education: A Documentary History*, Vol. 1. Chicago: University of Chicago Press, 1961.

Hollis, Daniel W. *The University of South Carolina*, Vols. 1 and 2. Columbia: University of South Carolina Press, 1951, 1956.

Hoover, Thomas N. *History of Ohio University*. Athens: Ohio University Press, 1954.

Hope, Arthur J. *Notre Dame: One Hundred Years*. South Bend, IN: Icarus Press, 1978.

Horowitz, Helen L. *Campus Life*. New York: Knopf, 1987.

Humphrey, David C. *From King's College to Columbia, 1747–1800*. New York: Columbia University Press, 1976.

Jaffe, A. J. and Walter Adams. *Negro Higher Education in the 1960's*. New York: Frederick A. Praeger, 1968.

Jencks, Christopher and David Riesman. *The Academic Revolution*. Garden City, NY: Doubleday, 1968.

Johnpoll, Bernard K., ed. *Norman Thomas on War, An Anthology*. New York: Garland Publishers, 1974.

Johnson, Donald. *The Challenge to American Freedoms: World War I and the Rise of the American Civil Liberties Union*. Lexington: University of Kentucky Press, 1963.

Johnson, Walter. *The Battle Against Isolation*. Chicago: University of Chicago Press, 1944.

Kelley, Brooks M. *Yale: A History*. New Haven: Yale University Press, 1974.

Kendrick, Alexander. *The Wound Within*. Boston: Little, Brown & Co., 1974.

Kennedy, Gail., ed. *Education at Amherst*. New York: Harper & Row, 1955.

Kinnear, Duncan L. *The First 100 Years: Virginia Polytechnic Institute*. Blacksburg: Virginia Polytechnic Institute Educational Foundation, 1972.

Knepper, George W. *New Lamps for Old*. Akron, OH: The University of Akron, 1970.

Koelsch, William A. *Clark University: 1887–1987*. Worcester, MA: Clark University Press, 1987.

Ladd, Everett C. and Seymour M. Lipset. *The Divided Academy*. New York: McGraw-Hill, 1975.

Leary, Lewis. *That Rascal Freneau*. New Brunswick, NJ: Rutgers University Press, 1941.

Lee, Calvin B. T. *The Campus Scene: 1900–1970*. New York: David McKay, 1970.

Leitch, Alexander. *A Princeton Companion*. Princeton, NJ: Princeton University Press, 1978.

Levine, Arthur. *When Dreams and Heroes Died*. San Francisco: Jossey-Bass, 1980.

Lindsay, Julian I. *Tradition Looks Forward: The University of Vermont, A History*. Burlington: University of Vermont, 1954.

Lipset, Seymour M., and Gerald M. Schaflander. *Passion and Politics: Student Activism in America*. Boston: Little, Brown & Co., 1972.

Lipset, Seymour M. *Rebellion in the University*. Chicago: University of Chicago Press, 1976.

Lipset, Seymour M. and Philip C. Altbach, eds. *Students in Revolt*. Boston: Houghton Mifflin, 1969.

Lipset, Seymour M. and David Riesman. *Education and Politics at Harvard*. New York: McGraw-Hill, 1975.

McCormick, Richard P. *Rutgers: A Bicentennial History*. New Brunswick, NJ: Rutgers University Press, 1966.

McDevitt, Gerald. *The University of Santa Clara*. Stanford, CA: Stanford University Press, 1979.

McGill, William J. *The Year of the Monkey: Revolt on Campus, 1968–1969*. New York: McGraw-Hill, 1982.

McGrane, Reginald C. *The University of Cincinnati*. New York: Harper & Row, 1963.

MacPherson, Myra. *Long Time Passing: Vietnam and the Haunted Generation*. Garden City, NY: Doubleday, 1984.

Malone, Dumas. *Jefferson the Virginian*. Boston: Little, Brown & Co., 1948.

Marriner, Ernest C. *The History of Colby College*. Waterville, ME: Colby College Press, 1963.

Marston, Philip M., ed. *The History of the University of New Hampshire*. Durham: The University of New Hampshire, 1941.

May, Arthur J. *History of the University of Rochester*. Rochester: University of Rochester, 1977.

Meigs, Cornelia. *What Makes a College? A History of Bryn Mawr*. New York: Macmillan, 1956.

Meiners, Fredericka. *A History of Rice University.* Houston: Rice University Studies, 1982.

Menashe, Louis and Ronald Radosh eds., *Teach-Ins, U.S.A.* New York: Frederick A. Praeger, 1967.

Michener, James A. *Kent State: What Happened and Why.* New York: Random House, 1971.

Miller, Howard. *The Revolutionary College.* New York: New York University Press, 1976.

Miller, James A. *Democracy in the Streets.* New York: Simon and Schuster, 1987.

Miller, Russell E. *Light on the Hill: A History of Tufts College.* Boston: Beacon Press, 1966.

Morgan, Edmund S. *The Gentle Puritan: A Life of Ezra Stiles.* New Haven: Yale University Press, 1962.

Morgan, James H. *Dickinson College: The History of One Hundred Fifty Years, 1783–1933.* Carlisle, PA: Dickinson College, 1933.

Morison, Samuel E. *Three Centuries of Harvard.* Cambridge, MA: Harvard University Press, 1936.

Nollen, John S. *Grinnell College.* Iowa City: The State Historical Society of Iowa, 1953.

Notestein, Lucy L. *Wooster of the Middle West*, Vol. 2. Wooster, OH: The College of Wooster, 1971.

Novak, Stephen J. *The Rights of Youth.* Cambridge, MA: Harvard University Press, 1977.

Oliphant, James O. *Rise of Bucknell University.* New York: Appleton-Century-Crofts, 1965.

O'Neill, William L. *Coming Apart: An Informal History of America in the 1960s.* Chicago: Quadrangle Books, 1971.

Osborne, James I. and Theodore G. Gronert. *Wabash College: The First Hundred Years.* Crawfordsville, IN: R.E. Banta, 1932.

Osborne, Newell Y. *A Select School: The History of Mount Union College.* Alliance, OH: Mount Union College, 1967.

Peckham, Howard H. *The Making of the University of Michigan: 1817–1967.* Ann Arbor: University of Michigan Press, 1967.

Perrett, Geoffrey. *A Dream of Greatness: The American People, 1945–1963.* New York: Coward, McCann, & Geoghegan, 1979.

Pierson, George W. *Yale College: An Educational History, 1871–1921.* New Haven: Yale University Press, 1952.

Pollard, James E. *A History of the Ohio State University.* Columbus: Ohio State University Press, 1952.

Powers, Thomas. *The War at Home.* New York: Grossman Publishers, 1973.

Price, Carl F. *Wesleyan's First Century.* Middletown, CT: Wesleyan University, 1932.

Pyre, James F. A. *Wisconsin.* New York: Oxford University Press, 1920.

Ragan, Allen E. *History of Tusculum College: 1794–1944.* Bristol, TN: Tusculum Sesquicentennial Committee, 1945.

Rammelkamp, Charles H. *Illinois College: A Centennial History, 1829–1929.* New Haven: Yale University Press, 1928.

Reid, J. Juan. *Colorado College: The First Century*. Colorado Springs: The Colorado College, 1979.

Richardson, Leon B. *History of Dartmouth College*, Vol. 2. Hanover, NH: Dartmouth College Publications, 1932.

Robson, David W. *Educating Republicans: The College in the American Revolution*. Westport, CT: Greenwood Press, 1985.

Roche, John F. *The Colonial Colleges in the War for American Independence*. New York: Associated Faculty Press, 1986.

Rorabaugh, W. J. *Berkeley at War: The 1960s*. New York: Oxford University Press, 1989.

Rosenberger, Jesse L. *Rochester: The Making of a University*. Rochester, NY: University of Rochester, 1927.

Ross, Earl D. *A History of the Iowa State College*. Ames: Iowa State College Press, 1942.

Roszak, Theodor. *The Making of a Counter Culture*. Garden City, NY: Doubleday, 1969.

Rudy, S. Willis. *The College of the City of New York: A History*. New York: The City College Press, 1949.

Sagendorph, Kent. *Michigan: The Story of the University*. New York: Dutton, 1948.

Scanlon, James E. *Randolph-Macon College: A Southern History, 1825–1967*. Charlottesville: University Press of Virginia, 1983.

Schmidt, George P. *Princeton and Rutgers: The Two Colonial Colleges of New Jersey*. Princeton: Van Nostrand, 1964.

Schrecker, Ellen W. *No Ivory Tower: McCarthyism and the Universities*. New York: Oxford University Press, 1986.

Sears, Louis M. *Purdue University*. Indianapolis: The Hollenbeck Press, 1925.

Sellers, Charles C. *Dickinson College: A History*. Middletown, CT: Wesleyan University Press, 1973.

Sellers, James. *History of the University of Alabama*. University: University of Alabama Press, 1953.

Servin, Samuel P. and Iris H. Wilson. *Southern California and its University*. Los Angeles: The Ward Ritchie Press, 1969.

Sheldon, Henry D. *History of the University of Oregon*. Portland: Binfords & Mort, 1940.

Skillman, David B. *Biography of a College: The First Hundred Hears of Lafayette College*, Vol. 1. Easton, PA: Lafayette College, 1932.

Starrett, Agnes L. *Through One Hundred and Fifty Years: the University of Pittsburgh*. Pittsburgh: University of Pittsburgh Press, 1937.

Statera, Gianni. *Death of a Utopia*. New York: Oxford University Press, 1975.

Stenehjem, Michele F. *An American First*. New Rochelle, NY: Arlington House, 1976.

Strietelmeier, John. *Valparaiso University's First Century*. Valparaiso, IL: Valparaiso University, 1959.

Sullivan, Mark. *Our Times*, Vol. 5. New York: Scribner's, 1933.

Summerscales, William. *Affirmation and Dissent*. New York: Teachers College Press, Columbia University, 1970.

Sweet, William W. *Indiana Asbury-DePauw University, 1837–1937*. Cincinnati, OH: Abingdon Press, 1937.

Theiss, Lewis E. *Centennial History of Bucknell University, 1846–1946*. Williamsport, PA: Bucknell University, 1946.

Topping Robert W. *A Century and Beyond: The History of Purdue University*. West Lafayette, IN: Purdue University Press, 1988.

Tucker, Louis L. *Puritan Protagonist: President Thomas Clap of Yale College*. Chapel Hill: University of North Carolina Press, 1962.

Tyler, Lyon G. *The College of William and Mary in Virginia*. Richmond: Whittet & Shepperson, 1907.

Tyler, Lyon G. *Williamsburg: The Old Colonial Capital*. Richmond: Whittet & Shepperson, 1907.

Veysey, Laurence R. *The Emergence of the American University*. Chicago: University of Chicago Press, 1965.

Vogelgesang, Sandy. *The Long Dark Night of the Soul*. New York: Harper & Row, 1974.

Weaver, Glenn. *The History of Trinity College*, Vol. 1. Hartford: The Trinity College Press, 1967.

Weigley, Russell F., ed. *Philadelphia: A 300-Year History*. New York: W.W. Norton, 1982.

Wertenbaker, Thomas J. *Princeton, 1746–1896*. Princeton: Princeton University Press, 1946.

Willard, Julius T. *History of the Kansas State College of Agriculture and Applied Science*. Manhattan: Kansas State College Press, 1940.

Wilson, Louis R. *The University of North Carolina: 1900–1930*. Chapel Hill: University of North Carolina Press, 1957.

White, Marian C. *A History of Barnard College*. New York: Columbia University Press, 1954.

Wittner, Lawrence S. *Cold War America*. New York: Holt, Rinehart and Winston, 1978.

Wolters, Raymond. *The New Negro on Campus*. Princeton, NJ: Princeton University Press, 1975.

Woodburn, James A. *A History of Indiana University*, Vol. 1. Bloomington: Indiana University Press, 1940.

Yankelovich, Daniel. *The Changing Values on Campus*. New York: Washington Square Press, 1972.

Articles

Adler, Renata. "The Price of Peace is Confusion." *New Yorker* (11 December 1965): 195–202.

"After Kent." *The Nation* (25 May 1970): 610–11.

"All Out for Defense." *School and Society* (24 May 1941): 660–61.

Alsop, Stewart. "The Intellectuals and Vietnam." *Saturday Evening Post* (5 June 1965): 18–19.

Altbach, Philip C. and Patti Peterson. "Before Berkeley." *Annals of the American Academy of Political and Social Science* 395 (1971): 1–14.

Angeloff, Sam. "Go to the V.D.C. House, Say I Sent You." *Life* (10 December 1965): 109–10.

"As President Hadley Sees the War's Lesson." *Literary Digest* (7 April 1917): 984.

"ASU Committee." *New Republic* (5 February 1940): 183–84.

"Battle of Vietnam Day." *Newsweek* (25 October 1965): 98.

Bayer, Alan E. and Astin, Alexander W. "Violence and Disruption on U.S. Campuses, 1968–1969." *Educational Record* 50 (1969): 337–50.

Beisner, Robert L. "1898 and 1968: The Anti-Imperialists and the Doves." *Political Science Quarterly* 85 (1970): 187–216.

Brooks, Thomas R. "Voice of the New Campus Underclass." *New York Times Magazine* (7 November 1965): 25–26; 134–40.

Brown, Eric. "Anti-War Demonstration at Columbia." *New Yorker* (25 April 1970): 30–31.

Carpenter, J. H. "Peace Congress Meets in Capital." *Christian Century* (11 June 1941): 790–91.

Cass, James. "After Kent State." *Saturday Review* (20 June 1970): 71.

"Cease-fire on Campus." *Newsweek* (19 October 1970): 79–80.

"Civil War Divided Princeton Undergraduates." *Princeton Alumni Weekly* (17 May 1931): 1–4.

Cohen, Sheldon S. and Larry R. Gerlach "Princeton in the Coming of the American Revolution." *New Jersey History* 92 (1974): 69–92.

"College Mobilization." *Literary Digest* (7 April 1917): 984–85.

"Collegiate Ignorance of the War." *Literary Digest* (22 January 1916): 177.

"Compulsory Conscription Arouses Discussion." *School and Society* (27 July 1940): 53–54.

Conant, James B. "How Can a Democratic Nation Fight a War and Still Stay Free?" *School and Society* (18 October 1941): 313–15.

Crane, Theodore R. "Francis Wayland and the Residential College." *Rhode Island History* 19 (1960): 75–7.

Crawford, Kenneth. "Egghead Soufflé." *Newsweek* (31 May 1965): 30.

"The Demonstrators: Why?" *Newsweek* (1 November 1965): 25–26; 31–34.

"Draft in the Ivory Tower." *Saturday Review* (20 January 1968): 61–62.

"Draft Riots on College Campuses?" *School and Society* (13 November 1965): 420–22.

Duncan, Richard R. "The Impact of the Civil War on Education in Maryland." *Maryland Historical Magazine* 41 (1966): 37–51.

Edwards, Allen R. "Military Training in our Colleges." *Columbia University Quarterly* 21 (1919) 217–24.

"Effigy Burning Among The Princeton Students." *Princeton Alumni Weekly* (7 April 1909): 406–7.

"Facing Draft Soon: Thousands of Married Men and College Students." *US News & World Report* (8 November 1965): 11.

Feuer, Lewis S. "Student Unrest in the United States." *Annals of the American*

Academy of Political and Social Science 404 (1972): 170−82.

Fisher, Arthur. "From the College Pacifists." *New Republic (15 May 1915): 43−44.*

"Freedom of Speech at Harvard University." *School and Society* (8 May 1915): 668.

Gannon, Thomas M. "A Report on the Vietnam Moratorium." *America* (1 November 1969): 380−83.

Gitlin, Todd. "Home Front Resistance to the Vietnam War." *Vietnam Reconsidered: Lessons from a War*. Ed. Harrison E. Salisbury. New York: Harper & Row, 1984, 71−76.

"Go Back, Go Back!" *Newsweek* (17 November 1969): 79−80.

Graham, Gene. "Turmoil in the Graduate Schools." *New York Times Magazine* (7 April 1968): 46−65.

Hamill, Clarence T. "The University and Preparedness." *Journal of Education* 83 (1916): 314−15.

"Harvard and Beyond: The University Under Siege." *Time* (18 April 1969): 47−50; 55−56.

"Harvard University and the War." *School and Society* (7 April 1917): 408−9.

"Have the Young Gone Sour?" *New Republic* (13 January 1941): 39.

"Heads of Junior Colleges Vote on the Reduction of the Draft-Age to Eighteen." *School and Society* (7 June 1941): 741−42.

Henderson, Yandell. "Universities and Unpreparedness." *Science, n.s.* (18 February 1916): 241−42.

Hilberry, Conrad. "Civil Disobedience at Oberlin." *Educational Record* 49 (1968): 133−38.

Hunt, Theodore W. "College and Civil War Reminiscences." *Princeton Alumni Weekly* (23 May 1917): 757−60.

Jordan, David Starr. "Arming College Men is not the Best Thing to Do." *New York Times* (25 February 1915): 8.

Kaufman, Arnold S. "Teach-ins, New Force for the Times." *The Nation* (21 June 1965): 666−70.

"Keep it Rolling!" *The Nation* (31 May 1965): 575.

"Keep Out of War." *Newsweek* (30 December 1940): 9.

Kenniston, Kenneth. "The Agony of the Counter-Culture." *Educational Record* 52 (1971): 205−11.

"Kent State: Martyrdom that Shook the Country." *Time* (18 May 1970): 12−14.

Kerr, Clark. "Student Dissent and Confrontation Politics." *Protest! Student Activism in America*. Eds. Julian Foster and Durward Long. New York: William Morrow, 1970, 3−7.

Kirk, Russell. "Students for Victory." *National Review* (31 May 1966): 535.

Kolko, Gabriel. "Untangling the Alliances." *The Nation* (18 December 1967): 645−47.

Knoll, Erwin. "Revolt of the Professors." *Saturday Review* (19 June 1965): 60−61.

Ladd, Everett C. "Professors and Political Petitions." *Science* 163 (1969): 1425−30.

Langer, Elinor. "National Teach-ins." *Science* 148 (1965): 1075−77.

Langer, Elinor. "Vietnam." *Science* 150 (1965): 1567–70.

Lasch, Christopher. "New Curriculum for the Teach-Ins." *The Nation* (18 October 1965): 239–41.

Levitas, Mitchel. "Vietnam Comes to Oregon U." *New York Times Magazine* (9 May 1965): 24–25; 89–92.

Levitas, Mitchel. "2-S—Too Smart to Fight?" *New York Times Magazine* (24 April 1966): 27; 125–32.

Lipset, Seymour M. "The American University, 1964–1974." *Universities in the Western World*. Ed. Paul Seabury. New York: Free Press, 1975, 333–36.

Lowell, A. Lawrence. "Military Training in the College." *School and Society* (26 February 1916): 317–21.

McCaughey, Robert A. "American University Teachers and Opposition to the Vietnam War: A Reconsideration." *Minerva* 14 (1976): 307–29.

MacCauley, Clay. "The College During the Civil War." *Princeton Alumni Weekly* (25 October 1916): 84–87; (22 November 1916): 180–83.

McCormick, Richard. "Rutgers and the Civil War." *Aloud to Alma Mater*. Ed. George J. Lukac. New Brunswick, NJ: Rutgers University Press, 1966, 60–63.

Meiklejohn, Alexander. "A Schoolmaster's View of Compulsory Military Training." *School and Society* (1 July 1916): 9–13.

Molnar, Thomas. "D-Day at Brooklyn College." *National Review* (30 January 1968): 86–87.

"More in Sorrow than Anger." *The Nation* (13 March 1967): 324–25.

Meuller, Marti. "Opposition to the War Put on Record." *Science* 166 (1969): 352.

Murphy, Mary E. "War and the Woman's College." *Journal of Higher Education* 12 (1941): 143–45.

"New Campus Mood: From Rags to Reform." *Time* (30 November 1970): 38–40.

"New Campus Rebels: Women." *Newsweek* (10 December 1973): 120–24.

Nisbet, Robert A. "Who Killed the Student Revolution?" *Encounter* (February 1970): 17–19.

Obear, Frederick W. "Student Activism in the Sixties." *Protest!* Eds. Foster and Long, 14–19.

O'Brien, James P. "The Development of the New Left." *Annals* 395 (1971): 15–25.

"Pasadena Meeting of the Association of American Colleges." *School and Society* (25 January 1941): 124–25.

Peckham, Howard. "*Collegia Ante-Bellum*: Attitudes of College Students and Professors toward the American Revolution." *Pennsylvania Magazine of History and Biography* 95 (1971): 50–72.

Perrin, Noel. "College Seniors and the War." *New Yorker* (20 July 1968): 56–60.

Peterson, Patti M. "Student Organizations and the Anti-war Movement in America: 1900–1960." *Peace Movements in America*. Ed. Charles Chatfield. New York: Schocken Books, 1973, 116–32.

"President Johnson vs. the Intellectuals." *Life* (25 June 1965): 4.

"President Roosevelt Emphasizes the Need for College Training." *School and Society* (30 August 1941): 134.

Redding, Saunders. "The Black Youth Movement." *American Scholar* 38 (1969): 585–87.

Riesman, David. "A Changing Campus and a Changing Society." *School and Society* (April 1969): 215–22.

Roberts, Derrell. "The University of Georgia and Georgia's Civil War G.I. Bill." *Georgia Historical Quarterly* 49 (1965): 418–21.

Ross, Irwin. "Youth Goes to Washington." *New Republic* (26 February 1940): 275–76.

Ross, Irwin. "What they Really Think, and Why." *Harper's Magazine* (January 1941): 127–32.

Ross, Irwin. "The Student Union and the Future." *New Republic* (8 January 1940): 48–49.

Ross, Irwin. "College Students and the War." *New Republic* (15 July 1940): 79–80.

Samuelson, Robert J. "War on Campus." *Science* 158 (1967): 1289–94.

Sartre, John Paul. "Up All Night." *Nation* (31 May 1965): 574.

Schick, Edgar B. "Campus Ferment and Tranquility, 1970–71." *School and Society* (February 1972): 93–95.

Schott, Webster. "Teach-in: New Forum for Reason." *The Nation* (31 May 1965): 573–79.

Schreiber, E. M. "Opposition to the Vietnam War among American Students and Faculty." *British Journal of Sociology* 24 (1973): 288–302.

Seidman, Harold. "The Colleges Renounce War." *The Nation* (17 May 1933): 554–55.

Seymour, Charles. "War's Impact on the Campus." *New York Times Magazine* (29 September 1940): 3–4; 15.

Silber, John R. "Respect for the Law on the Campus." *Educational Record* 51 (1970): 130–33.

"Students in Military Training Camps." *School and Society* (2 September 1916): 306.

"Tame Spring, Troubled Stanford." *Time* (19 May 1971): 62–63.

"Teach-ins." *New Republic* (17 April 1965): 9.

"Teach-ins and Walk-outs." *The Nation* (12 April 1965): 378.

"They March, Doubting they will Overcome." *New Republic* (30 October 1965): 9.

Thomson, Robert P. "The Reform of William and Mary, 1763–1800." *Proceedings of the American Philosophical Society* 115 (1971): 187–213.

"Training Soldiers at College." *Literary Digest* (6 February 1915): 242–43.

"Turmoil at the Harvard Semitic Museum." *Biblical Archeology Review* 20 (1994): 64–66.

"U.S. Campus Mood, a *Newsweek* Poll." *Newsweek* (22 February 1971): 61–63.

Walsh, John. "Confrontation at Stanford: Exit Classified Research" *Science* 164 (1969): 534–37.

Walton, Richard J. "The Last March." *The Nation* (5 February 1973): 164.

Weissman, Stephen R. "No Retreat from Commitment." *The Nation* (18 June 1973): 781–85.

Wechsler, James. "Politics on the Campus." *The Nation* (30 December 1939): 732–33.

"Wild in the Streets: Mark Rudd." *Newsweek* (20 October 1969): 42–43.

Wilkins, Ernest H. "The College Faces War and Peace." *School and Society* (6 January 1940): 1–7.

Williams, Donald T. "The Awesome Effectiveness of Confrontation." *Educational Record* 51 (1970): 130–33.

Woodward, C. Vann. "What Became of the 1960s?" *New Republic* (9 November 1974): 18–25.

Index

253